Library of
Davidson College

POLITICS IN AUSTRIA:
STILL A CASE OF
CONSOCIATIONALISM?

POLITICS IN AUSTRIA: STILL A CASE OF CONSOCIATIONALISM?

Edited by

KURT RICHARD LUTHER
and
WOLFGANG C. MÜLLER

FRANK CASS

First published 1992 in Great Britain by
FRANK CASS & CO. LTD
Gainsborough House, Gainsborough Road,
London E11 1RS, England

and in the United States of America by
FRANK CASS
c/o International Specialized Book Services, Inc.,
5602 N.E. Hassalo Street,
Portland, Oregon 97213

Copyright © 1992

British Library Cataloguing-in-Publication Data

Politics in Austria : still a case of consociationalism?
I. Luther, Kurt Richard II. Müller, Wolfgang C.
320.9436
ISBN 0-7146-34611

Library of Congress Cataloging-in-Publication Data

Politics in Austria : still a case of consociationalism? / edited by
Kurt Richard Luther and Wolfgang C. Müller.
  p.   cm.
  'This group of studies first appeared in a special issue,
Politics in Austria : still a case for consociationalism?, of West
European Politics, Vol. 15, No. 1 (January 1992)' – T.p. verso.
  Includes bibliographical references and index.
  ISBN 0-7146-3461-1 (cl : alk. paper)
  1. Austria – Politics and government – 1945–   I. Luther, Kurt
Richard, 1956– . II. Müller, Wolfgang C., 1957–
DB99.2.P56   1992
943.605'23 – dc20   91-46216
                                                                  CIP

This group of studies first appeared in a Special Issue on 'Politics in Austria: Still A Case of Consociationalism?', *West European Politics*, Vol. 15, No. 1 (January 1992), published by Frank Cass & Co. Ltd.

All rights reserved. No part of this publication may be reproduced in any form or by any means, electronic, mechanical, photocopying, recording or otherwise, without the prior permission of Frank Cass and Company Limited.

Printed in Great Britain by
Antony Rowe Ltd, Chippenham

Contents

Notes on Contributors	*page*	vii
Consociationalism and the Austrian Political System *Kurt Richard Luther and Wolfgang C. Müller*		1
The Decline of '*Lager* Mentality' and the New Model of Electoral Competition in Austria *Fritz Plasser, Peter A. Ulram and Alfred Grausgruber*		16
Consociationalism, Parties and the Party System *Kurt Richard Luther*		45
Austrian Governmental Institutions: Do They Matter? *Wolfgang C. Müller*		99
A Farewell to Corporatism *Peter Gerlich*		132
Changing Priorities in Austrian Economic Policy *Volkmar Lauber*		147
Austria in the International Arena: Neutrality, European Integration and Consociationalism *D. Mark Schultz*		173
Austrian Consociationalism: Victim of Its Own Success? *Kurt Richard Luther and Wolfgang C. Müller*		201
Appendices:		
1. Distribution of Votes at National Council Elections (1945–1990)		207
2. Distribution of National Council Seats (1945–1990)		208
3. Presidential Elections Since 1945		209
4. Austrian Cabinets Since 1945		210
5. English Language Sources for the Study of Austrian Politics		211
Abstracts		224
Index		227

Notes on Contributors

Peter Gerlich is Professor of Political Science at the University of Vienna. He has published widely on Austrian politics. His books include *Parlamentarische Kontrolle im politischen System* (1973) and (as co-editor) *The Politics of Economic Crisis* (1989) and *Handbuch des politischen Systems Österreichs* (1991).

Alfred Grausgruber is Lecturer in Political Sociology at the Department of Sociology at the University of Linz.

Volkmar Lauber is Professor of Political Science at the University of Salzburg. His area of expertise is economic policy, on which he has published widely. His books include *The Politics of Economic Policy* (1983) and *The Political Economy of France* (1983). He is also co-editor of *Handbuch des politischen Systems Österreichs* (1991).

Kurt Richard Luther is Senior Lecturer in European Politics at Lancashire Polytechnic. His research relates in the main to parties, party systems and federalism, on which he has published contributions to previous issues of this journal, as well as to edited volumes. He is currently working on a co-edited volume to be entitled *Austrian Parties and the Austrian Party System*.

Wolfgang C. Müller is Reader in Political Science at the University of Vienna. He has published widely on Austrian politics and is co-editor of *Zwischen Koalition und Konkurrenz. Österreichs Parteien seit 1945* (1983), *Sozialpartnerschaft in der Krise* (1985) and *Handbuch des politischen Systems Österreichs* (1991). His current projects include a volume to be entitled *Austrian Parties and the Austrian Party System*.

Fritz Plasser is Associate Professor of Political Science at the University of Innsbruck. His books include *Parteien unter Stress. Zur Dynamik der Parteiensysteme in Österreich, der Bundesrepublik Deutschland und den Vereinigten Staaten* (1987) and (as co-editor) *The Austrian Party System* (1989) and *Staatsbürger oder Untertanen? Politische Kultur Deutschlands, Österreichs und der Schweiz im Vergleich* (1991).

D. Mark Schultz received his doctorate in politics from the University of Oxford in 1989 for a thesis comparing Austria-EC integration with Canada-US trade and is now the European analyst in the Country Strategies department of the Royal Bank of Canada in Toronto.

Peter A. Ulram is Lecturer in Political Science at the University of Vienna. His books include *Hegemonie und Erosion. Politische Kultur und politischer Wandel in Österreich* (1990) and (as co-editor) *Staatsbürger oder Untertanen? Politische Kultur Deutschlands, Österreichs und der Schweiz im Vergleich* (1991).

Acknowledgement

The editors wish to express their appreciation to the Austrian Federal Ministry of Science and Research for the latter's support of this project. They also gratefully acknowledge the assistance of the European Consortium for Political Research, which awarded them a Research and Mobility Grant for their work on consociationalism in Austria.

Consociationalism and the Austrian Political System

KURT RICHARD LUTHER AND WOLFGANG C. MÜLLER

THE NINETEENTH CENTURY ORIGINS OF MODERN AUSTRIAN POLITICS

The origins of modern Austrian politics can be traced back to the decades following the unsuccessful bourgeois revolution of 1848, during the initial years of which the Habsburgs stoutly resisted all pressure on them to grant serious constitutional reform. It was not until the 1860s that they were finally obliged to agree to even modest liberal constitutional reforms, which were introduced by means of the 'Oktober Diplom' of 1860, the 'Februar Patent' of 1861, but above all through the so-called 'December Constitution' of 1867.[1] In 1867 Austria also embarked on an experiment to apply liberal principles to its economy. However, this venture lasted only until May 1873, when the Vienna stock exchange collapsed as a result of excessive speculative activity. This not only signalled the end of Austria's first venture in *laissez-faire* economics, but was instrumental in permanently discrediting economic liberalism in the eyes of the overwhelming majority of Austrians.[2] Their negative evaluation of *laissez-faire* economics was strengthened by the economic crises of the First Republic and helps to explain the weakness of economic liberalism in Austria since.

The more immediate, but no less significant, impact of Austria's failed experiment with *laissez-faire* and the intra-parliamentary groups' lack of democratic legitimacy was the development of three main extra-parliamentary political groupings, which began to crystallise around more-or-less distinct political subcultures or *Lager*.[3] Austria's rural peasantry and its *petite-bourgeoisie* formed the backbone of the Catholic-conservative *Lager*, which found its political expression in the Christian-Social Party.[4] The second major subculture drew its support predominantly from the emerging urban proletariat, but also included amongst its leading personalities disproportionately large elements of the assimilated Jewish and secular intelligentsia. It was headed by the anti-clerical Social Democratic Workers' Party (SDAP).[5] Both *Lager* controlled extensive networks of auxiliary associations, ranging from interest groupings to sporting and cultural associations, which together served to ensure not only that rival *Lager* members were characterised by their mutually exclusive and antagonistic ideological orientations, but also that their lives were increasingly lived within the encapsulated realms of their respective subcultures. Notwithstanding these similarities, there were important differences between the two *Lager* in at least two important respects.

First, though the socialist and Catholic-conservative *Lager* were both primarily 'externally created',[6] differences relatively soon emerged in terms of their relationship to Austria's dominant social, economic and bureaucratic elite. Though the Catholic-conservative *Lager* has traditionally been regarded as having operated above all in Austria's small towns and rural areas, the fact is that its initial political strength lay in the capital city of Vienna, where its greatest moment came when its leader was elected Lord Mayor in 1897. Such successes helped make this previous 'outsider' party more acceptable in conservative circles and helps explain why, in 1907, the Christian-Socials decided to join forces with the mainly rural conservatives. By 1911, the Christian-Social Party's fortunes had waned in Vienna, but in view of its incorporation of aristocratic and business elements, it had largely succeeded in becoming identified as a representative of the status-quo. Accordingly, the elites of the two main *Lager* were henceforth differentiated not only in terms of religion and political ideology, but also in terms of 'insider' versus 'outsider' status.[7]

A second important factor distinguishing the two main *Lager* relates to the principles underpinning their attempts to extend the scope and increase the cohesion of their respective subcultures. From a relatively early stage, the *Lager* placed differing degrees of emphasis on political and on socio-cultural factors. The socialists sought to integrate their predominantly urban, industrial subculture primarily by means of appeals to political ideology and by party-political organisation. Once the Christian-Socials had passed the highpoint of their success in urban Vienna, the prime attention of their Catholic-conservative *Lager* turned to an altogether different target, namely, the rural and small-town areas of Austria. These were characterised by small, face-to-face communities with socially and geographically immobile populations, amongst whom religious values and clerical influence were still high, and where socio-economic structures still bore the imprint of guild-like occupational groupings.

In such conditions, it is easier for traditional social elites to maintain social control and it is thus not surprising that the Catholic-conservative *Lager*'s increasing emphasis, in its attempts at subcultural expansion, penetration and integration, upon Catholic-integrationalist principles appealing for social hierarchy and solidarity, proved highly successful. Reliance upon such socio-cultural principles appears to have facilitated an ever greater degree of subcultural penetration and integration than was the case in the socialist camp, whose appeal was more purely political.[8]

Accordingly, the scope and control of the Catholic-conservative *Lager* may be considered to have been somewhat greater than was the case with the socialist camp.

The third of Austria's historic *Lager* was the secular, anti-clerical, but also anti-socialist 'national-liberal', or 'German-national' grouping,[9] support for which derived in the main from white-collar employees, bureaucrats, and elements of the non-Jewish German-speaking intelligentsia. Also significant for it were its student associations, important especially in providing elite recruitment and in ensuring the *Lager*'s support among persons who were later to become members of Austria's bureaucracy. It was different from the two *Lager* that we have so far discussed in at least three respects. First, whilst the latter certainly were initially predominantly externally-created, important elements of the 'Third *Lager*' were from the outset drawn from 'insider-groups' and in particular from among the liberal circles of the Austrian political and administrative elite. One of the significant factors that helped unite them with the 'outsider' elements of the nascent Third *Lager* was a commitment to German nationalism.

Accordingly, and this is the second feature distinguishing the German-nationals, the *Lager* was much more of a party of notables (in Duverger's terms a cadre party) than was the case with the party-political expressions of the other two *Lager*, which were clearly 'mass parties' in Duverger's terms.[10] Third, the German-national *Lager* was from the outset characterised by a significantly higher degree of ideological ambiguity and social heterogeneity, which was reflected in that it never attained the size, nor the political cohesion of the socialist and the Catholic-conservative *Lager*. This was true both at the mass level, where the *Lager*'s auxiliary associations were less extensively organised and at the elite level, where it proved impossible to form a single and united party.

At both levels, there were significant ideological conflicts between on the one hand those who retained a commitment to both liberal and German-national principles and on the other hand those such as Schönerer, whose nationalism was characterised by an irrational and anti-Semitic rascism. Though the latter type of ideas were also present in the other parties – and particularly amongst the Christian-Socials – in the Third *Lager* they helped fuel the internal conflict between government and anti-system protest orientations. They were later of course also to make the Third *Lager* especially vulnerable to the appeal of National Socialism.

THE FIRST REPUBLIC, 1918-34

With the advent of universal male suffrage in 1907 and especially after the introduction of republican government pursuant to the fall of the Habsburg dynasty in 1918, the *Lager* became the main actors in the Austrian political system, the political life of which was decisively shaped by the nature of the political parties and of their interaction. For a start, it was the two main *Lager* parties which were the architects of the constitution of the First Republic. The state building process that occurred was no easy task for two groupings with such different ideas as to how a political system should be structured.

There were three significant differences. First, they disagreed over the power which the central executive authority should possess, with the Christian-Socials preferring a far stronger executive than the socialists were willing to countenance. Second, the Christian-Socials were in favour of a decentralised federal state, whilst the socialists' preferred option was a centralised unitary state. Finally, there was fundamental disagreement over the role to be ascribed to the parliament, with opinions varying from Socialist calls for sovereignty to be located in parliament, to Christian-Social demands for a relatively weak system of bicameralism, coupled with a strong head of state. In the event, the compromise constitution adopted included a weak federal president, a centralised federal system and a bicameral system in which the territorial chamber lacked any significant powers.[11]

Overall, the constitution that finally emerged clearly reflected the socialists' demands more fully, as was perhaps to be expected since the socialists appeared to be in the political ascendent at that time. However, after an initial period (1918-20) of grand coalition federal government, the SDAP was relegated to main opposition party, a role which it continued to exercise for the remainder of the First Republic, while the Christian-Socials and the two parties of the Third *Lager* (the Greater German People's Party and the Agrarian League), formed a series of bourgeois coalitions. While influential elements of the Catholic-conservative *Lager* perceived themselves to be operating within the confines of a political system, about the constitutional structure of which they had significant reservations, but whose rigidity did not permit of easy revision, the socialists also felt little commitment to a political system in which they were effectively relegated to the role of opposition.

This lack of democratic legitimacy of the First Republic was exacerbated by a lack of an Austrian national identity and by the new state's questionable economic viability. Indeed, before the new regime was even born there was virtually unanimous agreement between the parties that Austria should join the German Reich, rather than attempt to establish from the mainly German-speaking rump of the previous empire a state which had no obvious political identity. All significant groups therefore openly advocated *Anschluss*, though the strength of individual parties' commitment obviously varied over time, in a manner not unconnected to changes in the relative strength of political forces within Germany.[12] Indeed, the fact that the parties sought to forge links with like-minded political groupings outside the fledgling state was a factor that further exacerbated the centrifugal tensions in a political system, the two westernmost constituent *Länder* of which were actively pursuing negotiations in an attempt to secede.[13]

Those who maintained that the new republic was not economically viable felt their arguments confirmed by the burdens which faced the republic at its birth, as well as by economic developments during its lifetime. The First Republic certainly faced severe economic handicaps. The dismemberment of the old empire into independent states that harboured little goodwill to the formerly dominant German-speaking areas had resulted in Austria losing access not only to significant sources of foodstuffs and of raw materials for its industry, but also to a large proportion of its previous market. What was left was thus a rather disjointed economic structure with a disproportionately large tertiary sector, a large part of which comprised the state bureaucracy.[14] The fact that large numbers of civil servants had eventually to be dismissed did little to enhance the support of a group from whom one would normally expect high levels of loyalty to the constitution.[15] A third problem faced by the postwar Austrian economy was of course the substantial reparations placed upon it by the victors of the First World War. These problems, combined with a severe downturn in the business cycle from the late 1920s, resulted in a downward adjustment of the Austrian economy. The state did not intervene, partly out of a commitment to *laissez-faire* by key economic policy-makers, but also partly out of a feeling of helplessness.[16]

Bearing all these factors in mind, one can perhaps view the history of the First Republic as a struggle over who was to bear the cost of Austria's economic problems. In a zero-sum conflict over the distribution of shares of a declining 'cake', the issue was whether the costs were to be borne by the interests of capital and its allies, or by those of labour. At the risk of oversimplification, hyperinflation and large-scale redundancies among white-collar workers in the oversized tertiary sector meant that in the early 1920s the costs of economic dislocation were borne disproportionately by members of the bourgeois *Lager*. In the 1930s the situation changed. It was above all blue-collar workers, but also low level clerks and others who were hit by the mass unemployment of those years. These economic problems were to lead to a political radicalisation of members of all three *Lager*.

In other words, the First Republic's clear failure to resolve either the crisis of legitimation, or that of distribution meant that it was fatally undermined.[17] It is therefore perhaps not surprising that throughout its lifetime (1918–34), the adherents of the *Lager* felt significantly greater loyalty to their respective political parties than they did to the political system. Political interaction between the parties increasingly became zero-sum conflict in which each feared total annihilation by the other and each sought to dominate the other and thus impose its alternative vision of society. As Diamant puts it, 'Austria's "morbific" politics were characterised not only by a lack of ideological consensus, but also by the fact that each of the two major *Lager* viewed the other as lacking a commitment to the "rules of the game" '.[18] Andics' designation of the First Republic as 'the state that no-one wanted' is thus rather apposite.[19]

Matters were not helped by the tactics of the two *Lager*. For their part, though they were *de facto* reform-orientated, the socialists maintained a radical Marxist rhetoric.[20] While this certainly facilitated *Lager* cohesion, as demonstrated by the creation of the *Kommunistische Partei Österreichs* (KPÖ) in November 1918 not resulting in a significant split on the left of Austrian politics and the new party remaining politically relatively insignificant, the socialists' 'Austromarxism' made political co-operation with the representatives of the bourgeois *Lager* difficult, but not impossible. Confirmed in their opposition role at the federal level, the socialists used the scope provided by a federal constitution, which they had originally opposed, to concentrate on developing an extensive social welfare system in the socialist stronghold of Vienna.[21]

Meanwhile, the political ideology of the Catholic-conservative *Lager*, the political strength of which lay largely in the rural *Länder*, moved increasingly towards a corporate-clerical state, some of the features of which were 'imported' from Mussolini's Italy.[22] It was not so much this ideological linkage, however, but above all the political alliances that the Christian-Socials increasingly forged with Mussolini that served to underscore the problems caused by the absence of a specifically Austrian identity. Not that an absence of a commitment to an independent Austria was a characteristic unique to the Catholic-conservative *Lager*, or even to the German nationals. Symptomatic of the radicalisation of the two main *Lager* was their establishment of paramilitary organisations, the clashes between which were increasingly bloody. These centrifugal pressures were accompanied by rising support for the National Socialists. As already mentioned, because of its ideological ambiguity and its commitment to pan-Germanism, the German-national *Lager* was the most vulnerable to incorporation by the Nazis, but it would be wrong to overlook the fact that the Nazis were able to penetrate substantially all three political *Lager*.

Using a procedural loophole, the bourgeois government in office in 1933 unconstitutionally suspended the parliament of the First Republic.[23] It then took further steps in its long-running campaign not only to destroy the Social Democrats' capacity to engage in armed resistance through their paramilitary organisations, but also to remove their remaining opportunities to engage in lawful political action. However, this just gave a further twist to a spiral of violence that saw the *Republikanischer Schutzbund* (the Social Democrats' armed formation) engage not only the paramilitary groupings of the right, but also the security forces of the bourgeois-dominated state apparatus. The outcome was a short, but sharp civil war in February 1934, which resulted in all Social Democratic party organisations being banned and many of the leaders of the party fleeing into exile, or being imprisoned.[24] In May 1934 the Christian-Social government unilaterally announced the introduction of a new constitution.

This self-styled *Ständestaat* was a dictatorship that promised to introduce a corporatist political structure, though in the event it never got around to implementing many of its declared aims.[25] Nonetheless, the structures which it created on paper were to be significant in the Second Republic as the embryonic corporatist institutions that came to form the bases of what has since become known as 'social partnership'.[26] As for the *Ständestaat* itself, it proved to be but a temporary phenomenon. In March 1938 came the *Anschluss*, (i.e., the annexation of Austria and its incorporation into Hitler's Third Reich) and thus the end of a tragic episode in Austria's political history that had commenced with its first attempt at republican government.[27]

Our discussion of that first attempt should not, however, end by implying either that the political process in the First Republic was bereft of any attempts at accommodation, or that the Republic's demise was in some way inevitable. While the political hostility between the *Lager* certainly made compromise difficult, it did not make it impossible, as a number of examples of attempts at co-operation between the two *Lager* testify. These include the grand coalition government of 1918 to 1920, the co-operation in some of the *Land* governments (particularly in Lower Austria), as well as *ad hoc* co-operation on a number of policy issues. Even after the conflict between the *Lager* had escalated considerably, in 1933 and 1934 there were still attempts at overarching elite co-operation intended to maintain the democratic system, as well as last ditch efforts in 1938 to create an anti-Nazi coalition.

That these attempts ultimately failed is perhaps an indication of the political and economic problems of the First Republic, but it does not mean that they were insignificant. First, they constituted a basis, at least at the level of personal relationships, for the construction of more successful inter-elite co-operation in the Second Republic. Second, they suggest an alternative perspective on the development of the First Republic, namely, to see it as an ultimately unsuccessful attempt at co-operation, rather than as an exclusively confrontational episode in Austria's political history.

AUSTRIAN CONSOCIATIONALISM IN ITS CLASSIC PHASE

Nonetheless, the development of Austrian politics in the period following the establishment of the Second Republic does indeed stand in striking contrast to the failure of Austria's first attempt at democratic government. Among the many factors that have significantly improved are first, that in comparison to the political violence of the First Republic, post-war Austria has been characterised by domestic peace and political stability. Second, Austria has experienced unprecedented and sustained levels of economic prosperity that compare favourably not only with its own interwar experience, but also with the post-war experience of most Western states. Indeed, its position has been apparently so positive that when Federal President Franz Jonas visited the Pope in the early 1970s, the latter was moved to comment that Austria had succeeded in establishing an 'island of the blessed'.

From a more academic perspective, what is perhaps most surprising is that Austria's post-war successes have occurred *despite* the fact that some of the key determinants of its political system remained unchanged from the interwar period. First, the establishment of the Second Republic in 1945 was largely undertaken by the same parties — and indeed by some of the very same individuals (e.g., Karl Renner) — that had been involved in setting up the abortive First Republic in 1918–20. Second, they gave Austria essentially the same political structure as in the First Republic, for it was decided at the outset that the new state would revert to the constitution of the First Republic, as amended in 1929. Third, Austria remained a *Kleinstaat* that still had substantial economic problems and an imbalanced industrial structure. Although it had experienced a considerable process of industrialisation under Nazi rule, the investments made were geared above all to the requirements of the German Reich (and its war machine) rather than to those of the Austrian republic. Fourth, though it must be acknowledged that there had been some significant changes in the parties' ideologies — there was now, for example, an unequivocal commitment by the Christian-Social Party's successor (the Austrian People's Party – *Österreichische Volkspartei* – ÖVP) to democratic government – the post-war *Lager* were substantially the same as in the First Republic, as were their party political organisations.

On the other hand, certain important factors had indeed altered. First, as had become apparent as early as the 1945 state-building process, there was now much a greater degree of commitment to the restored republican system than had been been the case in 1918. This and the more co-operative orientation of the parties was due in large measure to their respective centrist wings having assumed a controlling position in their parties. Some have attributed this to many of the party elite finding themselves in prison during Nazi rule alongside their counterparts from the opposing *Lager* and thus coming to believe that they did perhaps have some common interests. Second, unlike in the First Republic, the end of the war did not result in the imposition of reparations by the victors. Instead, the United States decided to instigate what became known as the Marshall Plan, the result of which was a Europe-wide economic upturn from which Austria also benefited substantially.

Finally, among the significantly altered environmental factors with which the new republic was confronted, one of the most obvious was that the country was, for the first ten years after the war, under foreign occupation. Though one can argue that Austria's sovereignty and thus its territorial integrity were seriously undermined by foreign occupation, seen from another perspective this proved to be a uniting element. Not only did it give Austrians a common aim, namely, that of getting rid of the occupying forces, but except for localised problems such as Carinthia's border with Yugoslavia, the territorial boundaries of the Second Republic were much more certain, especially with regard to the possibility on a renewed incorporation into Germany. The experience of Nazi incorporation from 1938 to 1945 helped ensure that the overwhelming majority of Austrians now desired an independent Austria.

It is undeniably the case that much of the rest of Western Europe also experienced a marked improvement in its political and social relations in the post-war period. However, one factor that singled out Austria from many of those countries was the apparent coexistence in Austria of on the one hand a segmented society with apparently still quite mutually hostile subcultures, and on the other hand, social, political and economic stability. This was, of course, the paradox which motivated certain political scientists to investigate and write what has since become an enormous literature on consociationalism.[28] It cannot be our task here to undertake a detailed review and evaluation of this literature.[29] Our purpose is both more modest and more practical. First, we intend to provide a brief outline of consociational literature's basic concerns. Second, we wish to establish what that literature held to be the empirical features that qualified the Austrian political system of the 1950s and 1960s for inclusion in the category of consociational democracies. The purpose of that endeavour is to proceed to structure the empirical examination, which this volume will offer, of the extent to which Austria still exhibits those features and thus still merits the designation of a consociational political system.

The basic proposition of the consociational literature is in fact rather straightforward. It contends that in certain subculturally segmented (or 'encapsulated') societies in which one might expect to find political immobilism, or instability, these characteristics are avoided as a result of a certain type of political response. At its core lies the willingness and capacity of political elites to engage in overarching behaviour to stabilise the system. The factors which exponents of consociationalism have advanced to explain why elites in some systems, or at particular times, should decide to engage in such accommodative behaviour have varied. They include the argument that it stems from deliberate attempts by elites to co-operate in order to preserve a political system which they see as under imminent threat. It is also argued that such accommodative elite behaviour is primarily a product of accommodative traditions ingrained in the role culture of the relevant country's political and administrative elite.[30]

Whichever explanation one prefers – and the Austrian case offers material that could be used to argue both propositions – the fact remains that the Second Republic was widely regarded by the exponents of consociationalism as being one of the best examples of a consociational system. The assertions which the consociational literature made in respect of Austria were based in the main on developments in the country between 1945 and 1966, which may thus be termed the 'classic' phase of Austrian consociationalism. Though they have varied somewhat in their terminology and in the manner in which they have addressed the issue, the following six phenomena have been consistently prominent in their descriptions of Austria's consociationalism.

First, there has been an emphasis on the persistence of encapsulated subcultures, held together by their so-called *Lagermentalität* (*Lager* mentality). This was deemed important both in maintaining high levels of political incorporation and especially in ensuring high levels of partisan attachment and ultra-stable electoral behaviour.[31] A second feature held to be characteristic of 'classic' Austrian consociationalism was the nature and interaction of its main political parties. The party system was dominated by two huge parties: the ÖVP and the Socialist Party of Austria (*Sozialistische Partei Österreichs* – SPÖ). They were distinctive not only by virtue of their sheer size and organisational penetration of their respective *Lager*, but also by the fact that they operated in an essentially accommodative manner.[32]

Third, Austria was seen as an almost archetypal case of corporatism, with all major socio-economic decisions being the subject of co-operation between the major interest groups and between them and the government.[33] The subject matter of this co-operation ranged from industrial relations and prices and incomes policy, through to participation in the initiation, formulation and implementation of legislation, especially social and economic policy. Fourth, in large measure as a result of the parties' extensive roles and the corporate system, Austria's formal governmental institutions were seen as lacking political salience with their prime role being merely to endorse decisions made elsewhere.[34] Fifth, during 'classic' consociationalism, Austria was held to have a distinctive approach to economic policy. Though it came to be labelled 'Austrokeynesianism', it was in fact a genuine mix of demand-side and supply-side measures. In light of the First Republic's above mentioned economic problems, it is perhaps not surprising that a principal goal of 'Austrokeynesianism' was to ensure not only a healthy economy, but also that its benefits and costs would be seen to be shared more equitably among the population.[35]

A final aspect considered to be significant for Austrian politics during the 'classic' consociationalism phase, albeit one given somewhat less attention than those mentioned above, was the nature of its external relations in general and their economic and security dimensions in particular. For academic observers this aspect included the interrelationship between Austria's internal and external politics and especially the extent to which political elites' willingness to engage in overarching domestic co-operation is fostered by external threat. It poses the question whether or not consociationalism is only possible in small states that allegedly have only a relatively 'light' international role.[36]

One of the most evocative manifestations of Austrian consociationalism in its 'classic phase' was of course the grand coalition federal government, which ruled the country for the 21 years from 1945 to 1966.[37] This practice came to an end in 1966 and was followed by an almost equally long period of single-party governments (first by the ÖVP and then a series of SPÖ governments), and then by three years of a less broadly based coalition, namely, that between the SPÖ and the Freedom Party of Austria (*Freiheitliche Partei Österreichs* – FPÖ), which governed Austria from 1983 to 1987. Though most observers acknowledged the importance of the end of grand coalition government and some spoke of the 'decline of consociationalism', or a change towards 'depoliticised democracy',[38] no change in the direction of adversarial elite behaviour was found. Austria continued to be referred to in some of the literature[39] as an example of consociational democracy.

The aim of this volume is to assess the extent to which this remains an appropriate characterisation of the Austrian political system. We shall attempt to answer this question by means of six contributions, one on each of the six above-mentioned core characteristics of Austrian politics during the phase of 'classic' consociationalism. These contributions will each provide an overview of the relevant aspect during the 'classic' phase, before proceeding to consider, on the basis empirical evidence, the nature and extent of change in the subsequent period. In the final chapter of this volume, we shall seek to draw the various threads together and to offer some conclusions as to whether the overall character of Austrian politics in the early 1990s justifies the assertion that Austria is still a case of consociationalism.

NOTES

1. See K. Ucakar, *Demokratie und Wahlrecht in Österreich* (Vienna: Verlag für Gesellschaftskritik, 1985).
2. See E. März, *Österreichische Industrie- und Bankpolitik in der Zeit Franz Josephs I.* (Vienna: Europa Verlag, 1968); K. W. Rothschild, 'Wurzeln und Triebkräfte der Entwicklung der österreichischen Wirtschaftsstruktur', in W. Weber (ed.), *Österreichs Wirtsschaftsstruktur. gestern—heute—morgen* (Berlin: Duncker & Humblot, 1961), Vol. 1, pp. 1–157; H. Matis, *Österreichs Wirtschaftspolitik vom Josephinismus zum Ständestaat* (Vienna: Jupiter, 1965) and *Österreichs Wirtschaft 1848–1913* (Berlin: Duncker & Humblot, 1972); A. Brusatti (ed.), *Die wirtschaftliche Entwicklung* (is Vol. I, of *Die Habsburgmonarchie 1848–1918*) (Vienna: Verlag der österreichischen Akademie der Wissenschaften, 1973); D. F. Good, *The Economic Rise of the Habsburg Empire 1750–1914* (Berkeley, CA: California UP, 1984).
3. The term *Lager* denotes an (armed) camp and is a not inappropriate term, since Austria's political parties came to form competing paramilitary organisations (see C. A. Macartney, 'The Armed Formations in Austria', *Journal of the Royal Institute of International Affairs*, Vol. 8 (1929), pp. 617–32); on the formation of the *Lager*, see A. Wandruszka, 'Österreichs politische Struktur: Die Entwicklung der Parteien und politischen Bewegungen', in H. Benedikt (ed.), *Geschichte der Republik Österreich* (Vienna: Verlag für Geschichte und Politik, 1954), pp. 289–485; A. Fuchs, *Geistige Strömungen in Österreich 1867–1918*, repr. of 1949 ed. (Vienna: Löcker, 1977); W. B. Simon, *The Political Parties of Austria* (Ann Arbor, MI: Reprint of Columbia Univ. Ph.D., 1957), esp. pp. 15–79 and P. Pulzer, 'The Legitimising Role of Political Parties: The Second Austrian Republic', *Government and Opposition*, Vol. 4 (1969), pp. 324–44.
4. See Wandruszka, 'Österreichs politische Struktur', pp. 301ff; J. W. Boyer, *Political Radicalism in Late Imperial Vienna. Origins of the Christian Social Movement 1848–1897* (Chicago, IL: Chicago UP, 1981); R. Knoll, *Zur Tradition der christlich-sozialen Partei* (Vienna: Böhlau, 1973); G. Lewis, *Kirche und Partei im Politischen Katholizismus* (Vienna: Geyer, 1977); W. Sauer, *Katholisches Vereinswesen in Wien* (Salzburg: Wolfgang Neugebauer, 1980).
5. See L. Brügel, *Geschichte der österreichischen Sozialdemokratie*, 5 vols. (Vienna: Verlag der Wiener Volksbuchhandlung, 1922–25); P. Kulemann, *Am Beispiel des Austromarxismus. Sozialdemokratische Arbeiterbewegung in Österreich von Hainfeld bis zur Dolfuß-Diktatur* (Hamburg: Junius, 1979); V. J. Knapp, *Austrian Social Democracy, 1889–1914* (Washington, DC: UP of America, 1980); W. Maderthaner (ed.), *Sozialdemokratie und Habsburgerstaat* (Vienna: Löcker, 1988).

6. M. Duverger, *Political Parties* (London: Methuen, 1959), pp. xxxff.
7. Cf. H. Daalder, 'Parties, Elites, and Political Development in Western Europe', in J. LaPalombara and M. Weiner (eds.), *Political Parties and Political Development* (Princeton UP, 1965), pp. 43–77.
8. We are of course not wishing to suggest that socio-cultural factors were not relevant in mobilising the socialist camp, but merely pointing to a different degree of emphasis and to the fact that the Catholic-conservatives' use of mobilising principles consonant with and reinforced by traditional social values helped ensure a somewhat greater potential for subcultural control.
9. See Wandruszka, 'Österreichs politische Struktur', pp. 369–421; Fuchs, *Geistige Strömungen in Österreich*, pp. 165–96; A. Whiteside, 'Austria', in H. Rogger and E. Weber (eds.), *The European Right* (Berkeley, CA: California UP, 1965), pp. 308–63; A. G. Whiteside, *The Socialism of Fools. Georg Ritter von Schönerer and Austrian Pan-Germanism* (Berkeley, CA: California UP, 1975).
10. Duverger, *Political Parties*, pp. 63ff.
11. See B. Skottsberg, *Der österreichische Parlamentarismus* (Gothenburg: Erlanders Boktryekeri, 1940); A. Pelinka and M. Welan, *Demokratie und Verfassung in Österreich* (Vienna: Europa Verlag, 1971), pp. 23–38; A. Ableitinger, 'Grundlegung der Verfassung' in E. Weinzierl and K. Skalnik (eds.), *Österreich 1918–1938* (Graz: Styria, 1983), pp. 147–94; R. Walter, *Die Entstehung des Bundesverfassungsgesetzes 1920 in der Konstituierenden Nationalversammlung* (Vienna: Manz, 1984).
12. See A. D. Low, *The Anschluss Movement, 1931–1938, and the Great Powers* (NY: Columbia UP, 1985).
13. For a comparative discussion from the *Länder* perspective of the state-building processes at the outset of the First and Second Republics, see P. Pernthaler, *Die Staatsgründungsakte der österreichischen Bundesländer. Eine staatsrechtliche Untersuchung über die Entstehung des Bundesstaates* (Vienna: Braumüller, 1979). See also K. R. Stadler, *Hypothek auf die Zukunft. Die Entstehung der österreichischen Republik 1918–1924* (Vienna: Europa Verlag, 1968).
14. See E. März, *Österreichische Bankpolitik in der Zeit der großen Wende 1913–1923* (Vienna: Verlag für Geschichte und Politik, 1981); F. Butschek, *Die österreichische Wirtschaft im 20. Jahrhundert* (Stuttgart: Gustav Fischer, 1985); H. Kernbauer, E. März and F. Weber, 'Die wirtschaftliche Entwicklung' in Weinzierl and Skalnik (eds.), *Österreich 1918–1938*, pp. 343–79.
15. We have already mentioned that state bureaucrats were disproportionately represented in the 'Third *Lager*'. When the government that included Third *Lager* parties decided to dismiss large numbers of civil servants, this therefore had particular impact on the willingness of important elements of this *Lager* to give the republic unqualified support.
16. Kernbauer et al., 'Die wirtschaftliche Entwicklung'; D. Stiefel, *Die große Krise in einem kleinen Land. Österreichs Finanz- und Wirtschaftspolitik 1929–1938* (Vienna: Böhlau, 1988).
17. See P. Pulzer, 'Legitimising Role of Political Parties'.
18. A. Diamant, 'The Group Basis of Austrian Politics, *Journal of Central European Affairs*, Vol. 18. (1958), pp. 134–55, here p. 135f.
19. H. Andics, *Der Staat, den keiner wollte. Österreich von der Gründung der Republik bis zur Moskauer Deklaration* (Vienna: Molden, 1968).
20. See N. Leser, *Zwischen Reform und Bolschewismus* (Vienna: Europa Verlag, 1968) and A. Rabinbach, *The Crisis of Austrian Socialism* (Univ. of Chicago P., 1983).
21. See C. A. Gulick, *Austria from Habsburg to Hitler* (Berkeley, CA: California UP, 1948), Vol. I, pp. 354–582 and A. G. Frei, *Rotes Wien* (Berlin: DVK-Verlag, 1984).
22. See A. Diamant, *Austrian Catholics and the First Republic–Democracy, Capitalism and the Social Order 1918–1934* (Princeton UP, 1960) and A. Staudinger, 'Christlichsoziale Partei', in Weinzierl and Skalnik (eds.), *Österreich 1918–1938*, pp. 248–76.
23. See E. Fröschl and H. Zoitl (eds.), *Der 4. März 1933. Vom Verfassungsbruch zur Diktatur* (Vienna: Verlag der Wiener Volksbuchhandlung, 1984), and P. Huemer,

Sektionschef Robert Hecht und die Zerstörung der Demokratie in Österreich (Vienna: Verlag für Geschichte und Politik, 1975).
24. See E. Fröschl and H. Zoitl (eds.), Februar 1934. Ursachen – Fakten – Folgen (Vienna: Verlag der Wiener Volksbuchhandlung, 1984).
25. See E. Tálos and W. Neugebauer (eds.), 'Austrofaschismus'. Beiträge über Politik, Ökonomie und Kultur 1934–1938 (Vienna: Verlag für Gesellschaftskritik, 1984).
26. See G. Stourzh and M. Grandner (eds.), Historische Wurzeln der Sozialpartnerschaft (Vienna: Verlag für Geschichte und Politik, 1986).
27. See, e.g., Low, Anschluss Movement; R. Neck and A. Wandruszka (eds.), Anschluss 1938 (Vienna: Verlag für Geschichte und Politik, 1981) and G. Stourzh and B. Zaar (eds.), Österreich, Deutschland und die Mächte (Vienna: Verlag der österreichischen Akademie der Wissenschaften, 1990). On the National Socialist era in Austria see E. Tálos, E. Hanisch and W. Neugebauer (eds.), NS-Herrschaft in Österreich 1938–1945 (Vienna: Verlag für Gesellschaftskritik, 1988).
28. See, e.g., H. Daalder, 'The Consociational Democracy Theme', World Politics, Vol. 26, No. 4 (1974), pp. 604–21; G. Lehmbruch, Proporzdemokratie: Politisches System und politische Kultur in der Schweiz und in Österreich (Tübingen: Mohr, 1967); G. Lehmbruch, 'Consociational Democracy in the International System', European Journal of Political Research, Vol. 3, No. 4 (1975), pp. 377–91; A. Lijphart, 'Typologies of Democratic Systems', Comparative Political Studies, Vol. 1, No. 1 (1968), pp. 3–44; idem, 'Consociational Democracy', World Politics, Vol. 21, No. 2 (1969), pp. 207–25; idem, Democracy in Plural Societies: A Comparative Exploration (New Haven, CT: Yale UP, 1977); V. R. Lorwin, 'Segmented Pluralism. Ideological Cleavages and Political Cohesion in the Smaller European Democracies', Comparative Politics, Vol. 3 (1971), pp. 141–75; K. D. McRae (ed.), Consociational Democracy. Accommodation in Segmented Societies (Toronto: McClelland & Stewart, 1974); J. Steiner, 'The Principles of Majority and Proportionality', British Journal of Political Science, Vol. 1, No. 1 (1971), pp. 63–70; idem, Amicable Agreement versus Majority Rule. Conflict Resolution in Switzerland (Chapel Hill, NC: Univ. of North Carolina P., 1974).
29. For reviews and critiques of the consociational literature see, e.g., B. Barry, 'Political Accommodation and Consociational Democracy', British Journal of Political Science, Vol. 5 (1975), pp. 477–505; idem., 'The Consociational Model and Its Dangers', European Journal for Political Research, Vol. 3 (1975), pp. 393–412; Daalder, 'Consociational Democracy Theme'; S. Halpern, 'The Disorderly Universe of Consociational Democracy', West European Politics, Vol. 10, No. 2 (1987), pp. 181–97; R. A. Kieve, 'Pillars on Sand. A Marxist Critique of Consociational Democracy in the Netherlands', Comparative Politics, Vol. 13, No. 3 (1981), pp. 313–27; I. Lustick, 'Stability in Deeply Divided Societies: Consociationalism versus Control', World Politics, Vol. 31 (1979), pp. 325–44; A. Pappalardo, 'The Conditions for Consociational Democracy: a Logical and Empirical Critique', European Journal of Political Research, Vol. 9 (1981), pp. 365–90; J. Steiner, 'The Consociational Theory and Beyond', Comparative Politics, Vol. 13, No. 2 (1981), pp. 339–54.

Useful overviews of the issues are contained on the one hand in M. P. C. van Schendelen, 'Consociational Democracy: The Views of Arend Lijphart and Collected Criticisms', Political Science Reviewer, Vol. 14 (1985), pp. 143–83 (see also Acta Politica, Vol. 19 (1984), pp. 19–55), and on the other hand in Lijphart's Power-Sharing in South Africa (Berkeley, CA: Univ. of California Inst. of Int'l Studies, 1985) esp. pp. 83–117, where he responds to his critics.
30. These arguments are advanced in, e.g., Lijphart 'Consociational Democracy' and Lehmbruch, Proporzdemokratie respectively. For very useful discussion of the early literature's various approaches, see K. D. McRae, 'Introduction' in K. D. McRae (ed.), Consociational Democracy, pp. 1–27.
31. See, e.g., K. Blecha, R. Gmoser and H. Kienzl, Der durchleuchtete Wähler (Vienna: Europa Verlag, 1964); F. C. Engelmann and M. A. Schwarz, 'Partisan Stability and the Continuity of a Segmented Society: The Austrian Case', American Journal of Sociology, Vol. 79, No. 4 (1974), pp. 948–66; Lorwin, 'Segmented Pluralism'; G. B.

Powell, *Social Fragmentation and Political Hostility: An Austrian Case Study* (Stanford UP, 1970).
32. See, e.g., Pulzer, 'Legitimizing Role of Political Parties'; P. Pulzer, 'Austria', in S. Henig and J. Pinder (eds.), *European Political Parties* (London: Allen & Unwin, 1969), pp. 282–319; J. J. Houska, *Influencing Mass Political Behaviour. Elites and Political Subcultures in the Netherlands and Austria* (Berkeley, CA: Univ. of California Inst. of Int'l Studies, 1985); R. P. Stiefbold, 'Segmented Pluralism and Consociational Democracy in Austria', in M. O. Heisler (ed.), *Politics in Europe. Structures and Processes in Some Postindustrial Democracies* (NY: David McKay, 1974), pp. 117–77; idem, 'Elites and Elections in a Fragmented Political System', *Sozialwissenschaftliches Jahrbuch für Politik*, Vol. 4 (1975), pp. 119–228.
33. For contemporaneous descriptions of its late 1950s operation, see, e.g., H. P. Secher, 'Coalition Government: The Case of the Second Austrian Republic', *American Political Science Review*, Vol. 52, No. 3 (1958), pp. 791–808; and idem, 'Representative Democracy or "Chamber State": The Ambiguous Role of Interest Groups in Austrian Politics', *Western Political Quarterly*, Vol. 13 (1960), pp. 890–909. On corporatism see P. Gerlich, E. Grande and W. C. Müller (eds.), *Sozialpartnerschaft in der Krise. Leistungen und Grenzen des Neokorporatismus in Österreich* (Vienna: Böhlau, 1985).
34. See, e.g., W. Rudzio, 'Entscheidungszentrum Koalitionsausschuss – zur Realverfassung Österreichs unter der grossen Koalition', *Politische Vierteljahresschrift*, Vol. 12 (1971), pp. 87–118 and R. Preston, 'Austrian Parliamentary Democracy', *Parliamentary Affairs*, Vol. 10, No. 3 (1957), pp. 344–52.
35. See, e.g., E. Streissler, 'Die Fiktion des Austro-Keynesianismus. Zum real existierenden "Keynesianismus" im Schrifttum von Hans Seidel', *Wirtschaftspolitische Blätter*, Vol. 34, No. 5–6 (1987), pp. 714–25; and S. W. Arndt (ed.), *The Political Economy of Austria* (Washington, DC: American Enterprise Inst., 1982).
36. See, e.g., Lehmbruch, 'Consociational Democracy in the International System'; P. J. Katzenstein, *Corporatism and Change: Austria, Switzerland and the Politics of Industry* (Ithaca, NY: Cornell UP, 1984) and Lijphart, *Democracy in Plural Societies*, pp. 65–7.
37. From 1945 to 1947 there was in fact an all-party government. The withdrawal of the KPÖ in 1947 meant that henceforth the grand coalition comprised the two big parties: the ÖVP and the SPÖ.
38. Cf. respectively Lijphart, *Democracy in Plural Societies*, pp. 1f, 104f, and K. Steiner, *Politics in Austria* (Boston: Little, Brown & Co., 1972), pp. 416–24).
39. See, e.g., A. Pelinka 'Postklassischer Parlamentarismus und Sozialpartnerschaft', *Österreichische Zeitschrift für Politikwissenschaft*, Vol. 3 (1974), pp. 333–45 and P. Gerlich, 'Politisches System und Integration', in E. Bodzenta (ed.), *Die österreichische Gesellschaft* (Vienna: Springer, 1972), pp. 176–202.

The Decline of 'Lager Mentality' and the New Model of Electoral Competition in Austria

FRITZ PLASSER, PETER A. ULRAM AND ALFRED GRAUSGRUBER

The Austrian political system has often been regarded as a somewhat 'deviant case' among the family of Western European democracies because it was characterised by a very high degree of political stability. That perception was derived in large measure from looking at the Austrian *Lager*, which provided the socio-political underpinning of a highly stable party system. In recent years, however, a definite shift has taken place from what might be called the traditional perspective in the study of Austrian politics to a concentration of academic interest on problems of political change, electoral dealignment, etc. This new perspective is partly a response to fundamental changes within the attitudinal and electoral landscape and thus also in the party system, and partly a result of the rethinking of traditional political science concepts in the fields of party and electoral research.

Our main aim in this article is to describe and analyse the factors leading to the erosion of the traditional pattern of Austrian electoral behaviour and to discuss the consequences for future patterns of party competition. We shall examine long-term trends in the development of attitudes toward political parties and in voting behaviour in order to describe the changes in voter-party relationships over the last four decades. A detailed analysis of the 1990 general elections will facilitate the identification of different groups of voters and thus permit an empirically based perspective on the new structure of electoral competition in Austria.

THE TRADITIONAL AUSTRIAN CLEAVAGE STRUCTURE – A BRIEF HISTORY

The party system of post-1945 Austria was widely regarded as built around social cleavages with origins that can be traced back at least to the end of the nineteenth century.[1] Since its reduction in 1918 from a multi-national empire to a small, almost exclusively German-speaking state, Austria has been characterised by a high degree of ethnic homogeneity, so that at the restoration of democratic government in 1945 there were three main politically salient cleavages. These were, first, that between industrial labour on one hand and farming and enterprise on the other. The first of these groups was represented by the Socialist Party of Austria (SPÖ), while the second was represented by both the Christian-Democratic Austrian People's Party (ÖVP), and the Freedom Party of Austria (FPÖ). The second cleavage revolved around the antagonism between secular and agnostic orientations on one hand and Catholic-integrationalist orientations on the other. Here the line of conflict left the SPÖ and FPÖ together on the side of the former, whilst the ÖVP represented the latter group. Finally, the country's cleavage structure was characterised by a conflict between German and Austrian nationalism, with the ÖVP and SPÖ representing Austrian nationalism and the FPÖ being more committed to the notion of Austria having a German national identity.

FIGURE 1
THE TRADITIONAL AUSTRIAN PARTY SPACE

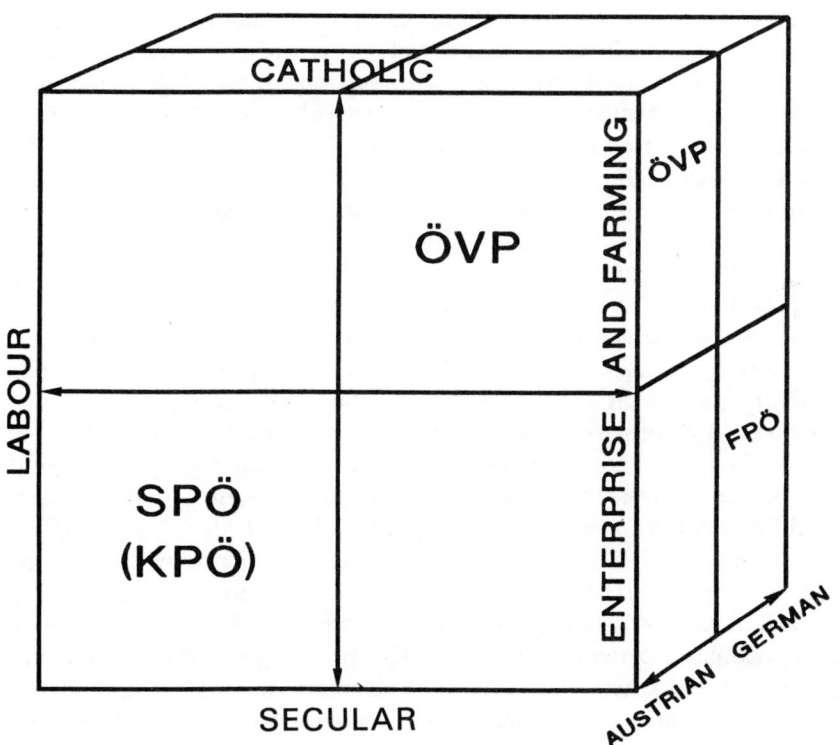

These cleavages were important factors differentiating the two main subcultures or *Lager*,² which in turn provided the social and cultural foundations for the two dominant post-war parties, the ÖVP and SPÖ. The Catholic-conservative *Lager* thus comprised farming and enterprise interests as well as other groups of the population with Catholic orientations. The socialist *Lager* encompassed industrial workers and voters with secular orientations.

These *Lager* not only provided their members with relatively uniform ideological attitudes and a feeling of 'political belonging', but also integrated them into larger networks of educational, cultural and occupational organisations, within the confines of which they could live their lives from womb to tomb. Within the *Lager*, there was a strong 'in-group' feeling, while the relationship to the outside world, was dominated by mutual animosity and distrust, especially as between lower- and middle-rank functionaries of the opposing parties. Accordingly, Austrian politics exhibited the classic signs of a fragmented or 'pillarised' political culture.³

This *Lager* encapsulation manifested itself in strong ties between the political parties and their respective electorates. As Table 1 indicates, in the 1950s more than eight out of ten voters for each of the leading parties were characterised by effective and willing partisanship, and about three out of ten were party members. In addition, nearly every employed person was a member of an interest group,⁴ which itself was closely related to and/or controlled by the parties.

In contrast to the encapsulated orientations of party adherents at the mass level and especially amongst the tens of thousands of lower and middle-rank functionaries, the political leadership groups showed significantly different patterns of behaviour. Partly as a result of the need to address overarching interests, contacts between the *Lager* elites did exist and their co-operation gradually contributed to the development of a feeling of qualified mutual trust that stood in sharp contrast to the style of their interwar interaction. The elite groups' prevailing political style became one of pragmatic bargaining and accommodation.⁵

This 'historical compromise' between once hostile elite groups found its political expression in the ÖVP-SPÖ 'grand' coalition governments until 1966 and in the division of the public administration system (at the communal, *Land* and national level), the educational system and the vast state-owned industrial sector into two separate spheres of influence and interest. This so-called *Proporz* system was based on dividing the spoils proportionately between the parties. The awarding of jobs, housing and government contracts was undertaken according to party affiliation and served to strengthen party loyalty and *Lager* culture. In fact, the personal living conditions of most of the population were strongly influenced by

TABLE 1

INDICATORS OF LAGER COHESION (1954–61)

	SPÖ	ÖVP	Total electorate
Party adherents living in labour households (for SPÖ respondents) and those living in self-employed, small trade, or farming households (for ÖVP respondents)	75	57	–
Party adherents going to church every Sunday	15	67	–
Party adherents in a party-politically extensively consonant network	86	78	–
Party adherents with affective party identification	89	85	73
Party adherents with conative party identification (subjectively bound traditional voters)	81	87	–
Party members			ca. 25
Readers of party newspapers	–	–	ca. 35

Source: Summaries of representative surveys of political indicators by Fessel and GfK between 1954 and 1961 (henceforth referred to as 'Political Indicators').

Note: Except where otherwise stated, all tables are based on representative surveys. The average sample size is N = 1,000–2,000.

the party, if not dependent on it. Work colleagues and neighbours belonged to the same party. The spoils system in the public sphere (and not only there) also helped create channels of advancement even for members of the lower social classes (e.g., farmers and workers). Together with the high organisational density of the parties and interest groups, this led to a high level of political participation.[6]

Political accommodation in government and administration was significantly buttressed by the system of social and economic corporatism (*Sozialpartnerschaft*), in which the economic interest associations took part in policy-making in the fields of economics, welfare politics and industrial relations. It was thus possible to integrate almost all relevant groups into the political system while, in turn, the political and especially the party system enjoyed high levels of stability and public support – from stable voting patterns to the almost complete absence of social unrest.[7]

THE EROSION OF THE *LAGER*'S STRUCTURAL AND CULTURAL FOUNDATIONS

Within the last three decades, Austrian society has undergone radical changes that have transformed a once partially 'pre-modern' society into a mature industrial and service society. While the agrarian sector, which in 1951 still accounted for every third employed person decreased rapidly, the tertiary sector grew constantly, employing more than half of the work-force by 1981 (see Table 2). A similar shift took place in the occupational structure, with a sharp decrease in the number of independent farmers, self-employed persons and professionals (the old middle classes), a stabilisation and later a decrease in the number of blue-collar workers and a concurrent increase of a new, white-collar middle class (see Table 3).

TABLE 2
EMPLOYED PERSONS ACCORDING TO ECONOMIC SECTOR (1951–81)

% of employed population working in	1951	1961	1971	1981	Change 1951–81
agriculture and forestry	31.6	23.0	15.0	8.5	−24.1
mining, industry and trade	37.6	41.4	42.0	41.0	+3.4
services	29.8	35.6	42.8	50.5	+20.7

Source: *Österreichisches Statistisches Zentralamt*, Census surveys (1951–81).

TABLE 3
OCCUPATIONAL STATUS OF LABOUR FORCE (1951–81)

% of employed population working as	1951	1961	1971	1981	Change 1951–81
self-employed	35	29	22	14	−21
blue-collar	45	44	43	44	−1
white-collar	20	27	35	42	+22

Source: *Österreichisches Statistisches Zentralamt*, Census surveys (1951–81).

These socio-structural changes had a strong effect on the *Lager* system, since the main social bases of the *Lager* (namely, farmers, old urban middle classes, and industrial blue-collar workers) were shrinking in absolute numbers, as well as in relative importance. The social structure of the major Austrian parties' vote today thus differs fundamentally from that of the historical *Lager* parties' 1950s electoral support: the social core groups which once formed the vast majority of the parties' electorates

TABLE 4

DECREASE IN THE TRADITIONAL CORE VOTER GROUPS OF THE MAJOR AUSTRIAN PARTIES (1961–90)

Declared party supporters (% of population)	SPÖ core section	ÖVP core section
1961	75	57
1969	68	48
1978	60	36
1990	51	35
Change 1961–90	−24	−22

Source: Fessel and GfK, Political Indicators (1961–90)
Note: SPÖ core section = SPÖ supporters living in working-class households;
ÖVP core section = ÖVP supporters living in self-employed, small trade, or farming households.

have become only a small majority (SPÖ) or have been reduced to a minority position (ÖVP) (see Table 4).

Changes in the socio-cultural system were of similar importance. In the last 30 years Austrian society has become predominantly secular. Even within the ÖVP's electorate, which always constituted the stronghold of religious attachment, there has been a loosening of church ties. Church attendance has decreased and the ÖVP has begun to break away from its traditional religious milieu. Although the Catholic milieu is still basically intact in rural regions, in urban centres the networks are breaking down and therefore losing their distinctiveness. Accordingly, the socio-political relevance of Catholicism is diminishing (see Table 5).

TABLE 5

SECULARISATION OF THE AUSTRIAN ELECTORATE (1955–90)

% of declared party supporters who go to church every Sunday, or did so the previous Sunday	1955	1972	1985	1990	Change 1955–90
ÖVP supporters	67	55	45	47	−20
SPÖ supporters	15	14	14	12	−3

Source: Fessel and GfK, Political Indicators (1955–90)

The third salient post-war political cleavage that we have identified is that between German and Austrian nationalism. This too has lost its divisive impact since the concept of an autonomous Austrian nation has for some time now been accepted by the vast majority of the country's citizens.[8]

While in 1956 only half of the population agreed that an Austrian national identity existed, in 1970 this opinion was shared by nearly three quarters of respondents and by more than 90 per cent in 1990 (see Table 6). The portion is somewhat smaller among FPÖ adherents but even their pan-Germanic sentiments are the province of an ever-diminishing minority (13 per cent in 1990).

TABLE 6
AUSTRIAN NATIONAL CONSCIOUSNESS (1956–90)

% agreeing that	1956	1964	1970	1980	1990	Change 1964–90
Austria is a nation		47	66	67	74	+27
Austria is beginning to feel like a nation	49	23	16	19	20	−3
Austria is not a nation	47	15	8	11	5	−10
No answer	4	14	10	3	1	−13

Source: Fessel and GfK, Political Indicators (1956–90)

Traditional milieus and their associated encapsulated subcultures have also been decisively undermined by other changes, the role of which has perhaps been less visible, however. Examples of such changes include the transformation of rural into suburban areas and of agricultural communities into tourist centres, as well as the increase in the proportion of those who enter higher education, higher social and geographic mobility and the spread of new life styles. In the early 1970s, for example, some 80 per cent of both SPÖ and ÖVP adherents still lived in a network of social contacts and personal relationships that were party-politically consonant. Two decades later this holds true for only half the voters of the two main parties. Increasing numbers of party adherents are now exposed to dissonant, or ambivalent political signals from their personal social environment (see Table 7).

Finally, the parties' formal networks of political information and communication have virtually dissolved. Whilst at the beginning of the 1960s about one third of the adult population read a party-owned newspaper, this once powerful means of communication is now a relic of the past. At the same time, television has not only established itself as the primary source of political information, but has it also come to be seen as the most trustworthy (see Table 8).[9]

TABLE 7
PARTY-POLITICAL CONSONANCE OF SOCIAL NETWORKS (1972–90)

	1972	1984	1990	Change 1972–90
% of SPÖ adherents				
in a largely consonant network	86	60	57	−29
in a largely dissonant network	4	7	17	+13
in a neutral, or unspecific network	10	33	23	+13
	100	100	100	
% of ÖVP adherents				
in a largely consonant network	78	60	48	−30
in a largely dissonant network	10	10	17	+7
in a neutral, or unspecific network	12	30	34	+22
	100	100	100	

Source: Fessel and GfK, Political Indicators (1972–90)

TABLE 8
CHANGES IN THE MEDIA SOURCES OF POLITICAL INFORMATION (1960s–90s)

Average % of population	Early 1960s	Early 1970s	Mid-1980s–90s	Change 1960s–90s
who read party newspapers	c. 35	c. 15	7	−28
who read independent newspapers	c. 45	c. 70	c. 85	+40
for whom TV was the primary source	11	–	67	+56

Source: Fessel and GfK, Media Surveys (1961–91)

ELECTORAL DEALIGNMENT

Although the erosion of the subcultural *Lager* identities undermined the established ties between the political parties and their electorate, it was a long time before the parties felt seriously affected. The first signs of a dealignment process became visible in political attitudes rather than political behaviour. One indicator of dealignment can be seen in the blurring of ideological orientations. The traditional *Lager* mentalities involved a relatively firm standpoint to the right or the left of the political spectrum and, even in the 1970s, nearly half of the electorate still claimed a clear position. Thereafter, however, voters at first showed an increasing tendency to identify themselves as in the middle, and later to avoid identification in terms of right and left all together (see Table 9).

TABLE 9
SELF-PLACEMENT OF LEFT OR RIGHT (1976–89)

Self-placement of the population and of party adherents in %	1976	1980	1985	1989	Change 1976–89
left or right	45	31	31	27	−18
centre	40	52	49	44	+4
no self-placement	15	17	21	28	+13
SPÖ-adherents defining themselves as 'left'	48	–	27	23	−15
ÖVP-adherents defining themselves as 'right'	48	–	41	41	−7

Source: Fessel and GfK, Political Indicators (1976–89)
Note: Based on a five-point scale (from 1 = very left to 5 = very right)

A similar development took place with the perceived ideological locations of the two main parties. Whereas the SPÖ and ÖVP were once clear reference-points for 'left' and 'right', they began to lose their ideological profile especially in the eyes of their respective party adherents.[10] As ideological orientations blurred, ideology became increasingly less important as a determinant of voting behaviour. In the 1970s most people believed that certain ideological standpoints were compatible only with voting for a particular party and the relationship was seen as a stable one. By the 1980s only a minority believed in a necessary accordance of the two factors (see Table 10).

TABLE 10
IDEOLOGY AS A DETERMINANT OF VOTING BEHAVIOUR (1972–90)

% of the population agreeing with the statement:	1972	1973	1984	1990
'if you have a particular ideology, there is only one party you can vote for and you must stay with it'.	59	60	37	37

Source: Fessel and GfK, Political Indicators (1972–90)

The first major shake-up in Austrian voting behaviour took place in the early 1970s.[11] The number of voters with average or weak party identification suffered a noticeable decline and there was a concomitant rise in the proportion of non-identifiers. However, the 'hard core' group with the strongest party identification remained more or less stable for another decade. This gave the parties, and especially the SPÖ, the possibility of forming new voter coalitions without the risk of losing their traditional strongholds (see Table 11).[12] The result of this shift in the pattern of distribution of party identification can be described as a partisan dealignment with concurrent electoral stability. In other words, changes in the affective foundations of Austrian voting behaviour were hidden by continuing stability at the macro level.

TABLE 11

PARTY IDENTIFICATION IN AUSTRIA (1954–90)

	% of the electorate with			
	total party identification	strong party identification	moderate, or weak party identification	no identification, or no opinion
1954	73	–	–	27
1957	71	–	–	29
1969	75	(31)	(44)	25
1974	65	–	–	35
1976	63	(31)	(32)	37
1984	61	(30)	(31)	39
1985	60	21	39	40
1986	60	23	37	40
1987	58	23	35	42
1989	51	15	36	49
1990	49	19	30	51

Source: Fessel and GfK, Political Indicators (1954–90)
Note: ( ) date not directly comparably due to modified scaling

In the 1980s, however, the dealignment process also reached the major parties' core groups, resulting in a major shake-up of voting behaviour and thus also of the party system. Between 1984 and 1990 party identification decreased by the same amount as it had during the three decades between 1954 and 1984. In 1990 only about one half of the Austrian electorate claimed some kind of party identification and strong identifiers accounted for a mere fifth of the adult population. The respective percentages are somewhat higher among SPÖ and ÖVP voters than is the case with minor parties' electorates, but even the two large parties can no longer count on a body of loyal party adherents big enough to shield them from the consequences of electoral desertion on the part of their fringe voters.

One outcome of de-identification with political parties can be seen in the decline of party membership. Austria's parties traditionally had a

TABLE 12

THE DECLINE OF PARTY IDENTIFICATION BY DEMOGRAPHIC GROUP (1954–90)

Party identification as % of relevant group	1954	1984	1990	Change 1954–84	Change 1984–90	Change 1954–90
Farmers	81	75	57	−6	−18	−24
Self-employed and professionals	63	48	42	−15	−6	−21
Blue-collar workers	78	65	45	−13	−20	−33
White-collar workers	69	57	45	−12	−12	−24
Overall	73	61	49	−12	−12	−24

Source: Fessel and GfK, Political Indicators (1954–90)

sound reputation for vast and even excessive organisational density, which they maintained in spite of considerable socio-structural change, a significant decline in their traditional voter segments, religious and political secularisation and a radical change in the political communication process. This extraordinary organisational capacity lasted until the late 1980s when the two major parties suddenly lost some 200,000 members within a few years (see Table 13).[13]

TABLE 13

DECLINE IN PARTY MEMBERSHIP (1969–89)

	1969	1979	1989	Change 1969–89
% of the adult population declaring themselves to be members of a political party	24	22	18	−6

Source: Fessel and GfK, Political Indicators (1969–89)

SIGNS OF CHANGE

At the time when political cleavages were frozen or petrified, subcultural identities and affective party ties were strong and when the political-organisational penetration of society was high it is not surprising that at least as far as the two major parties were concerned, it was possible to rely upon a stable electorate. Indeed during the 1950s the vast majority of Austrians not only always voted for the same party, but followed the principle of 'my party right or wrong'. In 1964 the pioneering volume on Austrian electoral behaviour stated that:

The stability of Austria's electoral outcomes is not the result of an accidental balance of numerous fluctuations, but the result of a real stability of 85 to 90 per cent of the Austrian voters. The truly fluctuating strata might amount to some 5 to 10 per cent of the electorate.[14]

Electoral change was restricted either to a small group of politically uninformed and uninterested people whom Kienzl termed 'political quicksand', or to new voters who were still not fully integrated into the *Lager*.[15] Even as recently as the 1970s, more than half of the adult population showed a fundamentally negative attitude toward shifting electoral allegiance.

The end of this 'golden age' for the traditional parties was, however, not only a consequence of political secularisation and the thawing of 'frozen' political cleavages. It also reflected growing criticism of and disappointment with the existing parties.[16] With the beginning of the 1980s there were already clear signals of anger and discontent *vis-à-vis* the traditional parties and a growing call for new political actors (see Table 14).

TABLE 14
PARTY WEARINESS AND THE SEARCH FOR POLITICAL ALTERNATIVES (1956–85)

% of the population who	1956	1976	1981	1985
have recently been angry about political parties	–	–	43	68
would like to see new parties in the political arena	12	10	17	47

Source: Fessel and GfK, Political Indicators (1956–85)

The idea of changing voting behaviour from one election to another is no longer as emphatically rejected, but is becoming acceptable to the majority of the population (see Table 15). Consequently, subjectively stable voter-party relationships (conative partisanship) are decreasing at an ever faster pace (see Table 16). This holds true not only for the electorate as a whole, but also applies to voters for the two major parties. In 1954 eight out of ten persons who expressed a preference for the SPÖ or the ÖVP consistently voted for that party. Nowadays, however, less than half of those expressing such a preference can be deemed to constitute reliable voters.

TABLE 15

DECLINE OF SUBJECTIVE PARTY TIES (1969–90)

% of the population who	1969	1972	1974	1976	1980	1990	Change 1972–90
Agree that: 'I have decided on a party and vote for it even if I am not in agreement with what it does, or plans to do.'	65	61	–	56	47	34	–34
Reject the proposition: 'There are more people today than before who don't always vote for the same party, but sometimes vote for one and sometimes for another.'	–	59	56	–	39	35	–24

Source: Fessel and GfK, Political Indicators (1969–90)

TABLE 16

CONATIVE PARTISANSHIP OF THE MAJOR AUSTRIAN PARTIES (1954–90)

% of party adherents with conotative party ties	1954	1990	Change 1954–90
SPÖ adherents	81	43	–38
ÖVP adherents	82	47	–35

Source: Fessel and GfK, Political Indicators (1954–90)

TRENDS IN AUSTRIAN VOTING BEHAVIOUR

Compared to most Western European democracies, Austrian voting behaviour[17] has until recently been characterised by above average turnout, a strong concentration of votes on the two major parties and low volatility. Until 1990 turnout at national elections was always above 90 per cent. On a long-term average, both major parties, the SPÖ and ÖVP, have together been able to mobilise the support of about 80 per cent of the electorate.

Until the late 1970s, volatility was unusually low by international standards.[18] Most voters were strongly tied to a political party by virtue of belonging to a certain occupational group and by traditional alignments to church, or trade union. Family tradition, emotional loyalties and a

TABLE 17

CONCENTRATION IN THE AUSTRIAN PARTY SYSTEM (1953–90)

	SPÖ+ÖVP	Others and invalid votes	Turnout	Non-Voters	Total net Volatility
1953	78.6	17.2	95.8	4.2	3.6
1956	83.9	12.1	96.0	4.1	5.8
1959	82.7	11.5	94.2	5.8	3.0
1962	82.9	10.9	93.8	6.2	1.7
1966	84.3	9.5	93.8	6.2	4.8
1970	84.7	7.1	91.8	8.2	6.9
1971	85.2	7.2	92.4	7.6	2.0
1975	85.9	7.0	92.9	7.1	0.5
1979	84.7	7.5	92.2	7.8	1.3
1983	83.0	9.6	92.6	7.4	4.6
1986	75.0	15.5	90.5	9.5	6.1
1990	62.6	23.6	86.1	13.9	9.9

Note: Figures represent percentage of electorate

strong *Lager* mentality in certain groups of the electorate prevented people from voting for a different party. Consequently, although social change was causing a continuous decline in both traditional parties' core occupational and attitudional groups, it was still possible for both the SPÖ and ÖVP to stabilise their voter potential.

This hyperstability in Austrian voting behaviour lasted up until the general election of 1970, when strong voter movements produced a reversal of the majority and the SPÖ for the first time gained a majority both of votes and of parliamentary seats. Largely because of the personal charisma of Chancellor Bruno Kreisky, the SPÖ became the dominant force within the Austrian party system throughout the 1970s, gaining an absolute majority of votes and seats in three consecutive general elections. The SPÖ was able to increase its vote to above 50 per cent by virtue of an electoral coalition comprising both traditional working class voters, as well as reform-orientated voters from amongst the new middle-classes. Meanwhile, the ÖVP maintained a level of support at between 42 and 43 per cent.

The SPÖ's hegemonic position within the Austrian party system ended with the general election of 1983. As a consequence of the electoral participation of two new Green parties and of the signs of wear on the SPÖ which had been in government for 13 years, the SPÖ failed to get an absolute majority and had to form a coalition government with the FPÖ.[19] Nevertheless, despite the higher mobility of the electorate and the candidacy of the Green parties which largely attracted younger, more educated, urban voters, the 1983 general election still reflected a high degree of continuity and stability. With a turnout rate of almost 93 per cent, Austria was again among those Western European democracies with the highest degrees of electoral participation. Despite the SPÖ's heavy losses, the two major parties combined were still able to gain 83 per cent of the electorate, and although the rate of party-shifters was, at 10 per cent, above average for Austrian standards, voter mobility compared to other Western European democracies was still astonishingly low. About 90 per cent of voters had already definitively decided to vote for a particular party long before the election campaign began. Party identification had definitely weakened compared to the previous decade and traditional electoral motivations had increasingly been superseded by questions of issue and candidate, but traditional patterns of voting behaviour could still be observed.

TABLE 18
TRENDS IN AUSTRIAN VOTING BEHAVIOUR (1979–90)

% of total electorate of parliamentary elections	1979	1983	1986	1990	Change 1979–90
Voter turnout	92.2	92.6	90.5	86.1	−6.1
Non-voters	7.8	7.4	9.5	13.9	+6.1
SPÖ + ÖVP voters	85	83	75	62.6	−22.4
Other parties	7.5	9.6	15.5	21.0	+13.5
Floating voters[1]	7	10	16	17	+10
Late deciders[2]	9	8	16	14	+5
Total volatility	1.3	4.6	6.1	9.9	+8.6

Source: Fessel and GfK, Post-Election Surveys 1979 and 1983 and Exit Polls 1986 and 1990
Notes: 1) Percentage of declared party-shifters on representative post-election survey, or exit poll
2) Percentage of those voters who made a definitive voting decision just before election day

The dealignment process which had been visible since the 1970s under the surface of voter stability found its first clear expression at the 1986 general election. As a result of the sharp increase in votes for the FPÖ (which under its new leader Jörg Haider had presented itself during the election campaign as a populist protest party) and due to the candidacy of a united Green party, the two traditional parties together were only able to poll 75 per cent. At the same time, the percentage of floating voters and late deciders rose to 16 per cent. Analyses of voting behaviour at the 1986 election pointed to profound changes from the well-known stability characteristic of the 1960s and 1970s:

- Socio-structural characteristics, such as belonging to a certain occupational group, now only explained a small proportion of voting behaviour.
- Issues and candidates had a much stronger influence upon individuals' voting decisions.
- There was a large increase in the percentage of protest voters or 'negative voters' who, being sceptical towards all political parties, decided to choose the 'lesser evil'.
- 1986 also manifested a new, generation-specific difference in voting behaviour, as those who turned away from the two main parties were primarily from the younger generation of voters. Thus it appeared that the older generation tended to support the traditional 'two-party system' of SPÖ and ÖVP, while electoral behaviour of the younger, better qualified voters suggested support for a competitive multi-party system.

The dissolution of encapsulated subcultural loyalties and identities has also resulted in a weakening of traditional voter alignments in Austria. Both the degree and the intensity of party identification have declined strongly during the 1980s. Between 1976 and 1988, party identification in the EC countries dropped by 11 per cent. More than 40 per cent of the electorate in the EC have no close ties to a political party; among younger voters, the percentage lies far above the average.[20] During the same period, however, party identification in Austria fell by 14 per cent. In 1990 only 49 per cent of Austrian voters identified with a particular political party. Twenty years ago it was 75 per cent. The degree and intensity of party identification among Austrian voters now corresponds to the Swiss level. In line with the international trend, the decline of party ties is strongest among the younger generation of Austrian voters, implying a progressive weakening of affective party ties. As of the early 1990s, about 60 per cent of voters under 30 years of age do not have any specific political attachments. The erosion of traditional party ties and affective party loyalties have resulted in an increase in volatility. Voter movements between political parties are increasing, the percentage of mobile and shifting voters (floating voters, wavering voters) is rising as is the total rate of volatility.[21]

The results of the 1990 general election clearly showed the profound changes taking place in Austrian electoral behaviour.[22] The process of deconcentration, visible since the end of the 1970s, accelerated. The traditional parties' reduced capacity for integration, as expressed by the decline of affective party ties, finally found its expression in actual voting behaviour, with the SPÖ and ÖVP together receiving only 62 per cent of

TABLE 19

CONSISTENCY IN AUSTRIAN VOTING BEHAVIOUR (1972–89)

% of eligible voters who have	1972	1979	1989	Change 1972–89
always voted for the same party	76	65	58	−18
sometimes voted for a different party	8	16	26	+18
voted only once	2	2	2	no change
never voted	13	16	14	+1

Source: Fessel and GfK, Representative Surveys (1972 and 1979) and Fessel-IFES, Politische Kultur in Österreich (1989)

the potential vote (i.e., of eligible voters, rather than of actual voters). However, not only has the traditional voting pattern of the Austrian electorate disintegrated, voting turnout has markedly declined. With about 14 per cent of non-voters, Austria still has a much lower rate of abstention than most other Western European democracies. However, the decline of voter participation remains an indicator of the reduced impact of social norms on traditional participation rituals in Austria.

To summarise, at the start of the 1990s, a growing percentage of the Austrian electorate is first unencumbered in its choice of which political party to support by any specific ties or sense of loyalty. Second, it is increasingly more mobile and willing to change its voting behaviour. Third, in deciding how to cast its vote, it is increasingly motivated by current issues and by the images of the top candidates. These images are of course formed by the mass media and have for many voters come to replace the traditional party images.

The dealignment of voting behaviour, the erosion of subcultural loyalties, and the transition to a multidimensional, individualised electorate have contributed significantly to increasing the major parties' vulnerability. They can no longer treat elections as an exercise in mobilising a reliable *Lager* vote. To avoid their further decline and a concomitant fundamental restructuring of the party system, the parties will have to pay much greater attention to their media image, to the electorate's perception of their competence and to their strategic decisions. Time will tell whether the parties prove to be able to compensate for their electoral vulnerability by means of appropriate strategies and organisational reform.

The trend to an even stronger personalisation of the political process seems to be irreversible. The strategic importance of an attractive top candidate, of a strong media performance and of professional image-building were clearly vital in the outcome of the 1990 general election.

They will decisively influence not only future campaigns but also candidate recruitment, the self-presentation of political institutions and the perception of politics among the population. The 'chancellor election' of 1990 will also affect other levels of political competition and ensure that *Land* and local elections also become further personalised.

The progressive tendency towards the individualisation of Austrian voting behaviour seem to be largely irreversible too. The general election of 1990 represents a further, but not a final step in the dealignment process. Austrian voters have become more mobile. Traditional motives (especially party ties and social-cultural background) play a less decisive role in the voting decision, even if the voter stays with the same party. On the other side of the coin, the importance of leading political personalities (in particular, their television image), is increasing, as is the role of political emotions, moods and issues. These factors are especially relevant among those groups which make their voting decisions relatively late, or are ready in principle to shift from one party to another. This development represents a new type of challenge for all political parties. Instead of a continuous programmatic and pragmatic adjustment to a slowly changing electorate, the parties now require fast and effective reactions.

In spite of the Austrian electorate's increasing mobility, some traditional determinants of voting behaviour do still exist, albeit in a weaker form. As shown in Table 20, a strong affiliation with the church is still a factor favouring the ÖVP: almost two thirds (61 per cent) of regular Catholic church attendants vote for this party, whereas only 22 per cent vote for the SPÖ and 10 per cent for the FPÖ. On the other hand, almost every second non-church-orientated Catholic (49 per cent) votes for the SPÖ and only one quarter of this group votes for the ÖVP. Among Austrians who claim no religious affiliation, one half votes for the SPÖ, one quarter for the FPÖ, one tenth for the Green Party, but only 9 per cent for the ÖVP.

Trade union membership also remains a reasonably good predictor of voting behaviour. Some 62 per cent of union members vote for the SPÖ, 19 per cent for the ÖVP, and 11 per cent for the FPÖ. Among non-union members, about one third each votes for the ÖVP (36 per cent) and SPÖ (33 per cent); 18 per cent vote for the FPÖ. More than half of all blue-collar workers vote socialist, with only one-fifth each voting for the ÖVP and the FPÖ. The Green groupings are also only weakly represented in this constituency. Among white-collar workers, the picture is much more diffuse: some 38 per cent vote SPÖ while one half vote for other parties (27 per cent ÖVP, 16 per cent FPÖ, 7 per cent Green Alternative Party).

The occupational environment, once an essential factor in maintaining the *Lager* culture, is of even greater relevance than the actual professional activity: two-thirds (65 per cent) of voters coming from households headed by self-employed persons or farmers vote ÖVP, 15 per cent FPÖ, and only 10 per cent SPÖ. On the other hand, 57 per cent of voters who come from a blue-collar milieu vote Socialist, 20 per cent ÖVP, and 17 per cent FPÖ.

TABLE 20
TRADITIONAL DETERMINANTS OF AUSTRIAN VOTING BEHAVIOUR (1990)

in %	SPÖ	ÖVP	FPÖ	Greens[1]
Religious Voting				
– regular church attenders (Catholics)	22	61	10	2
– distant from church (passive Catholics)	49	24	17	4
Class Voting				
– blue-collar workers	52	21	21	2
– white-collar workers	35	27	16	7
Union voting				
– union member	62	19	11	3
– not a union member	33	36	18	5
Lager Culture				
– voters living in blue-collar households	57	20	17	1
– voters living in self-employed, or farming households	10	65	15	4

Source: Fessel and GfK, Exit Poll, (N = 2,200 voters leaving the voting booth)
Note 1. The figures for the Greens constitute an aggregate of the respondents who voted for any 'green', or 'alternative' party.

Compared to the late 1960s, class voting in Austria has declined significantly.[23] In 1969 the Alford Index of class voting still registered 26 points; in 1990, it was only 14. The respective scores on the Lijphart Index of Religious Voting (1969: 30 points, 1990: 27 points) are, however, comparatively stable.

DETERMINANTS OF THE 1990 VOTING DECISION

Since the general election of 1990 reflects significant changes in Austrian electoral behaviour, its results deserve a closer examination.[24] Table 21 is based upon a multi-variate analysis of the 1990 data and shows the particular importance of the following motivations: first, candidate-orientated motives; second, protest motives and third, traditional socio-structural background characteristics. Of these three factors, candidate-orientated motives and protest motives were the strongest determinants, while the influence of traditional socio-structural characteristics such as age, occupation and level of education was definitely less significant. Issue-orientated motives were relatively much less important than those related to the candidates and to protest.

The data permit one to establish a picture of the primary motivations of those voting for each party. Thus the dominant motive for those casting their vote for the SPÖ was its top candidate, namely, the incumbent chancellor: Franz Vranitzky. This was followed by specific policy issues and by the SPÖ's perceived overall problem-solving competence, though these were significantly less important. A certain influence, albeit only weakly reflected, could also be attributed to affective partisanship towards the Socialist Party.

The central motives for electing the ÖVP were completely different. The determining factors were positive affective partisanship as well as a negative motive, that is to say, the decision to vote for the lesser of two evils. Candidate-orientated motives played a less important role for those deciding to vote for the ÖVP, while issue-orientated motives were only a marginal determinant. The data available suggests that the primary motive for those who voted for the FPÖ was in part a highly emotionalised protest orientation. Candidate-orientated motives followed in second place, but at a considerable distance. Those who voted for the Green parties explained their decision to a large degree by reference to issue-related motives. Protest motives played only a minor role.

Compared to the 1986 general election, the explanatory value of socio-structural characteristics has remained relatively stable. If the traditional determinants of Austrian voting behaviour such as frequency of church attendance and union ties are included in the analysis, however, socio-structural characteristics only explain about one quarter of the votes for the two large parties. Traditional determinants of voting behaviour only explain one sixth of the vote for the two Green parties. Finally, the FPÖ breaks the traditional structures of Austrian voting behaviour. Transformed under its leader Jörg Haider into a populist protest party, it attracts voters from different strata and social classes into a new populist voter coalition.[24]

The influence of age and educational level on voting behaviour has, however, increased in some respects over the 1986 election. Members of the younger voting generation show an even stronger inclination to support the opposition parties and voters with higher education have also increasingly turned away from the two main parties. Candidate-orientated decision motives had a much stronger influence on Austrian voting

TABLE 21

FACTORS INFLUENCING PARTY CHOICE AT THE 1990 GENERAL ELECTION

Influencing factors (part. corr. coeff. p < 0.05)	Party Choice				
	SPÖ	ÖVP	FPÖ	Greens[1]	Others
1. Socio-structural information					
Sex (male)	–	–	–.07	–	–
Age-groups					
up to 29 years	–.05	–	–	+.06	–
30–39 years	–	–	–.05	+.07	–
40–49 years	–	–	–	–	–
50–59 years	–	–	–	–	–
60–69 years	+.05	–	–	–.05	–
Educational level	–.12	+.07	–.08	+.15	–
Occupational Status					
self-employed / professional	–.13	+.11	–	–	–
senior employee / senior civil servant	–	+.06	–	–.06	–
white-collar	–	–.05	–	–	+.05
skilled worker	+.19	–.10	–	–	–
unskilled worker	+.09	–.06	–.04	–	–
farmer	–.12	+.15	–	–	–
Work Status					
employed	–	–	–	–.06	–
retired	–	–	–	–	–
unemployed	–.04	–	–	+.05	–
home-maker	+.06	–.05	–	–	–
in schooling	–	–	–.09	+.17	–
Religious Affiliation	–.05	+.13	–.04	–.08	–
Frequency of church attendance	–.18	+.24	–.05	–.05	–
Union membership	+.23	–.08	–.12	–.05	–
2. Motives					
Candidate-orientation	+.05	–.20	+.09	–.08	–.14
Protest motives	–.25	+.15	+.21	+.07	–.21
Issue-orientation	+.12	–.05	–	+.10	–.22
Party identification	+.06	+.17	–.16	–.10	–.06

Source: Fessel and GfK, Exit Poll 1990 (N = 2,200 voters)
Notes: Positive or negative values indicate the direction of influence on decision for a certain party. Other statistically controlled variables are: region, size and community, wavering, time of decision.
   1. The figures for the Greens constitute an aggregate of the respondents who voted for any 'green', or 'alternative' party.
   > Multiple R 0.8092   R Square 0.6548

behaviour in 1990, with this trend to personalisation extending to voters of all social classes. Both protest motives and candidate-orientated motives cut across traditional *Lager*-boundaries. Consequently, the *Lager* mentality, for decades a defining characteristic of Austrian voting behaviour, is now not only being undermined by social change, but is also being weakened by the increasing importance of candidates' images and protest voting. The increasing permeability of the political subcultures and the consequent progressive lack of correlation between social structure and voting behaviour, the transition from partisan voting to issue and image voting and the widespread trend toward negative voting have all combined to change the conditions of competition within the Austrian electorate.

TYPES OF VOTERS AND AREAS OF COMPETITION WITHIN THE AUSTRIAN PARTY SYSTEM AT THE BEGINNING OF THE 1990s

Voter segments still showing typical attributes of a *Lager* culture now only represent a minor part of the Austrian electorate and this has led to a transformation of the pattern of party competition. Traditional areas of competition and voter segments still showing typical attributes of a *Lager*-culture now only represent a minor part of the Austrian electorate. Traditional two-party competition is slowly being displaced by a new open multi-party competition in which the SPÖ and ÖVP have to fight against third and fourth parties for the votes of a mobile electorate without clear and binding party ties.

In the model of party competition developed by Richard Rose and Ian McAllister, the attempt is made to differentiate between a determined and an indetermined electorate. In a determined electorate, voting reflects the prevailing structure of society and competition between parties is limited. In an indetermined electorate, competition is open and intense. Short-term influences upon voters are much more important than social structure, or enduring party identification.[25] By means of a cluster analysis of the 1990 exit poll data, we have attempted a similar analysis, with the intention of dividing the Austrian electorate into optimal differentiated types and thus to define the typical voter segments and areas of competition that characterise Austrian voting behaviour in the early 1990s.[26]

The cluster analysis resulted in a total of eight voting types, each representing a specific competitive situation. Clusters 1 to 3 are characterised by pillarisation and the absence of significant electoral competition, whilst cluster 4 corresponds to the traditional two-party competition of the Austrian *Lager* democracy. Clusters 5 to 8 stand for an open market of voters and a competitive multi-party system. However, whilst the traditional *Lager* parties (ÖVP and SPÖ) retain a starting advantage in clusters 5 and 6, clusters 7 and 8 constitute segments in which there is completely open, multi-party electoral competition.

TABLE 22
VOTER CLUSTERS AND THE TYPES OF ELECTORAL COMPETITION IN AUSTRIA IN THE 1990s

Cluster	Characterisation of Clusters	% of electorate	Types of Party Electoral Competition	% of electorate	Combined share of SPÖ+ÖVP support (%)	Close Party Ties (%)	Waverers (%)	Late-deciders (%)	White-collar (%)	Blue-collar (%)
C1	social-democratic segment	23.2	No competition	33.6	90.2	55.3	15.8	7.2	25.3	55.4
C2	bourgeois segment	6.1								
C3	rural-catholic segment	4.3								
C4	traditional *Lager* competition	11.4	Traditional 2-party competition	11.4	90.6	51.8	21.5	12.3	35.9	55.8
C5	welfare-state-orientation new middle classes	28.1	Open, multi-party competition (with advantage for SPÖ and ÖVP)	46.1	66.6	2.5	42.1	21.5	80.8	2.0
C6	market-orientated dynamic middle-classes	18.0								
C7	populist blue-collar protest voters	5.8	Open, multi-party competition	8.9	47.6	4.7	58.6	29.3	48.2	37.2
C8	urban white-collar protest-voters	3.1								
		100.0		100.0						

Source: Fessel and GfK, Exit Poll 1990 (N=2,200 voters)

Cluster 1: The Social Democratic Lager *(23 per cent of the electorate)*

This relatively large electoral segment is characterised by the massive dominance of social democratic voters. About three-quarters of this segment voted for the SPÖ, with the rest evenly distributed among the two bourgeois parties (i.e., ÖVP and FPÖ). The political orientation of this segment is characterised by an especially strong motivational structure. The voters are quite content with political developments in general, are especially orientated to welfare-state goals, make their decisions based on long-standing affective party loyalty and are massively motivated in their voting decision by the top candidate of their party. As far as the potential for change is concerned, they are extremely immobile and have either never questioned their 'social democratic' voting decision, or have already made their choice long before the election day. Socio-structurally, they represent the classical environment of (skilled) labour, with almost two-thirds of the voters coming from this occupational group. They also exhibit strong union ties and a relatively strong distance from the Catholic Church. There is, furthermore, an above average percentage of older and retired people in this segment.

If these characteristics are viewed in relation to social trends, this type can easily be described as the classical social democratic faction of the post-war period. Being embedded in homogeneous blue-collar environments, this electoral segment is largely immune to conservative politics and bourgeois parties. The counterpart of the social democratic *Lager* consists of two smaller bourgeois *Lager*, which have, however, definite differences of content.

Cluster 2: Lager *of the 'Petty Bourgeoisie': Old Middle Class Bourgeoisie (6 per cent of the electorate)*

More than 80 per cent of this segment voted for the ÖVP. These voters are extremely unhappy with the present political situation, but nevertheless characterised by a strong affective party loyalty. They represent the discontented ÖVP core which fulfils its 'duties' with gritted teeth. As with the voters of the social democratic cluster, they are unlikely to be attracted to a different political party. They are conservative, stable and politically immobile voters. This segment further shows an extremely high religious alignment and only minimal contacts with representatives of union interests. From a sociological point-of-view, this group represents the shrinking segment of the old middle classes of the retail trade and the farming profession and contains a high percentage of older people.

Cluster 3: 'Rural-Catholic Lager*': Rural Conservatism/Rural Apathy (4 per cent of the electorate)*

There are two main differences between this segment and that of Cluster 2. First, in spite of ÖVP dominance (above 60 per cent), a permanent competitor also exists in the SPÖ (over 30 per cent are SPÖ-voters). Second, this voter segment can be described as a politically largely apathetic and immobile type, without any emotional identification with the chosen party. The type 3 voter either takes part in the election because of a powerful feeling of having to do his or her duty, or votes for a conservative party for reasons of religious ties. This segment has above average representation in smaller rural communities and is characterised by a large percentage of older, less well educated, or unskilled rural workers and farmers.

Cluster 4: Traditional Two-Party Competition: (Grand-) Coalitionary Lager *(11 per cent of the electorate)*

This segment represents the classical arena of competition between the two major parties, in which other political parties have few chances. It is the best example of the traditionally limited party competition between ÖVP and SPÖ up until the 1980s began. The votes are relatively balanced, with about 45 per cent each for the SPÖ and the ÖVP. A detailed investigation of this segment shows its motivation to be strongly dominated by traditional party loyalties, rather than by other political factors. Strong union ties and at the same time an above average confessional affiliation, as well as an almost symmetrical partition into qualified blue-collar workers, and white-collar workers are further indicators for the adherence of this segment to the political *Lager* of the Second Republic. As was the case in the voter segments described above, older persons are also slightly overrepresented within this cluster.

Cluster 5: Welfare State-Orientated, Open Party-Competition: Upwardly Mobile New Middle Classes (28 per cent of the electorate)

This is the largest segment of the electorate and is primarily characterised by the fact that here, unlike in the first four clusters, both the opposition parties (i.e., FPÖ and Greens) also have remarkably high support, representing considerable political competition, mainly for the ÖVP. The competition also affects the SPÖ, even though it (still) has an absolute majority of support within this cluster. For the Green parties, this group represents one of the two most important segments; about 40 per cent of all Green voters are concentrated here. These voters do not have strong party alignments. Only an above average proximity to unions could be interpreted as a potential tie to a political party. Structurally, this segment's voters differ from those above only in so far as they are exclusively white-collar workers, belong to the younger age groups and have an above average level of education, since 40 per cent have achieved an educational level sufficient to permit university access, whilst more than one third actually have a university degree.

Cluster 6: Market-Orientated, Dynamic Middle Classes (18 per cent of the electorate)

Within this third largest segment, the largest group is definitely represented by ÖVP voters (48 per cent), with only a small minority of SPÖ voters. More than 40 per cent vote for one of the opposition parties. High mobility, late voting decisions and low union ties make this segment a hard fought over terrain for the non-socialist parties in Austria. Due to an extremely high percentage of self-employed people, a broad base among white-collar workers and civil servants, as well as an above average level of better educated and younger age-groups, this type of voter represents a dynamic, growing electoral segment which will represent an even stronger arena of party competition in the future.

Cluster 7: Populist Blue-Collar Protest Voters (6 per cent of the electorate)

This is the cluster in which we find intensive party competition for voters prepared to shift between the two main parties, SPÖ and ÖVP, and their populist competitor, the FPÖ. The opposition has the majority of votes in this segment. A lack of party alignment, extreme political discontent and protest, as well as large-scale candidate orientation mark this segment out as one of the most mobile groups of the electorate and as one of the most receptive for populist politics. This segment is the most flexible and makes its voting decision extremely late. The high union ties are explained in that an above average number of voters belongs to the (skilled) labour groups.

Cluster 8: Urban White-Collar Protest Voters (3 per cent of the electorate)

The voters in this cluster are extremely discontented with the political situation. Contrary to the voter type of cluster 7, they are not, however, attracted to FPÖ populism. Voters belonging to this type are part of the Austrian educational elite, largely employed in public service and living in urban environments. An above average proportion of this segment has voted for a Green party. This cluster definitely represents a new political alternative culture which at the present time can neither be integrated by one of the two traditional parties nor by the FPÖ.

The patterns of Austrian voting behaviour outlined in the preceding discussion enables one to perceive the outlines of the bases of two party systems. While clusters 1 to 4 represent the traditional *Lager* democracy of the first decades of the Second Republic, clusters 5 to 8 represent a new type of 'competition democracy', albeit as yet with a residual starting advantage for the ÖVP and SPÖ in clusters 5 and 6. Thus while the SPÖ and ÖVP together have a strategic duopoly within the traditional pattern of competition within the Austrian electorate, having together a common vote of about 90 per cent, party competition within the mobile sector of the Austrian electorate is becoming increasingly more intense. Low party ties, a high percentage of 'wavering' voters and the increasing importance of issues and images are making voting behaviour less and less predictable.

The structure of the eight clusters clearly shows the continuing transformation of the Austrian electorate from closed subcultural *Lager* to an open, mobile and competitive electorate. The consequences for the Austrian party system are profound and complex. Only 45 per cent of the Austrian electorate can be attributed to one of the two traditional *Lager* as far as social background, party identification and voting behaviour is concerned. About 90 per cent of this traditional segment again voted for either the SPÖ, or the ÖVP in 1990. These voters are located in clusters 1 to 4 and represent the core of both major parties. They still show signs of a *Lager* mentality into the 1990s and largely represent the traditional two-party dominance of the Austrian post-war democracy.

These traditional, politically immobile voter segments are faced by new voter types, for whom both traditional parties still partially have certain starting advantages. Yet the characteristic of these new segments is a much more open, competitive situation offering reasonable opportunities to third and fourth parties to gain votes and thus to strengthen their positions. This open arena of competition already covers the majority of Austrian voters. The hyperstability of Austrian voting behaviour has given way to a new competitiveness and this transformation process is not yet over.

NOTES

1. See the introductory chapter to this volume.
2. How far the *Lager* theory can also be applied to the FPÖ and its predecessors during the monarchy and the First Republic is somewhat questionable. For a positive response see A. Wandruszka, 'Österreichs politische Struktur: Die Entwicklung der Parteien und politischen Bewegungen', in H. Benedikt (ed.), *Geschichte der Republik Österreich* (Vienna: Verlag für Geschichte und Politik, 1954), pp. 289–485. See also the introductory chapter to this volume by Luther and Müller.

3. These orientations were labelled *Lager* Mentalität (*Lager* mentality). For an extensive case study, see G. B. Powell, *Social Fragmentation and Political Hostility. An Austrian Case Study* (Stanford UP, 1970). See also G. Lehmbruch, *Proporzdemokratie: Politisches System und Politische Kultur in der Schweiz und in Österreich* (Tübingen: Mohr, 1967); R. Stiefbold, 'Segmented Pluralism and Consociational Democracy in Austria: Problems of Political Stability and Change', in M. O. Heisler (ed.), *Politics in Europe. Structures and Processes in Some Postindustrial Democracies* (NY: David McKay, 1974); and R. Steininger, *Polarisierung und Integration* (Meisenheim am Glan: Anton Hain, 1975).
4. These were predominantly the 'chambers' of labour, of agriculture and of business, membership of which has been compulsory for the relevant occupational groups, and the Austrian Trade Union Federation. See the contributions to this volume by P. Gerlich and K. R. Luther.
5. On this process see A. Diamant, 'The Group Basis of Austrian Politics', *Journal of Central European Affairs*, Vol. 18 (1958), pp. 134–55; F. C. Engelmann, 'The Pooling of Opposition', in R. A. Dahl (ed.), *Political Opposition in Western Democracies* (New Haven, CT: Yale UP, 1966), pp. 260–83; and H. P. Secher, 'Coalition Government: The Case of the Second Austrian Republic', *American Political Science Review*, Vol. 52 (1958), pp. 791–809.
6. See S. Verba, N. H. Nie and J. Kim, *Participation and Political Equality: A Seven Nation Comparison* (CUP, 1978).
7. See G. Lehmbruch, 'Consociational Democracy, Class Conflict and the New Corporatism', in P. Schmitter and G. Lehmbruch (eds.), *Trends Towards Corporatist Intermediation* (London: Sage, 1979), pp. 53–61.
8. See F. Kreissler, *Der Österreicher und seine Nation. Ein Lernprozeß mit Hindernissen* (Vienna: Böhlau, 1984); E. Bruckmüller, *Nation Österreich: Sozialhistorische Aspekte ihrer Entwicklung* (Vienna: Böhlau, 1984); P. Gerlich, 'National Consciousness and National Identity: A Contribution to the Political Culture of the Austrian Party System', in A. Pelinka and F. Plasser (eds.), *The Austrian Party System* (Boulder, CO: Westview Press, 1989), pp. 223–58. For recent developments, see G. Stourzh, *Vom Reich zur Republik. Studien zum Österreichbewusstsein im 20. Jahrhundert* (Vienna: Böhlau, 1990) and P. A. Ulram, *Hegemonie und Erosion: Politische Kultur und politischer Wandel in Österreich* (Vienna: Böhlau, 1990).
9. See F. Plasser, 'Elektronische Politik und politische Technostruktur reifer Industriegesellschaften', in F. Plasser, P. A. Ulram and M. Welan (eds.), *Demokratierituale. Zur politischen Kultur der Informationsgesellschaft* (Vienna: Böhlau, 1985), pp. 9–31.
10. See P. A. Ulram, *Hegemonie und Erosion*, pp. 88ff. and F. Plasser and P. A. Ulram, 'Politisch-kultureller Wandel in Österreich', in idem (eds.), *Staatsbürger oder Untertanen? Politische Kultur in der Bundesrepublik Deutschland, Österreich und der Schweiz* (Frankfurt: Lang, 1991).
11. C. Haerpfer and E. Gehmacher, 'Social Structure and Voting in the Austrian Party System', *Electoral Studies*, Vol. 3 (1984), pp. 25–46, here p. 43. See also P. Gerlich, 'Consociationalism to Competition: The Austrian Party System since 1945', in H. Daalder (ed.), *Party Systems in Denmark, Austria, Switzerland, the Netherlands and Belgium* (London, F. Pinter, 1987), pp. 61–106.
12. On the formation and subsequent dissolution of a voter coalition between the traditional social democratic core groups and the new middle classes, see F. Plasser and Peter A. Ulram, *Unbehagen im Parteienstaat: Jugend und Politik in Österreich* (Vienna: Böhlau, 1982) and Ulram, *Hegemonie und Erosion*.
13. Note that because of the well-known unreliability of party membership statistics, party membership is here measured in terms of 'subjective membership', i.e., according to poll-responses. For an extensive treatment see F. Plasser, *Parteien unter Stress: Zur Dynamik der Parteiensysteme in Österreich, der Bundesrepublik Deutschland und den Vereinigten Staaten* (Vienna: Böhlau, 1987), pp. 115ff.
14. Heinz Kienzl, 'Die Struktur der Wählerschaft', in K. Blecha, R. Gmoser and H. Kienzl, *Der durchleuchtete Wähler* (Vienna: Europa Verlag, 1964), p. 46.

15. See Kienzl, p. 55, and C. Haerpfer, 'Nationalratswahlen und Wahlverhalten seit 1945', in P. Gerlich and W. C. Müller (eds.), *Zwischen Koalition und Konkurrenz: Österreichs Parteien seit 1945* (Vienna: Braumüller, 1983), pp. 111–49.
16. For an extensive treatment of the subject see Plasser and Ulram, *Unbehagen im Parteienstaat*; idem, 'From Stability to Diffusion: Dealignment in the Austrian Party System', paper delivered at the 1985 APSA-meeting (New Orleans, 1985) and Ulram, *Hegemonie und Erosion*.
17. On long-term trends in Austrian voting behaviour, see among others: Haerpfer and Gehmacher, 'Social Structure and Voting in the Austrian Party System'; C. Haerpfer, 'Austria' in I. Crewe and D. Denver (eds.), *Electoral Change in Western Democracies* (London: Croom Helm, 1985), pp. 264–86; F. Plasser, 'The Austrian Party System between Erosion and Innovation', in Pelinka and Plasser (eds.), *Austrian Party System*, pp. 41–67; and K. R. Luther, 'Dimensions of Party System Change: The Case of Austria', *West European Politics*, Vol. 12, No. 4 (Oct. 1989), pp. 3–27.
18. Regarding a measure of total volatility see M. N. Pedersen, 'Changing Patterns of Electoral Volatility in European Party Systems', in H. Daalder and P. Mair (eds.), *Western European Party Systems* (London: Sage, 1983), pp. 29–66.
19. On the 1986 general election see K. R. Luther, 'Austria's Future and Waldheim's Past: The Significance of the 1986 Elections', *West European Politics*, Vol. 10, No. 3 (Oct. 1987), pp. 376–96; F. Plasser and P. A. Ulram, 'Major Parties on the Defensive: The Austrian Party and Electoral Landscape after the 1986 National Council Election', in Pelinka and Plasser (eds.), *Austrian Party System*, pp. 69–92.
20. See H. Schmitt, 'On Party Attachment in Western Europe and the Utility of Eurobarometer Data', *West European Politics*, Vol. 12, No. 1 (April 1989), pp. 122–39.
21. The dealignment process in the Austrian party system in empirically documented in Plasser, 'The Austrian Party System between Erosion and Innovation'.
22. For an analysis of the 1990 general election see F. Plasser, F. Sommer and P. A. Ulram, 'Eine Kanzler- und Protestwahl. Analyse des Wählerverhaltens und der Wählermotive bei der Nationalratswahl 1990', *Österreichisches Jahrbuch für Politik 1990*, pp. 95–149; D. Meth-Cohn and W. C. Müller, 'Leaders Count: The Austrian Elections of October 1990', *West European Politics*, Vol. 14, No. 2 (April 1991), pp. 183–88.
23. See Haerpfer, 'Austria', p. 280.
24. On the transformation of the FPÖ see among others: Luther, 'Austria's Future and Waldheim's Past' and idem, 'Die Freiheitliche Partei Österreichs', in H. Dachs, P. Gerlich, H. Gottweis, F. Horner, H. Kramer, V. Lauber, W. C. Müller and E. Talos (eds.), *Handbuch des politischen Systems Österreichs* (Vienna: Manz, 1991), pp. 247–62.
25. The empirical basis is provided by an election-day survey, the questionnaire was more or less identical with that used on the election day of 1986.
26. See R. Rose and I. McAllister, *Voters Begin To Choose. From Closed Class to Open Elections in Britain* (London: Sage, 1986). See also idem, *The Loyalties of Voters. A Lifetime Learning Model* (London: Sage, 1990), pp. 183–98.

Consociationalism, Parties and the Party System

KURT RICHARD LUTHER

As demonstrated in the introductory chapter, Austria's political parties have since their inception played an important role in the Austrian political system. First, they were twice the main actors in the state-building process which established the formal constitutional framework of the Austrian republic: once in 1918–20 and again in 1945.[1] Second, it was the parties who provided their adherents with the mutually hostile political identities which so determined political culture and political behaviour in both Austrian republics.[2] In the First Republic, these identities eventually formed the bases for the rival factions in Austria's short 1934 civil war and though such ideological conflict has been substantially attenuated during the Second Republic, it was still only relatively recently that partisan attachment to the two main political parties was overtaken by commitment to a common Austrian national identity.[3] Third, the political parties helped create, and were important in running, the extra-constitutional structures and procedures of Austria's system of corporatism (the so-called 'social partnership'), which played a central role throughout much of the Second Republic.[4] Fourth, for much of the same period, Austria's two main political parties were the principals in an elite cartel, whose domain ranged from a virtual monopoly of federal and regional government, to a duopoly over staffing in much of the civil service, as well as in Austria's extensive public sector industries and enterprises.[5]

The fact that Austria's political parties and their interaction have been crucial in determining the Austrian political system's overall character is one reason why parties and the party system have figured so prominently in the literature on Austrian consociationalism.[6] At least equally significant, however, is the central role which parties play in consociational theory in general.[7] At its simplest, consociational theory seeks to explain the existence of political stability in certain countries with deeply fragmented political cultures. It comprises a set of propositions concerning in the main two aspects of such political systems: their political sociology and the nature of their political elite's behaviour. In the first aspect, consociational theory emphasises socio-political pillarisation, namely, the existence of vertically encapsulated and mutually hostile political subcultures, which in Austria have come to be referred to as *Lager*.[8] For its part, elite political behaviour is seen as characterised above all by cooperation and accommodation, by means of which a bridge (or 'arch') is built over the gulf separating the political subcultures (or 'pillars') and thus the political system's stability is ensured. Political parties play a crucial role both in the political sociology and the 'overarching' elite behaviour of consociational political systems.

First, it is primarily the parties who mobilise their respective subcultures and it is through party structures that subcultural interests are aggregated and the subcultural political elite recruited. Second, it is above all between the elite of the political parties that the overarching accommodation occurs.[9] That accommodation must of necessity embrace not only the policy-making, but also the policy-implementation process, for unless the subcultural political elites are capable of ensuring that their organisations 'deliver' the side of the bargain which has been struck at the elite level, accommodative policy-making would be meaningless. Accordingly, in the highly segmented world of consociational politics, the party-political writ of one or other of the main subcultures runs not only in the key socio-economic interest groups, but also within many formal policy-implementation structures. To retain their control in these areas, the parties rely heavily on their penetration and incorporation of their subculture and its associated interest groups and auxiliary associations. In sum, in consociational systems, political parties provide the two-way linking mechanism between the mass and the elite of the encapsulated subcultures, as well as the personnel and policy-implementation structures that enable effective, or binding, overarching elite accommodation to take place.

The overall aim of this volume is to establish whether it is still appropriate to consider Austria an example of such a consociational system and to that end the volume investigates the nature and extent of changes to what were regarded as the six core features of Austrian politics during 'classic' Austrian consociationalism (i.e., from 1945 to 1966).[10] This essay's contribution is to examine changes in the nature and role of Austria's parties and party system. We shall start by looking at the political parties themselves, then move on to analyse the operation of the party system (i.e., of the nature of party interaction), consecutively, in the electoral, parliamentary, governmental, corporate and bureaucratic arenas.

THE LAGER PARTIES AND THEIR INTRA-SUBCULTURAL LINKAGES

After the Second World War, there were initially (1945–49) only three political parties licensed by the occupying powers. The traditional Catholic-conservative *Lager* was represented by the Austrian People's Party

(*Österreichische Volkspartei*, or ÖVP), while the Socialist Party of Austria (*Sozialistische Partei Österreichs*, or SPÖ) and the much smaller Communist Party of Austria (*Kommunistische Partei Österreichs*, or KPÖ) competed for the support of the traditional socialist *Lager*. Predictably, the Allies would at first not countenance a party of the German-national 'Third *Lager*'. In 1949, largely due to pressure from the SPÖ, which aspired to divide and thus weaken the bourgeois camp, the occupying powers relented and granted permission for the formation of the League of Independents (*Verband der Unabhängigen*, or VdU). The VdU's founders' intention was that the party would rally the traditionally anti-socialist and anti-clerical Third *Lager* by means of an appeal to the latter's liberal, as opposed to its discredited German-national principles. The 'national' elements soon asserted themselves, however, and in 1956 the VdU eventually succumbed to its internal ideological divisions and reconstituted itself as the Freedom Party of Austria (*Freiheitliche Partei Österreichs*, or FPÖ), in which national and conservative forces dominated.[11] Though the 1960s saw a number of new minor, often short-lived splinter parties, they had no lasting significance for the Austrian political system and thus do not merit further consideration here. During 'classic' Austrian consociationalism there were thus at most four 'relevant' *Lager* parties: the ÖVP, SPÖ, FPÖ and KPÖ.[12]

The intention of this section is not to discuss in detail the post-war development of these individual parties, but rather to analyse their respective intra-subcultural linkages since 'classic' consociationalism.[13] As explained above, consociational theory emphasises the party-subculture relationship's capacity to ensure sufficient intra-subcultural political cohesion to support overarching, inter-subcultural elite accommodation. In their interaction with their political subcultures, the political parties of consociational systems can thus be regarded as performing three main roles. The first is the *organisational penetration*, or *incorporation* of their subculture. The second has to do with the articulation and communication to the subculture of *values* that assist in its *political mobilisation*. The third major role is to ensure enough *hierarchical control* of the subculture to allow the subcultural political elite to engage in binding inter-*Lager* bargaining.

Subcultural Penetration and Incorporation

The significance of party-political penetration of Austria's subcultures is reflected by the consociational literature's consistent emphasis upon the sheer size and organisational density of Austria's political parties. During 'classic' consociationalism they successfully embraced – and penetrated deep into the lives of – virtually the whole potential membership of their subculture, the sociology of which showed significant continuity with the pre-war *Lager*.[14] This was achieved by a densely organised party structure, allied to a wide range of auxiliary associations. Accordingly, our assessment of whether the parties are still successful in this role will use two main indicators. The first will be their party membership's size and density, the second will relate to the size and scope of the parties' auxiliary associations. Finally, we shall turn to the subcultures' social composition and try to estimate the continuity in their sociological profile.

The size and density of party membership. The absolute size of a party's membership is a useful, albeit rough, measure of party size and of the political subculture it represents, while a party's organisational density helps indicate how successful that party is at mobilising its potential subculture.[15] Table 1 contains both figures for the SPÖ, ÖVP, FPÖ and KPÖ and shows that during 'classic' consociationalism, the parties differed substantially both in absolute membership and organisational density. In absolute size, by far the largest parties were the SPÖ and the ÖVP. Though immediately after the war the SPÖ had had a 'mere' 357,818 members,[16] by 1959 that figure had virtually doubled, and by 1979 SPÖ membership reached its peak, when the party embraced nearly 720,000 card-carrying members in a country whose total electorate amounted to just over five million persons. Since then, however, SPÖ membership has declined by just over 100,000, so that by 1990 the SPÖ had fewer members than at any time since just after the Second World War. SPÖ's organisational density tells a similar story. The proportion of the SPÖ's electorate that identified with the party sufficiently strongly to be party members declined from an average of 36 per cent at the elections held between 1949 and 1966, to 31 per cent at the elections since 1970. Were it not for the SPÖ's falling share of the electorate since its 1979 peak, that membership density figure would in 1990 have amounted to only about 26 per cent. Another way of interpreting these figures is to say that while in the 1970s the SPÖ was successful in extending its vote beyond its subculture, by 1990 the SPÖ's vote had shrunk back to nearer its 'natural' level, while the level of party membership had in the meantime also receded.

Unfortunately, the available data do not permit one to make as detailed statements about the number of individual ÖVP party members. In part because of the peculiar and uneven manner in which the party's various territorial and functional subunits assess their membership, but also because it is in those units' interests to maintain exaggerated figures, since membership size is one factor taken into account when intra-party resources are distributed, the official party figures present an inflated picture.[17] Informed sources suggest that actual individual members may have totalled approximately three quarters of the official figure. Moreover,

TABLE 1
MEMBERS, VOTERS AND ORGANISATIONAL DENSITY OF SPÖ, ÖVP, FPÖ AND KPÖ IN SELECTED ELECTION YEARS

Year	SPÖ			ÖVP				FPÖ			KPÖ		
	Members	Voters	Density (%)	Members[1]	Voters	Density (%) (Nominal)	Density (%) (Estimated)	Members	Voters	Density (%)	Members	Voters	Density (%)[2]
1959[3]	710,378	1,953,935	36.4	752,023	1,928,043	c.39	c.29	22,000	336,110	15.4	150,000	213,066	70.4
1970	719,389	2,221,981	32.4	819,397	2,051,012	c.40	c.30	28,000	253,425	11.0	29,000	44,750	64.8
1971	719,389	2,280,168	31.6	805,771	1,964,713	c.41	c.31	–	248,473	c.11.3	–	61,762	c.44.3
1975	693,156	2,326,201	29.8	776,629	1,981,291	c.39	c.29	33,000	249,444	13.2	–	55,032	c.37.6
1979	721,262	2,413,226	29.9	813,715	1,981,739	c.41	c.30	37,288	286,743	13.0	14,000	45,280	30.9
1983	694,598	2,312,529	30.0	836,284	2,097,808	39.9	c.28	37,233	241,789	15.4		31,912	c.38.2
1986	674,821	2,092,024	32.3	806,301	2,003,663	40.2	c.26	36,583	472,205	7.8		35,104	c.30.8
1990	620,141	2,012,787	31.7	813,331	1,460,392	c.56	c.35	40,629	754,379	5.4	9,000	25,685	35.0

Sources: Election results: as Appendix 1. Membership statistics as follows: SPÖ: K. Ucakar 'Sozialistische Partei Österreichs'; FPÖ: K. R. Luther 'Die Freiheitliche Partei Österreichs'; KPÖ: J. Ehmer 'Die Kommunistische Partei Österreichs', and ÖVP for 1983, 1986 and 1989: W. C. Müller 'Die Österreichische Volkspartei', all in H. Dachs *et al.* (eds.), *Handbuch des politischen Systems Österreichs* (Vienna: Manz, 1991), in print; remaining ÖVP statistics: W. Urban and E. Zeidner 'Vom Umfang und Nutzen der Parteimitgliedschaft' in P. Gerlich and W. C. Müller (eds.), *Zwischen Koalition und Konkurrenz. Österreichs Parteien seit 1945* (Vienna: Braumüller, 1983), pp.151–71, here 156.

Notes: 1. The figures comprise the total official membership of the ÖVP's three main *Bünde* (Leagues) in 1960, 1968, 1973, 1976, 1980, 1983, 1986 and 1989 respectively. They significantly overrepresent actual individual membership, but no accurate figures exist. Best estimates suggest that actual individual membership has until recently been about a third lower and that the disparity has grown larger in the last 10 to 15 years. The rubric entitled 'estimated' membership density assumes an overestimation in the formal figures of about 25 per cent until 1975 and then deducts 25,000, 50,000, 75,000 and 100,000 from the amended figure at the following elections. These estimates must of course also be treated with considerable caution (see text).
2. Figures for 1971, 1973, 1975 and 1986 are based on the assumption of an even decline in membership between the years for which statistics are available (i.e., 1970, 1979 and 1990).
3. The figures for the KPÖ relate to 1949.

whilst the official figure has remained fairly static over the last 15 years, insiders believe individual membership has declined to the tune of about 100,000 persons.

Table 1 thus contains both nominal membership and membership density figures, as well an estimated membership density figure, based on the aforementioned assumptions. What these figures suggest is that during 'classic' consociationalism the ÖVP's membership and membership density was about a fifth lower than that of the SPÖ and will have remained at about that level until the late 1970s, when membership started to decline. By 1990, the party may well have lost some 100,000 members, but in view of the even greater decline in voters (about 25 per cent), the membership density figure actually increased to about 35 per cent. Though these figures cannot be more than estimates, the general trend is clear: the size of the Catholic-conservative *Lager* appears to be declining in absolute terms and in its level of political mobilization at a faster rate than socialist *Lager*.

Largely due to its resistance role, but also because of active support from the Soviet occupation forces, the KPÖ's post-war membership figures rocketed from a mere 7,000 in 1931 to 150,000 in 1949. This not only made it the third largest party, but also meant that for much of 'classic' consociationalism it was the party with by far the highest level of organisational density, peaking at 70.4 per cent in 1949. Since then, however, the socialists successfully countered the KPÖ's threat to the left flank of their *Lager*, with the result that the KPÖ has suffered a sustained full in membership. By 1990 it stood at only 9,000, a mere six per cent of its 1949 figure, but given that its vote has fallen in the same period by nearly 90 per cent, the KPÖ's membership density is, at 35 per cent, still quite high. By contrast, during 'classic' consociationalism, the membership of the FPÖ and of its predecesor party, the VdU, was much lower in both absolute and relative terms than that of any of the three parties discussed so far. Yet while the membership of the latter has declined significantly in recent years, the overall trend for the FPÖ has been a gradual increase, with individual members rising from approximately 22,000 in 1959 to just over 40,000 in 1990. Given that the FPÖ's vote has more than trebled since 1983, its membership density figure has more than halved, however, and at the 1990 election stood at only 5.4 per cent.

The preceding comparison of the major parties' membership and organisational density during 'classic' consociationalism and since has made four points clear. First, despite the KPÖ's early challenge to the SPÖ's organisational hegemeony within the socialist *Lager*, by the early 1960s, Austria was indeed characterised by four distinct and politically consolidated subcultures: the two large Catholic-conservative and socialist *Lager* on the one hand and the minor German-national and communist subcultures on the other. Second, since 'classic' consociationalism, the two major *Lager* have witnessed a significant decline both in party membership and in membership density, while the decline within the communist subculture has in both respects been acute. Third, though the absolute size of the FPÖ's membership has doubled since the late 1950s, this has not narrowed the huge disparity with the two major parties. Such convergence as there has been cannot be attributed to a sizeable shift in *Lager* support, for the SPÖ and ÖVP's combined loss in the last 10–15 years of some 200,000 members cannot be accounted for by movement from one of the major *Lager* to the other, nor has it led to a corresponding rise in the membership of the other parties. Instead, a major cause of the decreased levels of political organisation in the ÖVP and SPÖ has been a general process of de-pillarisation, that is to say, a decline in the socio-political cohesion of the two major parties' subcultures. This itself stems from the significant socio-economic and socio-cultural changes analysed in this volume by Plasser *et al*, which have reduced the proportion of the population that lives within encapsulated *Lager* subcultures, and is also attributable to the parties' weakening linkages with their subcultures. This will be discussed later in this essay under the rubric of 'mobilisation and values'. Fourth, one should not forget that although the SPÖ and ÖVP appear since the mid-1970s to have had declining membership, by international standards they remain mass parties with membership levels and rates of organisational density that compare very favourably with other Christian-democratic and social-democratic parties in Western Europe. By contrast, the KPÖ is now clearly a cadre-party, while the FPÖ undoubtedly still remains a *Wählerpartei* (electoral party).

The Size and Scope of Auxiliary Associations. If the parties provide one main organisational base of subcultural political penetration in Austria, their auxiliary associations provide the other, though it is in some cases very difficult to distinguish between party organisations and auxiliary associations. One can, at the risk of over-simplification, identify three broad types of *Lager* auxiliary association. They differ in respect of four factors, between which there is a positive, albeit rough, correlation. The first relates to their closeness to the political party of their *Lager*; the second concerns their degree of direct significance for the political process; the third comprises their degree of formality; while the final criterion is the extent to which their prime rationale lies in representing the material interests of their members, as opposed to, for example, the promotion of their cultural, sporting, or other leisure-time activities.

The first type of auxiliary association is usually highly formalised, if not bureaucratic, and its membership is based upon occupation. The main function of this *Lager* auxiliary association relates to the (political) representation of the socio-economic interests of its members. Its relationship to its *Lager* party is so close that most associations, though not all, are constituent elements of one or other of the *Lager* parties and, or run by intra-party groupings. Their offices are usually in party buildings, their officials are almost invariably party members and their leaders are as a rule the party spokespersons in the relevant policy area. This first type of auxiliary association is thus a form of party/interest-group hybrid. All the main *Lager* parties have such auxiliary associations. In terms of size and political impact the most important are the various constituent *Fraktionen* (party-political groupings) of Austria's three key chambers: those of labour, business and agriculture.

The degree of party-group overlap is highest, indeed virtually complete, in the ÖVP. It is represented in the chambers by the three associations that constitute the three main functional 'Leagues' of the party; the minority grouping in the chamber of labour is the *Österreichischer Arbeiter- und Angestelltenbund* (Austrian League of Workers and Salaried Employees, or ÖAAB), while the ÖVP dominates business and agriculture chambers through the *Österreichischer Wirtschaftsbund* (Austrian Business League, or ÖWB) and the *Österreichischer Bauernbund* (Austrian Farmers' League) respectively. Moreover, these three associations' combined membership comprises the overwhelming majority of the ÖVP's party membership and currently officially stands at approximately 800,000 persons.

The chamber groupings of the socialist *Lager* are not as crucial in intra-party terms as those of the Catholic-conservative *Lager*. None the less, the *Fraktion Sozialistischer Gewerkschaftler* (the Fraktion of Socialist Trades Unionists), the *Freier Wirtschaftsverband Österreichs* (Free Business Association of Austria) and the *SPÖ-Bauern* (SPÖ-Farmers) not only respectively constitute the dominant grouping in the chamber of labour and the SPÖ's minority groupings in the business and agriculture chambers, but are also recognised by the SPÖ as socialist organisations. This at the very least means that they formally profess their support of the SPÖ and that their officials are required to be SPÖ party members. The combined membership of the socialist associations that could be considered to come under the rubric of this first type of auxiliary association also amounts to approximately 800,000 persons, many of course also individual party members.

By contrast, the FPÖ and its predecessor has since 1954 only had one chamber *Fraktion* of any significance, namely, that in the chamber of business. In 1990 its total membership amounted to a mere 5,000 persons.

This *Ring Freiheitlicher Wirtschaftstreibender* (Circle of Free Businesspersons, or RFW) has a much looser relationship to its party than the chamber groupings of the major *Lager*. Any greater independence which this entails is probably a function of its limited size and thus of political insignificance. Furthermore, the RFW is not formally a constiutent organisation of the FPÖ.

This first type of auxiliary association provides the main *Lager* parties with control of the three main chambers of Austria's distinctive system of corporatism and thus it is significant in terms of party interaction, as will be discussed below in our elucidation of the Austrian party system's corporate arena. However, it is also highly significant in terms of the organisational penetration of Austria's subcultures. This is a function first of these associations' size, kept very high not only because the chambers between them cover almost the complete spectrum of occupational groupings in Austria, but also because membership is obligatory for all those in the relevant employment categories. In other words, nearly all employed Austrians are chamber members, even if they never become activists within them. Second, this first type of auxiliary association is important by virtue of the scope of its activities. The Austrian political system has assigned important rule-making and rule-implementation functions to the chambers, the activities of whose *Faktionen* thus directly affect the working lives of their members. Each chamber is dominated by a single *Fraktion* and thus the working lives of employed persons are significantly influenced by socialist *Lager* politics, while those of the self-employed and of farmers are similarly organised by Catholic-conservative *Lager* politics. In sum, these associations help ensure not only the organisational incorporation, but also the penetration of their *Lager*.

The second type of auxiliary association differs from the first in degree rather than in kind. It enjoys greater informality in both its membership, which is voluntary rather than compulsory, and in its role in the political system. It too is often closely linked to the *Lager* party, albeit often primarily via overlapping leadership and financial support, rather than by direct incorporation. Thus while most of the associations' activists will be party members and their officials are likely also to be party functionaries, or office-holders, many members will not formally belong to the relevant *Lager* party. Estimates of party membership share in such associations vary from group to group, but may well be something between half and a quarter, depending on the nature of the group. The relatively low levels of party membership in this type of association, as compared with the first type, reflects not so much the weakness of *Lager* organisation, as its strength. For these associations, inevitably permeated by the *Lager*'s political values, embody the subcultures' capacity to incorporate not only the politically committed members of their *Lager*, but also persons whose political identification would not normally entice them into purely party activities. Although such associations are thus still within the *Lager* parties' sphere of influence, most are to be regarded not so much as direct party appendages, but as part of what is called in Austria their *Vorfeld* (i.e., domain) or *Umfeld* (i.e., part of their general political environment).[18] The role of many of these associations includes supporting their members in matters of material concern to them, but that of many others does not. Thus all parties have associations for senior citizens, whose role includes, for example, seeking to help members claim the state benefits to which they are entitled, but they also organise excursions and other cultural, or leisure-time activities. Examples of the diverse socialist associations that fall under this heading are the League of Socialist Freedom Fighters and Victims of Fascism (c. 3,400 members in 1970, c. 4,300 in 1982 and 1,982 in 1990); the Socialist Youth of Austria (c. 2,400 in 1959 and 42,000 in 1983) and the Working Group for Sport and Body Culture in Austria (c. 258,000 members in 1957, 968,000 in 1983 and 1,080,000 in 1990).[19]

The third type of auxiliary association is by far the most numerous. It has in the main only very loose organisational ties to the *Lager* parties, though there is in some cases financial support (which can flow in either direction). The nature of the bond linking these auxiliary associations to their *Lager* party is mainly the sharing of the latter's *Weltanschauung*. Though some can be regarded as interest groups (such as, e.g., associations of home-owners, or of rentiers), the prime orientation of the overwhelming majority is of a cultural, sporting, or otherwise primarily non-political, often leisure-time orientated nature. The character of the individual associations varies enormously and spans a spectrum that ranges from, for example, the 'Austrian Club for Automobilists, Motorbikers and Cyclists' (ÖVP-orientated), to the 'Central Association of Austria's Small Gardeners, Homecrofters and Pet Breeders', or the 'First Austrian Association of Worker Stamp-collectors' (both SPÖ-orientated). This third category of auxiliary association probably embraces a total of approaching two million members, though precise figures are simply not available.

The extensive networks of auxiliary *Lager* associations mean that an even larger number of individuals are incorporated in a subculture than suggested by the (albeit already very high) party membership figures alone. They assist the *Lager* parties in their efforts at vertical subcultural integration, since the main *Lager* duplicate not only the occupation-based auxiliary associations, but also those seeking to organise, for example, women, the youth and senior citizens. Despite their size and their significance for Austrian politics in general and Austrian consociationalism in particular, there is very little academic work on the auxiliary associations.[20] Accordingly, it is difficult to make definite statements about changes since classic consociationalism. What appears to have happened as regards the two main parties' auxiliary associations is that there has been a general decline in the importance and scope of their *Vorfeld*. In response, all *Lager* have since the 1970s at times sought to staunch the flow by investing considerable energy in organising auxiliary associations for their youth, but especially for their senior citizens. Estimates would put their total membership in 1990 at about 200,000 and about 600,000 persons respectively. In the FPÖ *Lager*, there has been a marked decline since the 1950s and 1960s in party recruitment from student associations with a pronounced German-national orientation. Instead, the late 1960s and the 1970s saw a rise in the less nationalist *Ring Freiheitlicher Studenten* (Circle of Free Students), through which many of the key party elite of recent years were recruited. The change of the FPÖ to a more populist party is perhaps seen in the recently formed 'Club 3', an auxiliary association whose prime activity lies in organising discos, at a number of which the current party leader makes an appearance.

Subcultural Sociology. Having established changes in the size and extent of incorporation of Austria's traditional subcultures, we shall consider the sociological profile of those subcultures. Regrettably, this is another topic on which direct information is scarce. The two *prima facie* most promising sources are the political parties and the major auxiliary associations, in particular those operating within the three chambers. However, not only do they not normally make the relevant data available, but in many cases they simply do not have it, either because it was never systematically collated, or because records have been lost. Accordingly, the following comments will in the main be predicated upon indirect sources.

First we shall consider the two major *Lager* parties, the sociological profile of the very highest levels of party activists of which, namely, of those holding public office, is quite easily established. To ascertain the sociological profile of the parties' rank-and-file membership and of their functionaries, one is, however, obliged to rely largely upon indirect sources, such as interviews with party insiders and on poll data.[21] A recent study on the sociology of rank-and file members and functionaries within the two main parties (see Table 2) suggests significant differences between the parties and between the different types of members. First, the data show that SPÖ members – and in particular their functionaries – are older than their ÖVP counterparts. Second, nearly half (47.3 per cent) of the SPÖ's members and over four in ten (41.8 per cent) of its functionaries are still drawn from the blue-collar labour-force, whilst the figures for

TABLE 2
SOCIOLOGY OF RANK-AND-FILE MEMBERS AND FUNCTIONARIES OF SPÖ AND ÖVP (1988)

	Age Under 40s (%)	Educational Level (%)				Occupation			
		Basic	Apprentice	Intermediate[1]	Higher	Self-employed and farmers	White-collar	Civil servants	Blue collar
SPÖ									
Rank-and-file	27.7	29.5	40.3	7.7	2.1	2.7	24.4	25.6	47.3
Functionaries	24.0	18.9	45.4	12.8	4.1	3.3	27.2	27.7	41.8
ÖVP									
Rank-and-file	30.1	38.0	22.9	12.7	4.1	39.8	15.1	22.3	22.8
Functionaries	40.8	22.1	31.0	15.5	3.8	51.3	13.5	19.2	16.1

Source: Poll data cited in E. Gehmacher 'SPÖ: Wähler und Mitglieder 1945 bis 1989' in E. Fröschl, M. Mesner and H. Zoitl (eds.), *Die Bewegung, Hundert Jahre Sozialdemokratie in Österreich* (Vienna: Passagen Verlag, 1990), pp. 520–30.
Note: 1. i.e., qualified for university entrance ('Matura').

the ÖVP are only 22.8 and 16.1 per cent respectively. Third, the self-employed and farmers constitute well over a third (39.8 per cent) of the ÖVP's membership and over half (51.3 per cent) of its functionaries.

The significant number of farmers among the ÖVP's members is reflected in the membership's educational profile, which shows not only a higher proportion than in the SPÖ of those with intermediate, or higher education, but also a significantly higher proportion (38.0 as opposed to 29,5 per cent) with just a basic education. The ÖVP continues to be successful in mobilising the traditional rural, less well educated farming element of its subculture. Finally, the 1988 figures point to the significant increase since classic consociationalism in the proportion of civil servants among the SPÖ's members; it rose from just under one in seven in 1955 to just over one in four in 1988 and reflects the success of *Proporz* in increasing socialists in Austrian public administration, which in the First Republic and also immediately after the Second World War had been the preserve primarily of Catholic-conservative and German-national *Lager* adherents.

Turning to the sociology of the minor parties, a recent publication has for the first time offered a detailed breakdown of the social composition of KPÖ activists and functionaries[22] and its findings point to substantial differences between the party's rank-and-file membership and its activists, who constitute a high proportion – estimated at between a quarter and a third – of the KPÖ's whole membership. First, the KPÖ has aged markedly since the height of its success in the post-war period. By 1990, over half the membership comprised persons over 60 years of age, but by contrast, over half of the party's activists are under 40 years of age. Second, there has been a concurrent decline of blue-collar workers (from 59 per cent to 13 per cent) and a corresponding rise in white-collar workers (from 31 to 56 per cent).

Though no detailed figures on the FPÖ exist, this author's recent research[23] suggests that since the 1960s, significant changes have taken place in the social profile of above all the FPÖ's functionaries and key political elites. First, although always disproportionately numerous at the party's higher levels, the FPÖ's liberalisation in the late 1970s and early 1980s led to an even greater significance of professionals and the self-employed. In 1985, for example, when the party was in government for the first time, the background of the members of the federal party executive (*Bundesparteivorstand*) was 61 per cent from the liberal professions, 22 per cent self-employed, 11 per cent farmers, and six per cent white-collar employees, while that of its narrower membership which together comprised the party's presidium, (*de facto* the politically most important body), was 83 per cent from the liberal professions and the rest from self-employed backgrounds. Since the 1986 re-orientation of the FPÖ towards a populist strategy under its young and charismatic new chairman, Jörg Haider, the average age of key party functionaries fell significantly, as Haider replaced many long-serving individuals – some at the very highest levels of the party's apparatus – with people who are predominantly young and in part self-employed entrepreneurs.

The overall message of these figures on the sociology of party membership is first, that the two main parties' membership still reflects the traditional core elements of their respective subcultures. The archetypal SPÖ member is still a male, blue-collar worker who has undergone an apprenticeship; the ÖVP's membership still contains a disproportionately high number of farmers, with basic levels of education, as well as significant numbers of self-employed and of persons with intermediate, or higher education. Second, since 'classic' consociationalism, these parties' social profiles have thus not kept pace with the substantial changes in Austria's overall social structure, prominent among which have been a radical decline in the number of farmers and a substantial decrease in the proportion of blue-collar workers.[24] Finally, it is interesting to note that the data also suggests that the the sociological profile differences of the two main parties' functionaries is – in key respects such as occupation – greater than the differences between the parties' rank-and-file.

That would be consistent with the widely-held perception of students of Austrian politics that inter-*Lager* hostility has persistently been highest between mid-level party functionaries, as opposed to between the subcultural 'masses', or between the party elite. As was long since observed,[25] both before and during 'classic' consociationalism, the socio-economic profiles of the political elite of the two main *Lager* were significantly less distinct than were those of groupings at other levels of the rival subcultures. That is not to say that their traditional differences – above all those of religiosity and political belief – were not, or are not still, important. First, the ÖVP party elite continues to have high levels of religiosity, while their SPÖ counterparts are likely to be at least secular, if not atheistic. However, religious distinctiveness has in recent years been primarily at an individual level; policy issues with an intrinsically religious, or clerical dimension have of late figured comparatively rarely on the Austrian political agenda. Second, while ideological differences also remain (see below), many years of political co-operation has brought about a significant decline in the levels of distrust between the party elites. Moreover, examinations of key SPÖ and ÖVP party elite groups such as members of parliament and government, as well as of the members of the parties' highest organs, show that their occupational and educational profiles are if anything even more alike than during 'classic' consociationalism.[26]

Information on subcultural sociology can also be gleaned from the various subcultural auxiliary associations. Relevant factors include the relative size of the *Lager*'s occupation-based auxiliary associations and the related returns of the elections to the main three chambers (see, e.g., Tables 4 and 5 below), as well as the different character of many third type auxiliary associations, still largely organised around the traditional *Lager* cleavages, namely, those relating to occupation; religion, or religiosity; and national identity. In the student world, for example, the socialist subculture organises its students into the 'Association of Socialist Students of Austria', while the various Catholic and German-national fraternities are still linked with the ÖVP and Third *Lager* respectively. Such evidence largely reinforces the picture of subcultural sociology provided by the party membership information.

To summarise, our investigation of Austrian subcultural sociology since 'classic' consociationalism clearly suggests that Austria has experienced a process of de-pillarisation. That process may perhaps best be likened to the peeling away of the subcultures' outer rings, the politically organised cores of which have (except in that of the KPÖ) as yet shrunk only slightly. Moreover, at mass level and in terms of mid-level functionaries, their sociological profile is substantially unchanged. At elite level, however, there has been a maintenance of differences in religiosity and political belief, but a general decline in previously already less pronounced levels of socio-economic differentiation. Accordingly, while Austria's demographic change since the 1950s and 1960s has in many ways passed the parties' mass memberships by and thus left them increasingly unrepresentative of Austrian society, the sociological profile of the parties' highest elites has if anything become more socially representative.[27]

Mobilization and Values

The preceding section has shown how the two major Austrian *Lager*'s successful organisational penetration and incorporation of their respective subcultures depended upon the combined efforts of very large political parties and a myriad of auxiliary associations. However, the ensuing plurality of intra-subcultural organisations is not necessarily an advantage in consociational political systems. First, it implies a potential for a divergence of political values and thus a certain risk to subcultural cohesion. Second, it provides potentially competing intra-*Lager* power centres and could therefore pose problems for (party-political) *Lager* control. The nature of *Lager* values and mobilization and the structures and techniques of intra-*Lager* organisational control have to meet the twin challenges of cohesion and control and thus to keep at bay latent intra-*Lager* centrifugal pressures. Organisational structure will be considered below under the rubric 'hierarchical control'. This section's focus is the nature and efficacy of values which the Austrian *Lager* use to achieve cohesive subcultural mobilisation.

Mass Political Participation. While many consociational political systems exhibit high levels of political participation, the latter is – even more so than in many other liberal democracies – often of an essentially symbolic, or acclamatory nature. It is not designed to enable individuals to affect significantly the political process. The high premium which such systems place upon the quantitative, as opposed to the qualitative aspects of participation has much to do with *Lager* elites' bargaining strength being greatly affected by the opposing *Lager*'s estimate of their subculture's size and how far they are able to mobilise it politically.[28] It is not surprising that the mobilisational efforts of *Lager* elites are usually intended to elicit from their respective subcultural masses compliant political behaviour, limited in the main to ritual demonstrations of *Lager* loyalty.

Since 'classic' consociationalism, there has been a significant decline in the Austrian *Lager*'s success at mobilising the uncritical support and passive political participation of their rank-and-file. First, there are falling levels of partisan attachment to the two main *Lager*. As the data analysed in the essay by Plasser *et al.* show,[29] partisan *Lager* attachment, or *Lagermentalität* has substantially decreased. For example, between 1954 and 1990, the proportion of party identifiers in the Austrian electorate declined from 73 per cent to 49 per cent, while the levels of conative partisanship of the major parties' adherents fell from 81 to 43 and from 82 to 47 per cent for the SPÖ and ÖVP respectively. Moreover, between 1969 and 1990 the proportion of Austrians expressing unconditional party support fell from 65 to 34 per cent. Second, Austria's previously consistently high level of voter turnout has declined. At national elections held during 1945–1966 inclusive, the proportion of non-voters averaged only 4.8 cent; between 1970 and 1983 it rose to an average of 7.6 per cent and by 1990 had increased to an all-time high of 13.9 per cent. Third, voters are no longer as loyal to their *Lager*, as indicated by, for example, changes in Austria's level of total net volatility, which at 1953–66 national elections had been one of the lowest in Western Europe.[30] As a result of a leftward shift of voter support, volatility initially jumped to 6.9 per cent in 1970 and though it fell back to very low levels for the rest of the decade, it again increased significantly during the 1980s, peaking at 9.9 per cent in 1990. Finally, there has undoubtedly been a reduction in respect of party and auxiliary association membership (see above).

Explanations of such changes in political attitudes and behaviour have to date been couched mainly in terms of political sociology, with an emphasis upon, for example, secularisation; urbanisation; changes in

Austria's occupational structure and its social and geographical mobility, as well as in its networks of political information and communication.[31] That these factors have contributed to change Austrian political culture into a more critical-participant orientation,[32] as well as reducing subcultural encapsulation and thus loosening *Lager* ties, is not in doubt. However, levels of political participation and the extent of uncritical *Lager* loyalty cannot be explained fully by reference solely to socio-economic, or socio-cultural factors, but must include the role of the *Lager* parties themselves.[33] Of particular significance is the nature and efficacy of the values underpining their efforts at mobilising their subcultures. Though they clearly overlap, it may be useful to consider those efforts by two broad types of values with a specific mobilising effect, namely, ideological values and material, or instrumental values.

Ideological Values. During 'classic' consociationalism, the three main *Lager* parties utilised ideological values to define their respective subcultures not only 'positively' (in terms of a distinct *Weltanschauung*), but also 'negatively' (by fostering hostility to opposing *Lager*). An analysis of formal party programmes[34] shows first, a trend for the ideological distinctiveness of the two main *Lager* to decline. Thus the SPÖ has continued to move away from the Austro-Marxism of the inter-war years, as articulated in, for example, the 1926 Linz programme, which was strongly anti-clerical and identified the party's role as leading the struggle to liberate the working class. Though that programme technically remained binding until 1958, the party had soon after the war shifted its ideological position towards mainstream West European social democracy. In 1958 it chose to describe itself as a 'party for all working people' and supported gradualist policies that emphasised the need for economic planning, industrial democracy and a dense social security net, but also explicitly accepted the idea of entrepreneurial initiative, competition and the price mechanism. In its 1978 programme the SPÖ rejected further nationalisation and by the mid-1980s had in fact come to champion selective privatisation and deregulation.

For its part, the ideology of the post-war Catholic-conservative *Lager* was also very much less radical. First, the party was now unequivocally committed to liberal democracy. Second, the role which the party ascribed to the Catholic church was far less pronounced and though it continued to emphasise Catholic social theory throughout 'classic' consociationalism, there has since been a further secularisation of both the language and substance of the party's ideology. Third, during the Second Republic's first three decades, the dominant strand of the ÖVP's economic policy was very similar to that of the SPÖ and can be summed up as a shared commitment to what has come to be known as 'Austrokeynesianism'.[35]

However, in the late 1970s and especially in the early 1980s, the ÖVP sought to improve its poor electoral position by enhancing its ideological distinctiveness *vis-à-vis* the SPÖ. It not only renewed its emphasis upon moral conservatism, but also adopted a range of neo-liberal economic policies, a mix that can be characterised as neo-conservatism.[36] In the event, the re-establishment in 1986 of grand coalition government has resulted in the ÖVP's moral conservatism being placed on the back-burner, while its commitment to economic liberalism has been all but matched by that of the SPÖ. Accordingly, the late 1980s witnessed the re-establishment, albeit on the basis of a revised economic policy, of substantial similarities in the ideological profiles of the SPÖ and ÖVP.

Second, there have been significant changes since the mid-1960s in the political ideology of the Third *Lager*. Most important has been a decided shift away from the markedly conservative and German-national values so typical of the party's 1950s and early 1960 platform. The FPÖ's greater emphasis on liberalism, articulated most clearly in its 1985 party programme, underpinned the party's participation in the 1983-86 coalition with the SPÖ, which one could argue paved the way for the above-mentioned new, more market-orientated economic consensus between the SPÖ and ÖVP. On the other hand, while the FPÖ's ideology has formally not changed since 1985, the election of Jörg Haider as party chairman in 1986 led to a much lessened FPÖ emphasis on liberalism. The FPÖ has always rejected Austria's elite political cartel, but since 1986 its opposition has been much more strident with vehement attacks on bureaucratization, as well as on various categories of 'social parasites' (*'Sozialschmarotzer'*). This has helped ensure that despite similarities in economic policy *vis-à-vis* the two main *Lager*, the FPÖ maintains a distinctive, protest-orientated ideological profile. It also suggests that its historical ideological ambiguity has yet to be resolved.

Third, while the SPÖ has largely been successful in maintaining a cohesive ideological identity, the Catholic-conservative *Lager* has always been plagued by ideological conflict, especially between its social and liberal wings, as represented particularly in the ÖAAB and the ÖWB respectively. In the early 1960s the ÖVP's ideological factionalism was sufficiently pronounced for Engelmann to cite it as one of the major features of political opposition in Austria.[37] Despite greater emphasis under the new grand coalition governments since 1986 upon deregulation and the market, ideological dissent within the Catholic-conservative *Lager* has if anything intensified. It currently not only hampers the ÖVP's bargaining capacity, but also threatens the persistence of a single party-political expression of the Catholic-conservative *Lager*.

Fourth, a major change in the ideological values employed by the three main *Lager* to promote the cohesion and mobilisation of their subcultures concerns the use of negative values designed to maintain inter-*Lager* hostility. During 'classic' consociationalism, the two main *Lager* parties called for subcultural solidarity against the 'threat' to the political system posed by the rival *Lager*.[38] However, the credibility of such attempts at ideological mobilisation was increasingly undermined by first, over two decades of inter-*Lager* co-operation in grand coalition government and second, by the series of single party governments that ruled Austria from 1966 to 1983 patently not abusing their position to bring about a fundamental change in the rules of the game. The two main *Lager* have therefore become much less strident in the ideological values they use for subcultural mobilisation and rely much less upon 'negative' values. However, the FPÖ is rather different, with the post-1986 populist style indicating a return to an ideological appeal that is at least as confrontational as during 'classic' consociationalism. The FPÖ's attack relates in part to the two main *Lager*'s *Weltanschauungen*, but is directed primarily at the material values which they have traditionally used to mobilise and retain the support of their subcultures.

Material Values. The mobilisational capacity of ideological values is of course closely related to how individuals believe the policies associated with those values will affect their material well-being. Indeed, material values themselves play a direct role in parties' attempts to attract and reward voters and members. One target of such material values are groups and prominent among the vehicles used to deliver such values are social and economic policy. A second target are individuals, whose political support is rewarded by direct political intervention on their behalf. Though they have not been the subject of detailed empirical investigation,[39] many observers of Austrian politics argue that both policy-based patronage and individual patronage have played a key role in maintaining *Lager* loyalty. In the case of the Catholic-conservative and socialist *Lager*, this has been because of the political control of material resources by the ÖVP and SPÖ respectively. Paradoxically, it has also played a role in the Third *Lager*, whose leaders were largely excluded from political power, in that opposing such patronage helped unite a *Lager* traditionally characterised by the absence of a single set of ideological values.

When considering the role of material values in mobilising support for the two main *Lager*, it is worth noting first, that policy patronage helped mobilisation during 'classic' consociationalism, when the parties provided not only high levels of economic growth, full employment and social welfare benefits, but also delivered their client groups specific material rewards. In the Catholic-conservative *Lager*, this included farming subsidies and regulative outputs designed to ensure restricted access to certain categories of trade and commerce. In the case of the socialists, it provided *et al.* job security and advantageous pension rights to workers in the nationalised industries. Second, among the recent economic downturn's effects have been substantial redundancies in public sector enterprises, cuts in public subsidies and a streamlining of the tax system that has removed various tax concessions. These developments have significantly reduced the policy patronage exercised by the two major *Lager*. Moreover, the latter's capacity to provide large-scale policy rewards is likely to decline even further if, as expected, Austria joins the European Community and the existing economic policy priorities are retained.[40]

Third, individual patronage has figured prominently in the mobilisation strategies of the main *Lager* throughout the Second Republic. Such patronage has been based in the main upon the introduction, soon after the war, of the principles of *Proporz* and of segmental autonomy. *Proporz* denotes the proportional distribution of posts in the state bureaucracy and public sector industries, as well as of public resources, between the two major parties in proportion to their relative strength, as defined primarily in terms of their relative share of the vote at the most recent national election. The main aims of *Proporz* and of segmental autonomy were to avoid the crises of distribution and legitimation of the First Republic, by ensuring first, that both major *Lager* would consider themselves to be equal beneficiaries of the new state and second, that they would be permitted the greatest possible latitude in the regulation of their own affairs. However, these principles also functioned to increase *Lager* mobilisation, since distribution of the material values allocated to subcultures was largely undertaken autonomously within the *Lager*, where the beneficiaries were chosen above all from among those persons who could demonstrate their *Lager* commitment through, for example, active party or auxiliary association membership. The material rewards which such people could expect included preferential treatment in housing, jobs and promotion, as well as in the granting of individual licences to trade.

Fourth, both policy-based material rewards and individual patronage are not only limited in their capacity to ensure *Lager* support, but are also costly. In the former case, the main problems are the macro-economic costs of such measures as well as the impossibility of preventing 'free-riders'. The latter problem is of course much reduced – though not eliminated – in individual patronage. However, the second form of mobilisation presents its own problems. First, allocation of posts by *Lager* loyalty fosters inefficiency. Second, for individual patronage to be effective in recruiting and retaining *Lager* support, there must be seen to be a relationship between *Lager* loyalty and material rewards. However, such a perception can also be counterproductive, as has become increasingly evident in Austria, where political clientelism now causes widespread public resentment. The well documented rise in recent years of 'party weariness', or negative affect appears to be strongly related to public dissatisfaction at what it increasingly perceives as a practice associated with political corruption. The significance of this development for Austria's traditional *Lager* structure is potentially serious, since it delegitimises not only the two main *Lager* as such, but the political class as a whole. In that this increases the salience of horizontal political cleavages, political patronage increasingly threatens, rather than supports, the vertical subcultural encapsulation upon which *Lager* loyalty rested.

To summarise, the reduction since 'classic' consociationalism in uncritical support for the two main *Lager* is the product of depillarisation brought about not only by general social and economic change, but also by the growing ineffectiveness of both the ideological and the instrumental values traditionally employed by subcultural elites seeking to mobilise support for their *Lager*. On the one hand, the two main *Lagers*' ideological distinctiveness has decreased and with it the mobilisational capacity of both positive and negative ideological values. On the other hand, there has been a decline in the scope for and success of strategies of fostering partisan attachment *via* material values based on either group, or individual patronage.

Hierarchical Control

While the organisational plurality within Austria's *Lager* has facilitated subcultural penetration and incorporation, a multiplicity of oligarchic subcultural organisations could undermine intra-*Lager* hierarchical control. This undermining could prevent the subculture performing as a single and decisive political actor externally. In turn, this could threaten the subcultural elites' capacity to engage in the binding inter-*Lager* accommodation central to consociational political systems. The final aspect of intra-subcultural linkages examined here thus concerns how and with what success the Austrian *Lager* have sought simultaneously to ensure the hierarchical nature of their subcultural organisations and their *Lager*'s political unity. That examination will first outline how this was achieved during classic consociationalism, before proceeding to identify examples of continuity and change in the post-1966 period.

Hierarchical Subcultural Organisations. The internal structure and operation of the parties and major auxiliary associations of above all the socialist and Catholic-conservative *Lager* traditionally shared at least three key characteristics.[41] First, they were essentially bureaucratic in nature, largely because of their size. Though no precise figures are available, it is clear that if one were to add up the numbers of persons employed more-or-less directly by the parties and auxiliary associations of each of the two main *Lager* during this period, one would arrive at a figure of many thousands. The sheer numbers of their employees placed inexorable pressure on these organisations to adopt bureaucratic structures and operating styles, which were then perpetuated by the principles of recruitment. On the one hand, recruitment of new members was undertaken by persons within those organisations, who had already been socialised into the types of attitude and behaviour valued by those bureaucracies. Consequently, candidates predisposed to such values were more likely to be successful.

On the other hand, the hierarchical operating style of the *Lager* parties and auxiliary associations was reinforced by criteria that effectively governed career progression within those organisations. These tended to value seniority and bureaucratic loyalty. Aware that both promotion within the bureaucracies and recruitment to subcultural political office depended upon them pleasing their superiors in the organisational hierarchy, functionaries were inclined to work more for their bureaucracies, than the needs of their membership subculture. In sum, *Lager* organisations were staffed in the main not by politically committed amateurs, but by professional bureaucrats, whose values were often orientated inwards to the organisations themselves. Due to this bureaucratisation, they became increasingly distant from the grassroots of their subculture. This applied not only to auxiliary associations, but also to the political parties. Indeed, the gap between the latter and their members was widened further by mid-1970s legislation on party finance, which reduced parties' financial reliance upon membership dues in favour of state subsidies. In turn, this lowered the parties' incentive to recruit and retain individual members and may thus in part help explain the recent decline of SPÖ and ÖVP membership levels.

A second feature of many of the most significant organisations of the two main *Lager* was their internal operation of technocratic, as opposed to ideological values. Partly a function of their aforementioned bureaucratic nature, it also related to the specialist role of the largest of the *Lager*'s auxiliary associations. During 'classic' consociationalism, when the two main *Lager* exercised a duopoly over national government, access to the expertise of such occupation-based associations was crucial to the *Lagers*' capacity to influence policy formulation and implementation processes in their favour. Indeed, the chambers in many respects gave more expert advice than even the state bureaucracies and since the socialist and Catholic-conservative subcultures exercised a virtual monopoly of control over access to the expert advice of 'their' chambers, this put them in a politically very powerful position. For their part, the party and auxiliary associations of the Third *Lager* were never as bureaucratically structured, nor as technocratically orientated as those of the two main *Lager*. On the contrary, they can be described as markedly amateur. This was due to first, the much smaller number of full-time equivalent party functionary posts available within an electorally and financially comparatively weak subculture. However, it was also a corollary of the *Lager*'s weak representation in the chambers, which reduced the role of technocrats within the subculture, a group in any event of less importance to a *Lager* excluded from government at the national level.

A third characteristic of Austria's subcultural organisations during 'classic' consociationalism was their tradition of oligarchic decision-making. It was evident in organisations of all four *Lager* and has been regarded as both a cause and a consequence of Austria's well documented subject political culture. As long as the political system's outputs were perceived to be satisfactory, most Austrians appear to have been content to restrict themselves largely to formal types of political participation and to leave 'real' politics to a more or less professional class of politicians,[42] which included political activists, functionaries and office holders. In turn, a high proportion of the activists and functionaries of the key *Lager* organisations shared orientations that could be described as a largely deferential. Organisational oligarchy was of course predicated not only upon attitudinal predispositions, but also upon structural factors, including, for example, the aforementioned dependence of party and auxiliary association functionaries and office holders upon the bureaucratic hierarchies of their respective organisations. Together, such factors help explain the disciplined nature of subcultural organisations, their tendency for centralised decision-making and the pre-eminence within them of what Panebianco terms 'horizontal', as opposed to 'vertical' power games.[43]

Subcultural Political Unity and Control. The existence within each Austrian subculture of numerous large, bureaucratic organisations, with hierarchical structures and oligarchic decision-making procedures made all the more critical the need to promote the overall political cohesion of the *Lager*. Among the structures and techniques employed to this end were first, appeals to the kind of ideologically-based values discussed above. A second key factor was that group politics in Austria was marked by not only the mutual exclusivity of membership of organisations of competing *Lager*, but also by the practice of intra-*Lager* organisational overlap. The combined effect of *Lager* encapsulation and membership of multiple intra-*Lager* organisations was to ensure both partisan *Lager* attachment and, by means of cross-cutting loyalties to intra-*Lager* organisations, a dampening of intra-*Lager* conflict.[44] Of considerable significance was the fact that *Lager* organisations also overlapped in their leadership, for as has been mentioned above, the statutes of the politically most significant *Lager* auxiliary associations obliged their officials to be at least party members, if not holders of party office.

Whilst overlapping membership and leadership undeniably helped reinforce *Lager* cohesion, this essay is also concerned with the extent of party-political control over the *Lager*. Whether political primacy within the subculture was exercised by the *Lager* party, or by one or more *Lager* auxiliary associations was greatly influenced by two factors. The first relates to the organisation of party membership. Where this was direct, as in the KPÖ, the SPÖ and the FPÖ, subcultural loyalty was orientated primarily to the party. Conversely, in the ÖVP, where party membership was indirect, the loyalty of many members of the ÖVP's constituent 'Leagues' remained directed mainly to the latter, rather than to the party as whole. The ÖVP was thus widely seen as comprising little more than the sum of its parts, which themselves frequently assumed divergent positions on key political issues. Despite the party's frequent attempts at reform, the basis of ÖVP membership remained unchanged, so the party continued to be beset by factionalism.

Second, the relative political strength of the various *Lager* organisations was critically influenced by the extent to which they controlled the subculture's reward structure. Though the *Lager*'s occupational auxiliary associations were always important in dispensing rewards, in the communist and socialist subcultures the party retained a significant degree of control over these associations, thus ensuring the party organisation's primacy within those *Lager*. By contrast, the experience of the Catholic-conservative subculture was of much greater auxiliary association independence and a concomitant relative weakness of the *Lager* party *vis-à-vis* the Leagues. To summarise, the most important organisations of the communist, socialist and German-national subcultures were their respective political parties, but the position in the Catholic-conservative *Lager* was less clearcut. Moreover, while *Lager* cohesion was traditionally very high within the socialist and the communist subcultures, it remained low in the Catholic-conservative and German-national *Lager*, where it was undermined by factionalism and ideological dissent respectively.

Continuity and Change. At first glance, there appears to have been little or no change since 'classic' consociationalism in the internal character of Austria's subcultural organisations, or in the nature and extent of *Lager* cohesion. Many *Lager* organisations are still highly bureaucratised and *Lager* parties are still easily classified as either mass parties (SPÖ and ÖVP), or notable-led parties (FPÖ). Moreover, if one investigates the structure and operation of Austria's subcultural organisations in recent years, one finds much evidence that the decision-making processes of many remain oligarchic and often highly centralised. This is especially true of the communist subculture, in which the greatest degree of hierarchical control is still to be found. Though the ideological underpinnings of that control are presently under severe threat, its structural foundations persist.

Thus there remains a pervasive system of overlapping leadership between the various subcultural organisations, control over which is centred firmly in the KPÖ. Notwithstanding the significant decline in recent years of communist support, the KPÖ still has access to considerable funds and relative to its size maintains a very large apparatus, with currently over 200 full-time functionaries on its payroll.

A recent study of leadership selection in Austrian parties[45] shows that oligarchic decision-making continues to characterise the internal workings of all three main *Lager* parties. The most centralised of the three parties has historically been the SPÖ. Though approximately ten per cent of its large number of individual members have usually been classified as '*Vertrauensleute*', or confidants and the majority of those will have participated in minor party activities, it has been estimated that only approximately a third of that group will have ever been in a position to influence important aspects of intra-party decision-making.[46] Moreover, despite organisational adjustments pursuant to a party reform in 1967 and notwithstanding a subsequent lively and long-running debate on internal democratisation, it appears that efforts to decentralise the party and reduce its oligarchic decision-making processes have met with only limited success. The persistence of oligarchic practices within the party and of the SPÖ's hierarchical control of the socialist *Lager* have been regarded by many as closely related to the SPÖ's almost continual presence in Second Republic governments. The SPÖ's role as a party of government for 42 of the last 46 years has resulted in what Müller and Phillip[47] have described as the 'governmentness' of the party. Many observers conclude that until the SPÖ becomes an opposition party again, it is doubtful whether any attempts at party reform can bring about significant changes to the SPÖ and to its relationship with the socialist subculture.

Meanwhile, the Catholic-conservative *Lager* in general and the ÖVP in particular continue to be far more decentralised than the socialist and communist subcultures. For its part, the FPÖ has remained a party of notables, with political power traditionally decentralised among the leaders of the *Land* organisations of Upper Austria, Styria, Carinthia and Salzburg, which together have consistently provided three quarter of the party's total membership. Except for Norbert Steger's chairmanship (1981–86), the party leader has always been drawn from one of these *Länder*. With Haider's assumption of the chairmanship in 1986, his Carinthian power base has predictably become more important. Though internal party conflicts are often presented as ideological conflict between national and liberal orientations, in reality they tend to be power struggles based on personalities and regional interests, for which ideology has often served as a useful rationalisation.

Despite such evidence of continuity in the major features of *Lager* organisation, there have in recent years been some quite significant changes. First, in part due to public resentment of role accumulation by 'multi-functionaries', there has been a decline in the practice of overlapping leadership. Thus the ÖVP Styrian and Salzburg branches formally pledged themselves to stop interest group functionaries being automatically elected to represent the party in parliament. For its part, the SPÖ has not as yet passed a formal resolution, but recent evidence suggests a reduction in overlapping membership at the *Lager*'s highest levels (see the later discussion of the corporate arena).

Reducing overlapping membership was meant to curtail individual political power and to promote the role within *Lager* organisations of formal structures and or their ordinary members. This has not happened because of a second key development, namely, a shift in power within political parties from their official organs to party leaders. This stems directly from the increased importance of personalities in Austrian electoral politics and is most pronounced in the SPÖ and the FPÖ, which have in recent years both been led by strong individuals. In the SPÖ, Kreisky and latterly Vranitzky were able to use the SPÖ's reliance upon their electoral popularity as chancellor candidate to exercise more influence within the party than previously. In the FPÖ too, the force of Haider's personality, upon which the party's recent substantial electoral successes appear to have largely been based, has led to a marked increase in the party leader's power and a concomitant decline in that of other party organs. The party's more monocratic nature can perhaps be illustrated by recent changes in its recruitment practices. The FPÖ has always relied much less than the other *Lager* parties upon seniority and bureaucratic loyalty as principles governing promotion within the *Lager*. However, of late the leader's involvement in staffing decisions has increased at both *Land* and federal level. Moreover, many such appointments have been made from among those with little or no previous service in the *Lager*. Such persons are variously labelled 'fast climbers' (*Aufsteiger*), 'vertical starters' (*Senkrechtstarter*), or 'lateral entrants' (*Quereinsteiger*). In that they all owe their high positions in *Lager* organisations to the party chairman's direct intervention, their loyalty naturally tends less to the subculture, and more to the incumbent leader.

A third significant trend since 'classic' consociationalism, and one to some extent contrary to those just outlined, has been the increased territorial dimension of Austrian politics. This is caused by a revitalised Austrian federalism,[48] but also, paradoxically, by elections to the provincial parliaments (the *Landtage*) tending to become national elections. The implications have included an increased significance of the territorial subunits of the subcultural associations and in particular of local party leaders' power. During the long period (1970–87) when the ÖVP was relegated to opposition at federal level, already significant ÖVP party decentralisation became even more pronounced, as successful *Land* party organisations, like those of Lower Austria and Tyrol, pursued strategies independent of the central party and made individual deals with SPÖ federal governments. In both main parties, leaders of *Land* groups now exercise a considerable hierarchical control over the party's territorial subdivisions, especially where they are simultaneously the *Landeshauptmann*, that is to say, head of the provincial government. In many such cases they aspire to be *Landesvater*, or to put it less charitably, to the position of the local party 'boss'.

The final development we shall mention here concerns *Lager* cohesion. Within the socialist, communist and German-national subcultures, *Lager* unity and control have remained relatively constant, despite temporary fluctuations, such as in the Third *Lager* during the early 1980s. However, the picture has been very different in the Catholic-conservative subculture. Throughout the Second Republic, it has been plagued by problems arising from the party's League-based structure. As vertically organised intra-party interest groupings, the Leagues have institutionalised factionalism within the *Lager*. Since 'classic' consociationalism ended, problems posed by lack of *Lager* unity have become acute. Seventeen years of opposition at national level and the party decentralisation of these years combined with the chronic problem of factionalism to ensure that the *Lager* now lacks not a only centrally controlled party, but also political cohesion between its various subcultural organisations.

Increasingly frequent calls for a radical reform of the party resulted in 1991 in agreement on a new party statute.[49] Its reform proposals are an attempt to re-assert central control within the party and thus also the *Lager* as a whole. Great emphasis is placed on the binding nature of decisions of the party's new, slimmed-down central institutions, on which representation is no longer according to League membership. Though it is too early to judge these new regulations' effect, there is every reason to be cautious about their potential for resolving the ÖVP's chronic difficulties. Indeed, their exhortations to abandon factionalism in favour of unity and central decision-making indicate the depth of the problem faced by the *Lager*. For many observers, there is a real threat to not only the present unity of the *Lager*, but to its very survival, with one possible scenario being a fractionalisation of the party into its constituent functional, or even territorial units. Were that to occur, it would spell the end of the Catholic-conservative *Lager* as we know it, and would most likely have a dramatic impact on Austrian politics, for so long conducted by interaction between politically-cohesive *Lager* blocks.

THE *LAGER* PARTIES' INTER-SUBCULTURAL INTERACTION: THE FIVE ARENAS OF THE AUSTRIAN PARTY SYSTEM

As indicated at the beginning of this essay, political parties' significance for consociational theory and practice is primarily twofold. First, it relates to the nature of their intra-subcultural linkages and especially the extent to which the latter foster the pillarisation that constitutes one of consociationalism's characteristic features. Of equal importance, however, is their role in the inter-subcultural accommodation that comprises the second defining characteristic of consociational political systems. Inasmuch as the interaction between Austria's subcultures is undertaken primarily by political parties, to investigate Austria's practice of overarching elite accommodation is to examine the country's party system. In order to understand that system, it is necessary to assess what Sartori would term its 'format', or structure, as well as its pattern of interaction, or 'mechanics'.[50] That is to say, one must consider for example, the actors' number and relative size, the nature of their interaction and in particular how competetive, or consensual it is.

During 'classic' consociationalism, the style of interaction between the party-political elite of Austria's rival subcultures used to be governed above all by two techniques of accommodation: mutual veto and *Junktim*. The first was especially evident in Cabinet decision-making, but also found in party interaction in other bodies, such as, for example, the conference of provincial governors (*Landeshauptmännerkonferenz*) and in the social partnership's structures. It usually meant an explicit or implicit requirement for unanimity in decision-making. The term *Junktim* designates the practice of log-rolling in two substantively unconnected areas of policy and can thus be regarded as a technique for resolving, by reciprocal sacrificing of 'holy cows', stalemates brought about by the rigid application of the mutual veto principle.

For its part, the structure of inter-subcultural party interaction up to the mid-1960s contained four main features. The first was a high level of concentration and the second comprised proportional distribution of the overwhelming majority of public sector posts and resources between the two major *Lager* (the system of *Proporz*). The third was segmental autonomy, applied both functionally and territorially,[51] which was as a rule qualified within the relevant area of activity by structures and techniques designed for monitoring from and on behalf of the other subculture. Fourth, due to the major subcultures' desire to maximise control of Austrian public life, the *Lager* parties interacted everywhere. It pervaded not only electoral, parliamentary and governmental arenas, but also corporate and bureaucratic arenas. Moreover, practices such as overlapping leadership ensured low levels of role differentiation between these various arenas.

The following sections will seek the extent of recent change in inter-subcultural interaction. That examination will be a consecutive analysis of Austrian party-system structure and operation in the electoral, parliamentary, governmental, corporate and bureaucratic arenas. We shall concentrate on these arenas at national level, though as argued elsewhere, analysis of party interaction at regional (i.e., *Land* or state) level can also be highly instructive.[52]

The Electoral Arena

During the last 25 years, Austria's has experienced radical changes in traditional electoral behaviour (analysed in this volume by Plasser *et al.*), but because voting behaviour is exogenous to the party system as such,[53] it will not be re-examined here. For our purposes, Austria has of late experienced much voter de-alignment, with a substantial decline in partisan attachment to the traditional *Lager* and concomitant increases in the previously very small pool of floating voters and thus in net electoral volatility also. These changes in voting behaviour had two consequences for inter-subcultural interaction in the electoral arena: changes to the structure of party competition and changes to the pattern of party interaction.

The structure of party competition in Austria's electoral arena used to be governed by stable and predictable electoral outcomes, characterised by only three 'relevant' parties, by two-party concentration of the national vote, by one-party hegemony in most *Land* level electoral arenas and by the Third *Lager*'s relatively weak position. Since the mid-1960s, there have been changes in all four respects. First, the number of 'relevant' actors has increased. As Table 3 shows, the Second Republic's relevant parties were initially the SPÖ, ÖVP and KPÖ, but in 1949 the KPÖ was replaced by the VdU, the FPÖ's predecessor party. Throughout 'classic' consociationalism and some years thereafter, only three relevant parties disputed the Austrian electoral arena. However, in 1983 the Greens emerged and they had a large impact upon not only the agenda of electoral competition, above all ecological issues, but also upon the structure and direction of party competition.[54]

Second, there has been a marked decline in the two main *Lager*'s dominance of electoral outcomes. The SPÖ and ÖVP's combined share of the national vote fell from an average of 88 per cent and rising at National Council elections held from 1953 (when the party system stabilised) to 1966 inclusive, to a mere 75 per cent in 1990 (see Table 3). This trend was mirrored at all recent *Landtag* elections. In Carinthia,

TABLE 3
MAJOR PARTIES' STRENGTHS AND THE PARTY SYSTEM (1945–1990)

Legislative Period	Combined ÖVP/SPÖ % Share of		Federal Government			Type of Party System According to Sartori[2]		
	National Council Vote	National Council Seats	Party Composition[1]	% Share of Vote	% Share of Seats	'Relevant' Parties	'Format of Party System	'Mechanics' of Party System
1945–47	94.4	98	*ÖVP*-SPÖ-KPÖ	99.8	100	ÖVP-SPÖ-KPÖ	Moderate Pluralism	Moderate Pluralism
(1947–49)			*ÖVP*-SPÖ	94.4	98	,,	,,	,,
1949–53	82.7	87	,,	82.7	87	ÖVP-SPÖ-FPÖ(VdU)[3]	,,	,,
1953–56	83.4	89	,,	83.4	89	,,	,,	,,
1956–59	89.0	95	,,	89.0	94	,,	,,	,,
1959–62	89.0	95	,,	89.0	95	,,	,,	,,
1962–66	89.4	95	,,	89.4	95	,,	,,	,,
1966–70	90.9	96	*ÖVP*	48.3	52	ÖVP-SPÖ-FPÖ	Moderate Pluralism	2 Party System with SPÖ as predominant party 1970–83
1970–71	93.1	96	*SPÖ*[4]	48.4	49	,,	,,	
1971–75	93.1	95	,,	50.0	51	,,	,,	
1975–79	93.0	95	,,	51.0	51	,,	,,	
1979–83	92.9	94	,,	51.0	52	,,	,,	,,
1983–86	90.8	93	*SPÖ*-FPÖ	5.26	56	ÖVP-SPÖ-FPÖ-Greens	Moderate Pluralism	Moderate Pluralism
1986–90	84.4	86	*SPÖ*-ÖVP	84.4	86	,,	,,	,,
1990–	75.1	77	,,	75.1	77	,,	,,	

Sources: Own calculations based on sources cited in Appendix 1.
Notes: 1. The party which held the chancellorship is in italics.
2. See G. Sartori, *Parties and Party Systems: A Framework for Analysis*, Vol.1 (CUP, 1976).
3. The *Verein der Unabhängigen* ('League of Independents') was the predecessor party of the FPÖ, by which it was replaced just prior to the 1956 election.
4. The 1970–71 minority SPÖ government received tacit parliamentary support from the FPÖ.

for example, the 1953–65 figure was 80 per cent and rising, as compared to 65 per cent in 1989, while the analogous Viennese results are 87 and 66 per cent.[55]

Third, the Third *Lager*'s position has changed. The VdU's initial successes were undermined by the two main parties' success at recruiting many VdU voters to their own ranks. Third *Lager* support slipped from 11.7 per cent in 1949, to an average of only 6.7 per cent for the FPÖ at the three national elections beteen 1959 and 1966 (see Appendix 1). At *Land* level, support was very uneven, but also in overall decline. The VdU's average support across all *Land* elections it contested was 12.2 per cent, but the average level of FPÖ support at *Land* elections held up to 1967 was nine per cent, albeit with variations from 3.7 per cent in Burgenland to 15.4 per cent in Vorarlberg. From the mid-1960s until the mid-1980s, the rate of decline in Third *Lager* support slowed. Nationally, its strength remained at about 5 per cent. *Land* results varied from 2.8 per cent in Lower Austria, to 15.1 per cent in Vorarlberg, but averaged only 7.4 per cent overall. By contrast, the party's fortunes have soared since Haider took over the leadership. At the 1986 and 1990 general elections, the FPÖ won 9.7 and 16.6 per cent of the vote respectively. The *Land* results since 1986 show an average FPÖ support of some 15.4 per cent, with returns in individual *Länder* ranging from 7.3 to 29 per cent (Burgenland, 1987 and Carinthia 1989 respectively). Not only has there been a dramatic increase in the absolute level of Third *Lager* support, but for the first time in the Second Republic, a major *Lager* party was relegated to third place in an electoral arena. Moreover, that has now happened twice: in Carinthia 1989 and in Vienna in 1991. On both occasions the victim was the ÖVP, which lost to the FPÖ by 29 to 21 and by 22.6 to 18.1 per cent respectively.

Fourth, the Third *Lager*'s substantial inroads into the electoral support of the two main *Lager* has substantially eroded the hegemony traditionally enjoyed by one or other of the two main *Lager* in most of the *Land* electoral arenas. In Tyrol, for example, always a bastion of support for the Catholic-conservative subculture, the ÖVP's average share of the vote at 1953–65 *Landtag* elections was 60 per cent and rising. Yet at the 1989 election, the party managed only 48.7 per cent of voters. Similarly, the SPÖ's average share of the poll at 1954–64 elections held in its Vienna stronghold was 54 per cent and rising, while at the November 1991 election, the party could only manage 47.7 per cent. The erosion of the major *Lager*'s hegemony in regional elections weakens the geographical concentration of their support and thus their capacity to sustain territorially-based segmental autonomy.

The style of party interaction in the electoral arena. As Hölzl's influential study demonstrates, party interaction in the electoral arena never featured the accommodation typical of the party system's other arenas, but produced highly emotional 'propaganda battles'.[56] Though Austria's electoral arena remains conflictual, that conflict has changed in several ways in recent years.

First, its direction has altered. Up to the mid-1960s, *Lager* efforts were directed almost exclusively towards mobilising their own subculture's vote. As Austria entered the 1970s and the number of strong party identifiers gradually decreased, the *Lager* parties increasingly sought to compensate by appealing to the growing band of floaters. Indeed, the SPÖ's 1970s electoral success was predicated upon their ability to convince such voters to 'go part of the way' with them. Since the start of the 1980s, partisan attachment has decreased further and the *Lager* parties have even begun to direct their attention at supporters of rival *Lager*.

Second, this redirection of electoral competition has required both main *Lager* parties to reduce significantly traditional appeals to *Lager* values and solidarity in their electoral messages and to alter radically the language in which they compete. Up to 1970, their campaigns were articulated primarily in terms of negative ideological values. These emphasised the danger allegedly posed to the political system's very survival by the rival *Lager* winning an absolute electoral majority. Thus the ÖVP evoked the 'red peril' of East European style socialism, whilst the SPÖ suggested, for example, that the Catholic-conservatives harboured a secret desire to dismantle welfare benefits and introduce unfettered market competition. In the last two decades, there has been a general shift away from such ideological messages and in particular from attempts to promote or maintain fear of the rival *Lager*.

Third, there has been increased emphasis upon modern methods of competition. The 1970s saw the introduction of television spots, of television debates, of commercial advertising and of other techniques that are often collectively labelled as the 'Americanisation' of campaigning. Austrian electoral competition is now not only slicker and more expensive, but also devotes greater attention to promoting the image of key party candidates. All these developments typify the increasingly volatile nature of Austria's electors and the resultant unpredictability of electoral outcomes. They can also be interpreted as symptomatic of the declining capacity of the traditional *Lager* organisations effectively to deliver the *Lager* vote.

Fourth, for the first two post-war decades, each major *Lager*'s stated electoral goal was to achieve a balance of power between the parties and it accused its rival of aspiring to an absolute majority. This widespread fear of absolute majorities is understandable. Austrians still had vivid memories of civil war and Fascism and they were kept alive by the

Lagermentalität of Austrian politics at this stage. Meanwhile, Austria's experiment with accommodation politics was still rather new and the depth of the rival *Lager*'s commitment to it uncertain. Much has changed since that time, throughout the 1970s the SPÖ openly and successfully aspired to absolute electoral majorities and single-party governments. Their success reflected increased Austrian faith in the major parties' democratic credentials. In turn, this was partly owed to the Austrian accommodative political system's success at reducing *Lager* hostility and fear.

Finally, however, one should not neglect the role which protest and anti-system orientations have played and continue to play in the Austrian electoral arena. At least since the advent of the VdU in 1949, strong criticism of most central features of Austria's consociational political system has been firmly on the agenda of electoral competition. It has been directed at, for example, the ubiquity and alleged omnipotence of Austria's main *Lager* parties, at mutual veto and *Junktim*, as well as the practices of segmental autonomy, overlapping leadership and *Proporz*. These are seen as linked to the recurring problem of political corruption. While such attacks are thus not new, they have increased in recent years in frequency, vehemence and currency, as recent FPÖ electoral successes testify. No longer the sole preserve of the FPÖ, they are also advanced by, for example, the Greens, albeit from a rather different political ideology.

The widespread acceptance of many of these criticisms could point to a certain malaise in Austrian politics, which appears to be becoming more susceptible to protest and anti-system parties. Alternatively, it may just be the political maturity of Austria's voters, who are less willing to be governed by oligarchic political structures predicated upon mass deference to assumed elite wisdom.

The Parliamentary Arena

The structure of party competition. As is only to be expected of an electoral system based on proportional representation, changes since 'classic' consociationalism in the *Lager* parties' relative electoral strengths have been faithfully reflected in parliament.[57] Accordingly, the Austrian parliamentary party system has in recent years also seen the entrance of new actors, deconcentration, increased representation of the Third *Lager* and an end to the hegemony previously exercised in individual *Land* parliaments by the ÖVP and SPÖ.

To be specific, first, the Greens succeeded in entering the National Council in 1986, where they now hold five per cent of the seats. At the end of 1991, they were also represented in four of the nine *Land* parliaments. Second, the ÖVP and SPÖ's combined share of parliamentary seats has also declined (see Table 3). At the national level, during 1953–66 it comprised on average 94 per cent, but by 1990 had shrunk to a mere 77 per cent, with an analogous decline in the *Land* parliaments. Third, the German-national *Lager* has increased its national parliament representation from an average of five per cent of seats (1953–83), to 10 per cent in 1986 and 18 per cent in 1990. Moreover, the FPÖ now holds ten of the 63 seats in the indirectly elected Bundesrat, which with minor exceptions (1949–57) had until the late 1980s always been an exclusive preserve of the two main *Lager*. Finally, five *Landtage* now no longer have a party with an overall majority of seats and of those that do, none have over 56 per cent of seats. By comparison, at the 1953–67 *Landtag* elections, only two *Länder* (Styria and Salzburg) usually failed to return a party with an overall majority and six of the nine always had a party with 50 per cent or more seats. Meanwhile, two *Länder* parliaments (in Vienna and Tyrol), regularly contained a party with 60 per cent or more of the seats and in 1953 the Tyrolean ÖVP even obtained 72 per cent of all seats.

The style of party interaction in the parliamentary arena has also changed substantially.[58] It used to exhibit a high degree of accommodation, it has of late become less quiescent. First, there has been a decline in the practice of passing legislation unanimously. Up to as late as the early 1980s, 70 to 80 per cent of acts were regularly passed in this way, but in the 1986–90 legislative period, it prevailed in only 47 per cent of laws. Second, parliament has become more active and greatly increased procedures such as question time, tabling written questions to ministers and committees of investigation designed to hold government and the administration to account. Some such committees of investigation have for the first time been held in public and they have not shirked from challenging very prominent *Lager* politicians (e.g., the Lucona Committee). Third, parliament's previously exceptionally high levels of party discipline has loosened. There has been the novel sight of members using the various techniques of parliamentary control and supervision against members of their own party. For instance, ÖVP members tabled a vote of no confidence in against their own minister of defence, a hitherto inconceivable event. Moreover, unorthodox parliamentary behaviour has grown, notably by the FPÖ and the Greens, who regard many parliamentray procedures as based on a cosy, but corrupt system of accommodation established by and for the interests of the two major *Lager*.

In sum, inter-subcultural interaction in the parliamentary arena has become much more important over the last two decades. Though the Austrian parliament still has some way to go to become an actor in its own right, it has seen greater levels of confrontation and thus started to shed its previous role as a primarily symbolic arena, in which subcultural interaction meant *Lager* party delegates obediently rubber-stamping decisions made elsewhere.

The Governmental Arena

The structure of party competition in the national government had three main features up to 1966. First, from 1947, access was shared jointly and exclusively by the parties representing the two major subcultures. Together they formed a series of 'grand coalitions', usually able to rely on the support of well over 90 per cent of the members of parliament (see Table 3). For many observers, these grand coalitions were the single most distinctive feature of 'classic' consociationalism. Indeed, one distinguished contributor has described grand coalition government as 'the primary characteristic ... of consociational democracy' in general.[59] However, Austria has not been ruled by grand coalitions for most of the last 25 years. Initially, it was ruled by single-party governments, first ÖVP (1966–70) and then SPÖ (1970–83). Except for the minority SPÖ government of 1970–71, they were all backed by just over half the seats in parliament. However, the SPÖ's three consecutive terms as a single party of government mean that from 1970 to 1983 the party assumed the role of what Sartori terms a 'predominant party'. Thereafter, there was a second phase, of rather shorter duration (1983–86), but constituting the first and as yet only example of Third *Lager* participation in national government. Finally, 1987 saw not only the return to national government of the ÖVP, excluded from it for seventeen years, but also the reappearance of grand coalition government between the SPÖ and ÖVP. The present grand coalition controls 'just' 77 per cent of parliamentary seats.

A second key feature was the principle of proportionality, used to decide the overall number and importance of cabinet portfolios which the coalition parties received and calculated according to the parties' relative shares of the vote at the preceding general election. In practice, however, that formula was modified by above all the relative bargaining skills of the rival party elites. During the single party governments (1966–70), subcultural proportionality in government was clearly no longer applicable, though it revived as a rough guide for coalition formation in 1983 (when the FPÖ obtained a disproportionately large share of posts) and again from 1987, to regulate the composition of the new grand coalition.

Third, party interaction in government was also shaped by segmental autonomy, applied in two ways. First, while a party's overall allocation of portfolios was decided by proportionality, which individuals were to hold those posts was left to the *Lager* to resolve. Notwithstanding the chancellor's constitutional responsibility for appointing ministers, reality restricted his role mainly to selecting his own party's governmental team, while that of his coalition partner was proposed by its own leader: the vice-chancellor. Moreover, the scope to select their own party colleagues was further limited by the intra-*Lager* groups. Thus, for example, the Minister of Social Affairs was always from the trade union wing of the socialist subculture. Similarly, the traditional ÖVP ministries of agriculture and of trade and commerce were always headed by representatives of the relevant party Leagues, who jealously guarded their right to appoint their own candidate.

Indeed, the factionalisation of the Catholic-conservative *Lager* meant that independent action by the head of the ÖVP government team was always considerably more restricted than that of his SPÖ counterpart. Second, the principle of segmental autonomy was reflected in ministers' autonomy. According to conventional political and constitutional wisdom, they cannot be overruled by the chancellor, or even by the combined vote of the cabinet, which is obliged to operate on the principle of unanimity. In practice, ministerial autonomy was undermined by the custom of allocating key ministers a secretary of state of the opposing party, who was to monitor the former's activities on behalf of the latter's party, but above all by the sway which the parties exercised over government decision-making during the 1950s and 1960s grand coalitions (see below).

The single-party nature of 1966–83 national governments meant segmental autonomy was irrelevant in this period. Moreover, though it has been used again subsequently, it has not assumed its previous significance. During the 1983–86 coalition, four state secretaries were appointed to ministries in which they could monitor the activities of their coalition partner. An SPÖ state secretary was allocated to the Ministry of Trade and Commerce, which was headed by FPÖ Vice-Chancellor Steger. For its part the FPÖ received state secretaryships in the SPÖ ministries of agriculture, health and of finance. In the new grand coalition (1987–90) there were initially only two and later four state secretaries. However, in each case only one was allocated to a ministry controlled by another party, namely, to the SPÖ-controlled finance ministry. This indicates the small amount of monitoring that now takes place, though the ministry of finance's central role makes the one state secretary who retains a monitoring role there especially significant.

It must be acknowledged that this system works two ways. While the party represented by the state secretary can 'spy' on its coalition partner, it also, first, makes the ÖVP share responsibility for finance ministry decisions and second, promotes co-operation between the latter and ÖVP-led ministries. The grand coalition has also restored segmental autonomy in selection of members of government and especially in ÖVP party factions' power to determine government composition. Accordingly, a trend for the chancellor's recruitment power to increase has been reversed.

Hitherto, party interaction in national government has been assessed. However, the situation at the *Land* level has in many respects been different. First, relatively high levels of two-party concentration persist, while SPÖ and or ÖVP-dominated all-party government remains the norm, albeit with caveats to be mentioned below. Second, in seven of Austria's nine *Länder*, all parties with significant *Landtag* representation still have a legal entitlement to be represented in *Land* governments. Third, that entitlement is not as generous as might appear. For one, many such *Landesräte* are allocated minor ministries. In addition, the dominant party always holds the governorship, and thus retains crucial powers, such as the budget and appointment of staff. Finally, unlike the national government, decision-making in *Land* cabinets is by majority voting. Accordingly, despite apparent grand coalition government at *Land* level, there has usually been one-party dominance and so a degree of territorial autonomy for the relevant subculture. This situation has in recent years been mitigated in two respects. First, decline in regional electoral and parliamentary hegemony of the two main *Lager* has led to greater concessions by the dominant *Land* party. Second, in 1989 Austria witnessed the first ever *Landeshauptmann* not from ÖVP or the SPÖ, namely, the FPÖ's Haider. With ÖVP help, Haider was elected governor in the traditional SPÖ stronghold of Carinthia. Though his term abruptly and prematurely ended following his remarks about the utility of Third Reich employment policies, this may well not be the only occasion on which the FPÖ will assume control over a *Land* government.

The style of party interaction in the governmental arena has altered since the old grand coalition ended in 1966, not least because of the varied governments formed since. Rather than map out the changes in all three types of government, this section will compare party interaction in the old and the new grand coalitions[60] to identify both elements of continuity and change.

Continuity is still seen in the considerable amount of consensus. First, though parties naturally disagree over some aspects of policy, an external observer might be struck by the degree of overall agreement on major lines of policy. Economic policy offers a good example.[61] Despite tension between the market-orientated elements of the *Wirtschaftsbund* and the more social-market concerns of the SPÖ and of the ÖVP left-wing, the old grand coalitions fundamentally agreed over economic policy. During the early 1980s, Austrian economic policy saw considerable conflict, at least rhetorical, between the incumbent SPÖ government and the ÖVP, then in opposition. However, since grand coalition government returned in 1987, there is again fundamental agreement on the major thrust of that policy. Indeed, the new economic priorities were one major reason for the return to coalition. Moreover, though frictions persist between the grand coalition parties, particularly over how economic reform costs are to be borne, the new priorities in economic policy are not seriously threatened.

A second continuity is cabinet decision-making itself. It remains essentially accommodative, governed by mutual veto and also, albeit much less than before, by *Junktim*. Official cabinet sessions are if anything even more meticulously prepared in prior meetings, where any item unlikely to receive unanimous approval is deferred. Accordingly, formal cabinet meetings remain quite ritualised, formally ratifying decisions previously arrived at.

There have, however, been important changes in how and by whom those prior decisions are made. Under old grand coalition governments, such decision-making took place primarily in the extra-constitutional Coalition Committee, composed of the key political elites of the rival *Lager*, many not members of the cabinet itself.[62] Yet Committee decisions were politically binding on the cabinet members, who were thereby effectively reduced to initiating and implementing policies, the decisions on which had been made not in the arena envisaged by the constitution, but in inter-subcultural party caucuses. By contrast, while the new grand coalition also has a Coalition Committee, the latter is a very different political animal. First, its membership excludes the chancellor, or the vice-chancellor and so it lacks the political clout of its predecessor. Second, the Committee has only two members (the chairman of the SPÖ and ÖVP parliamentary parties), who are not full members of the government. Government decision-making is thus much less determined in extra-constitutional fora by binding inter-subcultural agreements. In sum, Austria's national government has increasingly come to be a significant political actor in its own right, rather than an institution dominated by groups acting purely in a party capacity, whose decisions the cabinet merely rubber-stamps.[63]

The Corporate Arena

If grand coalition government was the most distinctive feature of Austrian politics up to 1966, the country's extensive system of corporate intermediation probably came a close second. Changes to the structure, operation and overall significance of that system are analysed in detail by Peter Gerlich elsewhere in this volume,[64] so the following discussion can be relatively brief.

The structure of inter-subcultural interaction in the corporate arena differs from the three arenas considered so far in at least one very obvious respect: it is has not been conducted by the parties as such, nor even by persons directly representing them. Instead, the main actors have been the five 'social partners': the Federal Chamber of Business (BWK), the Austrian Trade Union Federation (ÖGB), the Chamber of Labour (AK), the Chambers of Agriculture (LWK) and the Association of Austrian Industrialists (VÖI). Of these, the BWK and ÖGB have always played the most significant role. Party involvement in Austria's corporate arena has traditionally been mediated through these five institutions, though it remains disputed whether that has resulted in the latter's colonisation by their respective parties, or *vice-versa* (see endnote 9).

Before looking at interaction *between* the social partners, it is worth considering party competition *within* them. It is most pronounced in the BWK, ÖGB, AK and LWK, the internal politics of which has always been dominated by one party. Party interaction is most visible during their internal elections. Those to the regionally organised Chambers of Agriculture retain very high levels of ÖVP dominance and electoral stability. At the 1985–90 elections average levels of support for the ÖVP, SPÖ and FPÖ groupings (*Fraktionen*) were 81, 11 and 4 per cent respectively.[65] Within the BWK and AK, the dominant *Fraktion* has declined in recent years (see Tables 4 and 5). At AK elections up to and including 1964, the average SPÖ share of the vote was 67 per cent and the average gap between the SPÖ and ÖVP lay at some 49 percentage points. Corresponding averages for subsequent elections are 60 per cent and 33 percentage points respectively. In recent BWK elections, the ÖVP vote has been rather uneven. It fell from 86 per cent in 1975 to 78 per cent in 1980, revived to 84 per cent in 1985, before falling back again to 76 per cent in 1990. Unlike the LWK's socially homogeneous electors, those in the BWK are clearly much less likely to be strong party identifiers. That declining political commitment is also apparent in the BWK's levels of turnout, down from 79 per cent in 1975 to 62 per cent in 1990. The decline is even more marked in the AK, however, where turnout averaged 71 per cent at 1949–64 elections, but stood at only 48 per cent in 1991.

Lower levels of participation and reduced dominant party representation within 'its' chamber attest to a decline in vertical interest group integration. Moreover, that process of de-pillarisation is probably more advanced in the BWK than its electoral results suggest, especially among the self-employed and professionals, never as fully incorporated into the Austrian *Lager* as most other occupational groupings. Not only has this group grown in size, but it is increasingly dissatisfied with the cost and the compulsory nature of chamber membership. That this has not led to greater electoral change within the BWK is due to the latter's complicated electoral system strongly militating against small and non-established parties.

TABLE 4
PARTY REPRESENTATION IN CHAMBER OF LABOUR ELECTIONS (1949–1989)

	Turnout	Total Seats	SPÖ[1] Vote	SPÖ[1] Seats	ÖVP[2] Vote	ÖVP[2] Seats	FPÖ[3] Vote	FPÖ[3] Seats	KPÖ[4] Vote	KPÖ[4] Seats	GREENS[5] Vote	GREENS[5] Seats	OTHERS Vote	OTHERS Seats
1949	81.1	797	64.4	504	14.2	120	11.7	117	9.7	56			3.0	25
1954	72.5	810	68.6	569	16.0	139	2.5	19	9.9	58			2.7	15
1959	65.3	810	68.4	563	18.6	161	3.7	31	6.6	40			1.9	11
1964	63.3	810	66.4	555	21.4	180	3.6	27	6.7	37			0.9	4
1969	62.4	810	68.3	560	23.5	195	4.9	40	2.4	11			0.1	–
1974	64.4	810	63.4	531	29.1	239	4.7	29	2.4	1				
1979	61.1	810	64.3	534	31.0	252	3.2	20	1.2	4				
1984	63.6	840	58.7	502	36.5	317	2.5	13	1.4	5	0.8	3		
1989	48.0	840	59.8	510	29.1	258	7.7	63	1.7	4	1.6	5		

Source: Österreichisches Jahrbuch für Politik (1989), p. 112.
Notes: 1. Fraktion Sozialistischer Gewerkschafter.
 2. Österreichischer Arbeiter- und Angestelltenbund.
 3. Freiheitliche Arbeitnehmer; in 1949: Verein der Unabhängigen.
 4. Gewerkschaftliche Einheit; 1979–89: Gewerkschaftlicher Linksblock.
 5. Alternative Liste.

TABLE 5
PARTY REPRESENTATION IN CHAMBER OF BUSINESS ELECTIONS (1970–1989)

	Turnout (%)	Total Seats	SPÖ[1] Vote	SPÖ[1] Seats	ÖVP[2] Vote	ÖVP[2] Seats	FPÖ[3] Vote	FPÖ[3] Seats	OTHERS Vote	OTHERS Seats
1970	–	–	10	–	85	–	9	–	5	–
1975	78.6	–	9.3	1,092	86.1	10,133	–	–	–	–
1980	69.7	11,774	9.3	1,090	78.1	9,200	8.1	959	4.5	525
1985	–	12,083	8.4	1,014	84.0	10,148	3.1	376	4.5	545
1990	61.9	12,280	9.7	1,187	76.4	9,383	9.2	1,134	4.7	576

Sources: 1985 and 1990: *Österreichisches Jahrbuch für Politik* (1990), p. 179; 1975 and 1980: *Österreichisches Jahrbuch für Politik* (1980), p. 573; 1970: W. C. Müller, 'Das Parteiensystem' in H. Dachs *et al.* (eds.), *Handbuch des politischen Systems Österreichs* (Vienna: Manz, 1991), p. 192.

Notes: 1. Freier Wirtschaftstreibender Verein. 2. Österreichischer Wirtschaftsbund. 3. Ring Freiheitlicher Wirtschaftstreibender.

Furthermore, the changes to absolute and relative strengths of party groups *within* the social partners have to date had very little impact upon the interaction *between* them. This is above all due to the latter's highly centralised and oligarchic internal structure. Moreover, positions of authority within those organisations are not allocated on a *Proporz* basis and so internal hegemony by the dominant *Fraktion* persists.

Interaction *between* the main actors in the corporate arena has exhibited four structural characteristics: two-party concentration, proportionality, interconnectedness with other arenas and segmental autonomy. The first two aspects have changed little or not at all since the 1960s. The two major *Lagers*' monopoly of the highest levels of corporate interaction remains intact and proportional representation still applies to the various bodies in which the social partners meet to conduct their business. Examples include the highly influential Joint Commission and its three main sub-committees, as well as the hundreds of advisory bodies (*Beiräte*), which have legal consultation rights regarding the detailed application of legislation.

However, the remaining two features are not as clearcut. The first is the corporate arena's interconnectedness with other subcultural interaction arenas. There undoubtedly remains a fair degree of functional overlap between the corporate arena and, for example, the governmental arena. Thus the social partners are, for example, still regularly involved in the initiation and formulation of policy, often through the Joint Commission, attended by federal ministers and chaired by the federal chancellor. However, that forum is nothing like as influential as it was in the 1960s, when it was widely referred to as a second cabinet. Moreover, while the social partners remain an important source of technical expertise, their involvement in policy-making is of late neither as frequently sought, nor as seriously taken as it once was.[66] Second, a key practice keeping the corporate arena closely intertwined with wider inter-subcultural accommodation processes was overlapping leadership. The social partner organisations's leaders continue to rank high within their respective party hierarchies and be inescapably involved in other arenas of the party system, but there has been a decline in the practice of holding multiple public office. For example, ÖGB presidents have customarily also held the post of first president (i.e., chairman, or speaker) of the National Council. However, the current incumbent is merely an ordinary parliamentarian. Similarly, whilst his predecessors as a rule also had a seat in parliament, the current president of the AK national organisation does not. Though these are merely examples, they are two of the more important individual actors in the corporate arena.

Inasmuch as it denotes self-regulation by the subcultures of their own sphere of the socio-economic system, segmental autonomy is of course the *raison d'être* of Austrian corporatism. It has justified the *Lager* organisations' involvement in not only the initiation, formulation and making of policy, but also in its implementation. However, there has since the mid-1980s been a tendency (and as yet no stronger than that) for the commitment to segmental autonomy to decline. This is primarily a result not of intervention by one or other of the two main *Lager* into a realm, regulation of which had previously been reserved for its rival, but of a general trend in Austrian public policy for the state's role to be reduced. Since the corporate actors function not only as interest groups, but also as agents of the state, the rolling back of the state implies a narrowing scope for corporate intervention and a concomitant reduction in segmental autonomy. Another pressure for a reduced regulatory role of the social partners *vis-à-vis* their *Lager* comes from those very subcultures. Public resentment has grown since the mid-1980s at both the structure and the operating style of the corporate arena in general and of the chambers in particular.

The style of party interaction in the corporate arena retains both mutual veto and *Junktim*. However, though the latter is not popular, it is not so much because of these two operating principles that the corporate arena has come under attack, as because of other aspects of the social partners' behaviour. The perception is now widespread and frequently stated that the chambers are not only inefficient, legally and politically unaccountable and bureaucratic, but also high-handed and remote from the 'members' they are supposed to serve.

These criticisms are directed first, against the secrecy of much of their important decision-making. While such practices typified the first two or three decades of the Second Republic and were largely uncontested, processes not amenable to public scrutiny are now much less acceptable than they used to be. Second, decision-making appears to have been conducted in an extremely oligarchic manner, with many of the most important decisions apparently taken by just two key individual actors: the ÖGB and BWK presidents. Not only did they outlast politicians appointed via the electoral channel, but the chambers' powers to regulate many important aspects of millions of Austrians' working lives meant these two men arguably outweighed many politicians, who were at least in theory accountable to the public through the ballot box. Third, the chambers have increasingly been criticised for their bureaucratic and immobilist nature. They have come to be widely regarded as being more concerned with self-preservation, rather than with improving their members' lot.

Demands for reform of the corporate arena have grown apace, varying from calls for the chambers to be scrapped to suggestions for increasing their public accountability. A very popular demand is the abolition of the principle of compulsory membership that governs the AK, BWK and LWK. Should the latter demand be acted upon – and that cannot be dismissed out of hand – the outcome might possibly even be the wholesale abandonment of the corporatist structures and practices that so distinguished 'classic' Austrian consociationalism.

The Bureaucratic Arena

Throughout much of the Second Republic, the bureaucracy has been a site of considerable party activity and the target for the application of key consociational techniques. The politicisation of Austria's bureaucracy is not new. During the First Republic, the bureaucracy was staffed overwhelmingly by members of the Catholic-conservative *Lager*. Deliberate exclusion from its ranks of all members of the socialist subculture understandably seriously undermined the latter's belief in the neutrality and legitimacy of that state. The bureaucracy's political bias became more acute under first the Austrofascist regime (1934–38) and then the Nazi dictatorship (1938–45). When Austria's republican government was re-established in 1945, the parties agreed that the new republic's prospects of survival depended among other things upon a radical reform of how posts within both the state administration and Austria's extensive range of public sector enterprises were allocated. Above all, socialists had to be reassured about the neutrality of the new state by being included in these organisations.

The structure of party interaction in the bureaucratic arena has been influenced by two major principles.[67] First, in their various coalition agreements, the political elite of the major *Lager* committed themselves to public sector appointments being undertaken according to *Proporz*. Though these agreements only explicitly referred to posts in the numerous public sector firms, it was understood that *Proporz* would also apply within the civil service. Second, in the civil service *Proporz* was not applied across-the-board, but according to the principle of segmental autonomy. Appointments within each ministry were left to the party in charge of that ministry, so the departments each assumed the political 'colour' of their ministers. Within some public sector enterprises, *Proporz* was applied in an analogous manner, with each *Lager* running its own organisation independently. For example, the *Länderbank* is an ÖVP preserve, whilst the *Creditanstalt* is controlled by the SPÖ and staffed predominantly by persons from within its *Lager*. In other public sector organisations *Proporz* requires a single institution to have an equal share of employees from the rival *Lager* at every level of its organisation. A good example is the *Nationalbank*.

It is very difficult to quantify the outcome of these two structural principles on public sector employment, particularly in the myriad public sector enterprises. Accordingly, comment will be mostly confined to their impact in the state administration. Their combined effect on the party-political profile of Austria's federal civil service can be guaged from the results of the elections to the federal civil servants' representative body (see Table 6). First, there is a high concentration of support for the two main *Lager*. The combined ÖVP and SPÖ share of the vote has been very similar to that in National Council elections, though its recent decline has been less pronounced. Second, unlike at parliamentary elections, the ÖVP is still the strongest party among civil servants, even though its lead over the SPÖ has slightly declined (from 26 percentage points in 1967 to 22 in 1991). Third, the FPÖ has always been weak and even at the 1991 election received only about half the vote which it would have probably received at a national election.

TABLE 6

PARTY STRENGTHS AT ELECTIONS TO THE FEDERAL CIVIL SERVANTS' REPRESENTATIVE BODY (1967-1991)

	SPÖ[1]		ÖVP[2]		FPÖ[3]		OTHERS[4]	
	Vote	Seats	Vote	Seats	Vote	Seats	Vote	Seats
1967	32.4	–	58.5	–	–	–	9.1	–
1971	32.4	–	60.0	–	–	–	7.6	–
1975	32.3	–	61.1	–	–	–	6.6	–
1979	33.4	102	61.5	198	1.4	–	3.5	28
1983	32.6	107	61.9	214	1.6	–	3.6	26
1987	33.2	116	57.1	205	3.4	2	5.8	31
1991	30.2	107	52.3	196	7.9	12	9.5	40

Sources: 1967–75: P. Gerlich and W. C. Müller (eds.), *Zwischen Koalition und Konkurrenz*, p. 343; 1979–87: *Österreichisches Jahrbuch für Politik* (1987), p. 623; 1991: provisional results kindly supplied by Wolfgang Müller.

Notes: 1. Fraktion Sozialistischer Gewerkschaftler and various SPÖ-orientated lists.
2. Österreichischer Arbeiter- und Angestelltenbund and various ÖVP-orientated lists.
3. Arbeitsgemeinschaft Unabhängiger und Freiheitlicher and various FPÖ-orientated lists.
4. Includes various independents, KPÖ-orientated lists and FPÖ-orientated lists from 1967–75.

If one looks more closely at the election results, it is possible to see the effects of segmental autonomy. First, the aggregate figures conceal considerable variations of support between the different ministries and federal agencies. Moreover, those differences mirror the party-political 'colour' of the relevant department. In traditional ÖVP ministries such as those of agriculture, of defence and of finance, the ÖVP's average share of the vote has been proportionately higher than its overall level of support. Similarly, SPÖ support has been much greater in its 'natural' ministries and agencies. For example, during 1967–91 the party's average level of support among civil servants in the Interior Ministry stood at about 70 per cent, as compared to the ÖVP's 20 per cent, while in the Employment Agencies the figures were roughly 80 and 20 per cent respectively. Second, one can detect movements of support that appear to shadow changes in political control. For example, in 1967, 69 per cent of civil servants employed in the Federal Chancellor's Office voted for the ÖVP and only 20 per cent for the SPÖ. This was at a time of single-party ÖVP government. In 1987, after 17 years in which the SPÖ consistently held the chancellorship, the vote was 45 per cent for the ÖVP and 44 for the SPÖ. Finally, at the 1987 election, support for FPÖ lists in ministries in which an FPÖ minister or state secretary had served during the 1983–86 FPÖ/SPÖ coalition increased by between two and three times, albeit from a very low level.

However, these results must be treated with considerable caution. First, they contain a considerable 'democratic bias' in that they constitute but a tally of total votes cast. Since one person has one vote, but only a few such persons exercise a significant degree of influence within the civil service, these figures do not reveal the relative degree of party influence within the bureaucratic arena. The general consensus among informed observers, however, is that the figures underestimate the extent of influence which the SPÖ has been able to build up, especially during its period of single-party governments, when it placed its supporters in many strategic positions. Second, these results do not include the large numbers of civil servants employed at the *Land* level where political considerations have traditionally also been important in staffing decisions.

The style of party interaction in the bureaucratic arena. It is impossible to be precise about the extent to which interaction in the bureaucratic arena is governed by party considerations. Access to the relevant information is usually not available and it is notoriously difficult to make judgements on the motives underpining individuals' actions. None the less, there does appear to have been a general decline in the politicisation of the bureaucracy. First, since the 1970s growing emphasis has been placed on appointment on merit, rather than on the basis of party membership. Second, Austrian civil servants' loyalty to any party affiliation is often mitigated by departmental loyalty, or a commitment to the principle of a non-partisan civil service, a principle which *Proporz* has not eradicated.

To summarise, the Second Republic from birth had a predominantly Catholic-conservative state administration and a socialist subculture traditionally excluded from the state apparatus and from equal access to posts in the wider public sector. Since then, *Proporz* and segmental autonomy have been very effective in increasing socialist representation at all levels. From the 1970s there have been increasing calls for subcultural affiliation to be reduced as a factor determining appointment to the public sector in general and to the state administration in particular. Since about the mid-1980s those calls appear to be being answered and staffing decisions in the state administration now seem to emphasise expertise and efficiency more than ever before. In public sector enterprises the market is now stressed, so here too the political sociology of applicants is less significant than it used to be. Overall, decisions on bureaucratic arena staffing are now no longer made for system stability and the need to be seen to incorporate previously excluded political groups. The legitimacy deficit which the bureaucracy had in socialist *Lager* eyes during the immediate post-war years has largely disappeared. The recent shift to its efficiency deficit can be regarded in some respect the outcome of the success of the consociational techniques of *Proporz* and segmental autonomy.

CONCLUSION

The significance of political parties for Austrian consociationalism has primarily been twofold. First, they have played an important role in the internal structure and operation of the rival subcultures underpinning Austrian politics. Second, they have been key actors in inter-subcultural accommodation characteristic of consociational democracy in Austria and elsewhere. This essay has analysed changes first in the Austrian *Lager* parties' intra-subcultural linkages and second in their role in subcultural interaction.

Among conclusions for the former aspect are first, that by international standards the main *Lager* parties and their auxiliary associations are still very large and have a high degree of organisational density. Second, these structures have historically been very important for the organisational penetration, incorporation and vertical integration of their respective subcultures. This has been a function both of their size and their scope. Third, there has, however, been a significant organisational decline within the two main *Lager* and notably within the Catholic-conservative subculture. Were it not for the compulsory membership in the chambers associated with the two subcultures, that organisational decline would in all probability be even worse. Fourth, de-pillarisation has resulted in a peeling away of the *Lager*'s outer rings, leaving a sociologically largely unchanged politically organised core that is, however, increasingly unrepresentative of modern Austria's social composition as a whole. Fifth, decline in uncritical *Lager* support is not only a result of general social and economic change. It is mirrored in and fostered by changes in the mobilisational capacity of ideological and instrumental values. In particular, the scope for and success of the latter has in recent years declined. Sixth, Austria's political parties and their allied auxiliary associations remain very oligarchic and bureaucratic, increasingly regarded as distant from their grass-roots. Seventh, *Lager* political cohesion and party dominance within those subcultures are closely related to techniques of overlapping membership, the dependence of *Lager* activists on *Lager* organisations and the location within the two main subcultures of control over their reward structures. Where the latter is party-centred, as in the socialist and German-national subcultures, party dominance has been high. Conversely, in the chronically factionalised Catholic-conservative subculture, *Lager* cohesion is currently dangerously low.

Second, this essay examined the *Lager* parties in the five main arenas of subcultural interaction. It established first, that interaction has traditionally consisted of two-party concentration, *Proporz*, segmental autonomy and the ubiquitous nature of parties. Second, the style of interaction between the subcultures was governed by accommodation based above all on mutual veto and *Junktim*. Third, in recent years a clear trend for deconcentration has emerged, especially in the electoral, parliamentary and governmental arenas. Fourth, the traditional importance of *Proporz* for staffing decisions in the bureaucratic arena has been reduced, albeit by no means abandoned, with the new criteria being merit and efficiency. Fifth, segmental autonomy and the regional party hegemonies are also on the decline. Sixth, the style of interaction is now less dominated by pressure on subcultural leaders to produce unanimous decisions, as is especially evident in the parliamentary arena. Seventh, the relative political importance of the various arenas of subcultural interaction has altered. The most significant shift has been from the corporate to the parliamentary and governmental arenas. Finally, the overlap between arenas has declined as role differentiation has increased. Accordingly, there has been a concomitant decline in the ubiquity of party control of the political process.

Overall, the preceding analysis has shown that the establishment, maintenance and recent decline of the practices associated with 'classic' Austrian consociationalism cannot be understood solely in terms of attitudinal, or ideological factors. The mutually hostile and encapsulated subcultures upon which that system's overarching elite accommodation was based owe at least as much to organisational factors. First, the historic weakness of the Third *Lager vis-à-vis* the two main subcultures largely stems from an organisational deficit which that subculture has never succeeded in making good. Second, the post-war petrification of Austrian politics around the socialist and Catholic-conservative *Lager* was in large measure a consequence of their capacity for organisational penetration and hierarchical control of their subcultures This in turn gave them duopolistic access to and control over a system of material rewards which enabled them to maintain their dominant position. Third, the two main *Lager* parties' current problems in general and the Catholic-conservative subculture's in particular are without doubt related to partisan de-alignment and a general decline in *Lagermentalität*. However, these problems also arise from the structure and style of the large party and auxiliary associations of those *Lager*. Noteworthy has been their increasing distance from the grassroots of their respective subcultures and the perceived excesses of the *Lager*'s patronage practices. As yet, there is no convincing evidence that the parties have found adequate solutions to these and other problems related to their structure and operation. Accordingly, the chances are that the changes in the Austrian parties and the Austrian party system which this essay has detailed will continue for some time to come.

NOTES

1. See A. Pelinka and M. Welan, *Demokratie und Verfassung in Österreich* (Vienna: Europaverlag, 1971). For an alternative viewpoint which analyses the two state-building processes from the *Länder* perspective, see P. Pernthaler, *Die Staatsgründungsakte der österreichischen Bundesländer. Eine staatsrechtliche Untersuchung über die Entstehung des Bundesstaates* (Vienna: Braumüller, 1979)
2. See, e.g., A. Wandruszka, 'Österreichs politische Struktur: Die Entwicklung der Parteien und politischen Bewegungen', in H. Benedikt (ed.), *Geschichte der Republik Österreich* (Vienna: Verlag für Geschichte und Politik, 1954), pp. 289–485; W. B. Simon, *The Political Parties of Austria* (Ann Arbor: repr. of Columbia Univ. Ph.D, 1957), esp. pp. 15–79; P. Pulzer, 'The Legitimizing Role of Political Parties: The Second Austrian Republic', *Government and Opposition*, Vol. 4 (1969), pp. 324–44, and *idem*, 'Austria', in S. Henig and J. Pinder (eds.), *European Political Parties* (London: Allen & Unwin, 1969), pp. 282–319.
3. On the development of an Austrian national identity see, e.g., W. T. Bluhm, *Building an Austrian Nation. The Political Integration of a Western State* (New Haven CT: Yale UP, 1973) and F. Kreissler, *Der Österreicher und seine Nation. Ein Lernprozeß mit Hindernisses* (Vienna: Böhlau, 1984). For details of changes in levels of partisan attachment and of an Austrian national identity, see the article in this volume by Plasser *et al.*
4. On the origins of social partnership see W. C. Müller, 'Die Rolle der Parteien bei Entstehung und Entwicklung der Sozialpartnerschaft: Eine handlungslogische und empirische Analyse' in P. Gerlich, E. Grande and W. C. Müller (eds.), *Sozialpartnerschaft in der Krise. Leistungen und Grenzen des Neokorporatismus in Österreich* (Vienna: Böhlau, 1985), pp. 135–224 This also contains detailed analyses of the subsequent operation and significance of social partnership. For most recent developments see the essay by P. Gerlich in this volume.
5. For an Austrian journalist's insightful account of how this operated during classic Austrian consociationalism, see A. Vodopivec, *Wer regiert in Österreich?* (Vienna: Verlag für Geschichte und Politik, 1960).
6. This was the case both in the very earliest literature, e.g., G. Lehmbruch, *Proporzdemokratie: Politisches System und politische Kultur in der Schweiz und in Österreich*

(Tübingen: Mohr, 1967), as well as in later work, e.g., by Pulzer, 'The Legitimizing Role of Political Parties'; Pulzer, 'Austria'; G. B. Powell, *Social Fragmentation and Political Hostility: An Austrian Case Study* (Stanford UP, 1970); V. R. Lorwin, 'Segmented Pluralism. Ideological Cleavages and Political Cohesion in the Smaller European Democracies', *Comparative Politics*, Vol. 3 (1971), pp. 141–75; R. P. Stiefbold, 'Segmented Pluralism and Consociational Democracy in Austria', in M. O. Heisler (ed.), *Politics in Europe. Structures and Processes in Some Postindustrial Democracies* (NY: David Mckay, 1974), pp. 117–77; R. P. Stiefbold, 'Elites and Elections in a Fragmented Political System', *Sozialwissenschaftliches Jahrbuch für Politik*, Vol. 4 (1975), pp. 119–228 and J. J. Houska, *Influencing Mass Political Behaviour. Elites and Political Subcultures in the Netherlands and Austria* (Berkeley, CA: Inst. of Int'l Studies, 1985).

7. See, e.g., H. Daalder, 'The Consociational Democracy Theme', *World Politics*, Vol. 26, No. 4 (1974), pp. 604–21; Lehmbruch, *Proporzdemokratie*; G. Lehmbruch, 'Consociational Democracy in the International System', *European Journal of Political Research*, Vol. 3, No. 4 (1975), pp. 377–91; A. Lijphart, 'Typologies of Democratic Systems', *Comparative Political Studies*, Vol. 1, No. 1 (1968), pp. 3–44; idem, 'Consociational Democracy', *World Politics*, Vol. 21, No. 2 (1969), pp. 207–25; idem, *Democracy in Plural Societies: A Comparative Exploration* (New Haven, CT: Yale UP, 1977); Lorwin, 'Segmented Pluralism'; K. D. McRae (ed.), *Consociational Democracy. Accommodation in Segmented Societies* (Toronto: McClelland and Stewart, 1974); J. Steiner, 'The Principles of Majority and Proportionality', *British Journal of Political Science*, Vol. 1, No. 1 (1971), pp. 63–70; idem, *Amicable Agreement versus Majority Rule. Conflict Resolution in Switzerland* (Chapel Hill, NC: Univ. of North Carolina P., 1974). See also the discussion by K. R. Luther and W. C. Müller in the first chapter of this volume, as well as its note 29 for revisions, reviews and critiques of consociational theory.

8. On the *Lager* theory, see especially Wandruszka, 'Österreichs politische Struktur', as well as the other literature cited in note 2 above. See also the overview of *Lager* development provided in the first chapter of this volume by K. R. Luther and W. C. Müller. How far the *Lager* theory can also be applied to the FPÖ and its predecessors during the monarchy and the First Republic is debatable, as pointed out in, e.g.: H. Fritzl and M. Uitz, 'Kritische Bemerkungen zur sogenannten Lagertheorie', *Österreichische Zeitschrift für Politikwissenschaft*, Vol. 3 (1975), pp. 325–32.

9. This assumes the primacy of party, as opposed to interest-group control of the political process. An alternative perspective is that in consociational political systems such as that in Austria up to the late 1960s, it was above all a case of political parties having been 'colonised' by the interest groups of their respective subcultures. For such a corporatist approach see, e.g., E. Scholten (ed.), *Political Stability and Neo-Corporatism. Corporatist Integration and Societal Cleavages in Western Europe* (London: Sage, 1987). However, more recent developments suggest the (renewed) primacy of the political over the corporate channel. See, e.g., P. Gerlich's contribution to this volume.

10. The six 'core characteristics' are identified in the first chapter of this volume.

11. That liberalism and German-nationalism could go together may appear strange to an Anglo-Saxon reader. For the historical processes that caused the Third *Lager* to have this apparent ideological contradiction see, e.g., Wandruszka, 'Österreichs politische Struktur', pp. 369–421; A. Fuchs, *Geistige Strömungen in Österreich 1867–1918*, repr. of 1949 ed. (Vienna: Löcker, 1977), pp. 165–96; A. Whiteside, 'Austria', in H. Rogger and E. Weber (eds.), *The European Right* (Berkeley: Univ. of California P., 1965), pp. 308–63; A. G. Whiteside, *The Socialism of Fools: Georg Ritter von Schönerer and Austrian Pan-Germanism* (Berkeley: Univ. of California P., 1975). On the FPÖ, see, e.g., K. R. Luther, 'The Freiheitliche Partei Österreichs: protest party or governing party?' in E. J. Kirchner (ed.), *Liberal Parties in Western Europe* (CUP, 1988), pp. 213–51 and M. Riedlsperger, 'FPÖ: Liberal or Nazi?' in F. Parkinson (ed.), *Conquering the Past: Austrian Nazism Yesterday & Today* (Detroit: Wayne State UP, 1989), pp. 257–78.

12. 'Relevant' is used here in the Sartorian sense of parties that have either 'governing', or 'blackmail' potential. (See G. Sartori, *Parties and Party Systems: A Framework for Analysis*, (CUP, 1976) esp. pp. 122f.)
13. Our focus will be primarily on the three traditional *Lager* parties: the SPÖ, ÖVP and FPÖ. Though it endured a sharp decline both during and after classic consociationalism, reference will also be made to the KPÖ. For English-language sources with more detailed information on individual parties, see section 4 of Appendix 5. The latest German-language publications on the ÖVP, SPÖ, FPÖ, KPÖ and Greens are the following contributions to H. Dachs, P. Gerlich, H. Gottweis, F. Horner, H. Kramer, V. Lauber, W. C. Müller and E. Tálos (eds.), *Handbuch des politischen Systems Österreichs* (Vienna: Manz, 1991): W. C. Müller, 'Die Österreichische Volkspartei', pp. 227–46; K. Ucakar, 'Die Sozialdemokratische Partei Österreichs', p. 210–26; K. R. Luther, 'Die Freiheitliche Partei Österreichs', pp. 247–62; J. Ehmer, 'Die Kommunistische Partei Österreichs', pp. 275–85 and H. Dachs, 'Grünalternative Parteien', pp. 263–74.
14. See the opening chapter of this volume by K. R. Luther and W. C. Müller, as well as Simon, *Political Parties of Austria*.
15. An additional, though much less precise, measure of a subculture size is the size of vote which its party receives. This aspect is examined in this volume by Plasser *et al.*
16. Ucakar, 'Die Sozialdemokratische Partei Österreichs', p. 221. The relatively low postwar figure is explainable by the SPÖ having been a proscribed organisation since 1934.
17. For a discussion of the problem, see W. Urban and E. Zeidner, 'Vom Umfang und Nutzen der Parteimitgliedschaft' in P. Gerlich and W. C. Müller (eds.), *Zwischen Koalition und Konkurrenz. Österreichs Parteien seit 1945* (Vienna: Braumüller, 1983), pp. 151–71, here 155–59, who concluded that there were as yet no usable ÖVP membership statistics available.
18. Like the term *Lager*, both *Vorfeld* and *Umfeld* have military connotations.
19. Gottweis, 'Die Parteien und ihr politisches Umfeld. Versuch einer Bestandsaufnahme', *Politische Bildung*, Vol. 3, No. 4 (1984), pp. 2–7, here p. 3. 1990 figures supplied by Wolfgang C. Müller.
20. The few examples include Gottweis, 'Die Parteien und ihr politisches Umfeld', Houska, *Influencing Mass Political Behaviour* and Powell, *Social Fragmentation*.
21. On the SPÖ see, e.g., C. Haerpfer, 'Die Sozialstruktur der SPÖ' in *Österreichische Zeitschrift für Politikwissenschaft*, Vol. 18, No. 4 (1989), pp. 373–94 and E. Gehmacher, 'SPÖ: Wähler und Mitglieder 1945 bis 1989' in E. Fröschl, M. Mesner and H. Zoitl (eds.), *Die Bewegung. Hundert Jahre Sozialdemokratie in Österreich* (Vienna: Passagen Verlag, 1990) pp. 520–30. On elite sociology more generally, cf., V. Baumgartner, 'Pareteieliten zwischen Repräsentation und Technokratie', in Gerlich and Müller (eds.), *Zwischen Koalition und Konkurrenz*, pp. 173–200 and P. Gerlich, 'Consociationalism to Competition: the Austrian Party System Since 1945' in H. Daalder (ed.), *Party Systems in Austria, Switzerland, the Netherlands and Belgium* (London: Pinter, 1987), pp. 61–106, here 70–72. Also of use are the results of elections to the chambers and to the civil servants' representative body (see respectively tables 4, and 5 and 6 of this essay).
22. Ehmer, 'Die Kommunistische Partei Österreichs', from which the following information is taken.
23. See Luther, 'Die Freiheitliche Partei Österreichs', or *idem*, 'The Freiheitliche Partei Österreichs: protest party or governing party?'.
24. See the contribution to this volume by Plasser *et al.* and especially Tables 2–4.
25. See, e.g., F. C. Engelmann, 'Austria: The Pooling of Opposition' in R. A. Dahl (ed.), *Political Opposition in Western Democracies* (New Haven, CT: Yale UP, 1966), pp. 260–83, here p. 277.
26. See, e.g., Gerlich, 'Consociationalism to Competition', pp. 70–72, or Baumgartner, 'Parteieliten'.
27. As Gerlich says of the sociological profile of the members of the National Council, 'parliament has not so much become more representative of society, but ... society has become more akin to parliament'. ('Consociationalism to Competition', p. 71).

28. Indeed, during 'classic' consociationalism the two major Austrian *Lagers'* capacity to mobilise their subcultures directly influenced their share of power. The formula governing the distribution of political office within the grand coalition government, as well as of posts within the state bureaucracy and public sector industries was none other than the *Lager's* relative share of the vote at the preceding election.
29. See especially Tables 11, 12 and 15 and 16.
30. M. N. Pedersen, 'Changing Patters of Electoral Volatility in European Party Systems, 1948–1977: Explorations in Explanation', in H. Daalder and P. Mair (eds.), *Western European Party Systems: Continuity and Change* (London: Sage, 1983), pp. 29–66. See also C. Haerpfer, 'Austria', in I. Crewe and D. Denver (eds.), *Electoral Change in Western Democracies. Patterns and Sources of Electoral Volatility* (NY: St. Martin's Press, 1985) pp. 264–86, esp. 268–78. Austrian electoral volatility is usually presented from 1953, rather than from 1949, since the figure for the latter election was distorted by it being first occasion on which the Third *Lager* was first permitted to compete.
31. See the contribution to this volume by Plasser *et al.*, as well as, e.g., F. Birk and K. Traar, 'Der durchleuchtete Wähler - in den achtziger Jahren', *Journal für Sozialforschung*, Vol. 27, No. 1 (1987), pp. 3–74.
32. On Austria's political culture and the recent decline in its subject orientation, see, e.g., P. A. Ulram, *Hegemonie und Erosion: Politische Kultur und politischer Wandel in Österreich* (Vienna: Böhlau, 1990); *Österreichische Zeitschrift für Politikwissenschaft*, Vol. 13, No. 1 (1984); and K. R. Luther, 'Austria's Future and Waldheim's Past: The Significance of the 1986 Elections', *West European Politics*, Vol. 10, No. 3 (1987), pp. 376–99. For a plea that these changes continue, see P. Gerlich, 'National Consciousness and National Identity: A Contribution to the Political Culture of the Austrian Party System', in A. Pelinka and F. Plasser, *The Austrian Party System* (Boulder, CO: Westview Press, 1989), pp. 223–58.
33. See K. R. Luther, 'Dimensions of Party System Change: The Case of Austria', *West European Politics*, Vol. 12, No. 4 (1989), pp. 3–27.
34. See K. Berchtold (ed.), *Österreichische Parteiprogramme 1988–1966* (Vienna: Verlag für Geschichte und Politik, 1967); A. Kadan and A. Pelinka, *Die Grundsatzprogramme der österreichischen Parteien. Dokumentation und Analyse* (St.Pölten: Verlag Niederösterreichisches Pressehaus, 1979); F. Horner, 'Programme – Ideologien: Dissens oder Konsens', in H. Dachs *et al.* (eds.), *Handbuch*, pp. 197–209 and R. Kriechbaumer, *Parteiprogramme im Widerstreit der Interessen. Die Programmdiskussionen von ÖVP und SPÖ 1945–1986*, Sonderband 3 of *Österreichisches Jahrbuch für Politik* (1990).
35. For a detailed discussion of Austrokeynesianism and its development since 'classic' consociationalism, see Volkmar Lauber's essay in this volume.
36. See W. C. Müller, 'Conservatism and the Transformation of the Austrian People's Party', in B. Girvin (ed.), *The Transformation of Contemporary Conservatism* (London: Sage, 1988), pp. 98–119, and *idem*, 'Die Österreichische Volkspartei'.
37. F. C. Engelmann, 'The Pooling of Opposition', p. 269f.
38. See N. Hölzl, *Propagandaschlachten. Die österreichischen Wahlkämpfe 1945–1971* (Vienna: Verlag für Geschichte und Politik, 1974), as well as below under 'electoral arena'.
39. See Vodopivec, *Wer regiert in Österreich?* and W. C. Müller, 'Party Patronage in Austria', in Pelinka and Plasser (eds.), *Austrian Party System*, pp. 327–356. On Austrian political participation, see R. Deiser and N. Winkler, *Das politische Handeln der Österreicher* (Wiener Neustadt: Verlag für Gesellschaftskritik, 1982) and esp. p. 237 for data on the importance of material values in motivating party membership.
40. On economic policy and EC membership see the contributions to this volume by Volkmar Lauber and D. Mark Schultz respectively.
41. See, e.g., references listed under note 13 above and in the relevant section of the English-language literature cited in Appendix 5, as well as A. Stirnemann, 'Die innerparteiliche Demokratie in der ÖVP', *Österreichisches Jahrbuch für Politik* (1979), pp. 391–433; R. Wimmer, 'Zur innerparteilichen Demokratie in der ÖVP', *Österreichische Zeitschrift für Politikwissenschaft*, Vol. 3 (1974), pp. 25–41; L. Reichhold, *Geschichte der ÖVP* (Graz: Styria, 1975); Gerlich and Müller, *Zwischen Koalition und Konkurrenz*.

42. See, e.g., Deiser and Winkler, *Das politische Handeln der Österreicher*; F. Plasser and P. Ulram (eds.), *Staatsbürger oder Untertanen?* (Frankfurt: Peter Lang, 1991).
43. A. Panebianco, *Political Parties: Organisation and Power* (CUP, 1988).
44. See, e.g., Powell, *Social Fragmentation* and Stiefbold, 'Segmented Pluralism'. Organisational overlap did of course not mean a complete avoidance of intra-*Lager* conflict, especially as regards the Catholic-conservative *Lager*, as will be discussed below.
45. W. C. Müller and D. Meth-Cohn, 'The Selection of Party Chairmen in Austria: A Study in Intra-Party Decision-making', *European Journal of Political Research*, Vol. 20, No. 1 (1991), pp. 39–65. However, the internal decision-making processes of Austrian parties and auxiliary associations remains a subject for considerable research.
46. A. Pelinka, 'Struktur und Funktion der politischen Parteien', in H. Fischer (ed.), *Das politische System Österreichs* (Vienna: Europaverlag, 1977), 2nd ed., pp. 31–53, here 39.
47. W. C. Müller and W. Philipp, 'Parteienregierung und Regierungsparteien in Österreich. Empirische Anmerkungen zu den strukturellen Voraussetzungen der Parteienregierung und zur Bedeutung der Regierungstätigkeit für die Parteien (1945–1987)', *Österreichische Zeitschrift für Politikwissenschaft*, Vol. 16, No. 3 (1987), pp. 277–302.
48. See, e.g., K. R. Luther, 'Bund-Länder Beziehungen. Formal- und Realverfassung', in Dachs *et al.*, *Handbuch*, pp. 816–32.
49. Müller, 'Die Österreichische Volkspartei'.
50. Sartori, *Parties and Party Systems*, p. 128f. As will be aparant, this essay is also predicted upon Sartori's defintion of a party system as comprising 'the system of interactions' resulting from inter-party competition' op. cit., p. 44.
51. The latter was referred to as 'sectionalism' by Lehmbruch, *Proporzdemokratie*, pp. 33–37.
52. Luther, 'Dimensions of Party Systems Change: The Case of Austria', *West European Politics*, Vol. 12, No. 4 (1989), pp. 2–27. This is merely one of several perspectives. E.g., one could adopt a neo-institutional approach and regard some arenas examined, as actors in their own right, as is done in Wolfgang C. Müller's contribution to this volume. The latter form was referred to as 'sectionalism' by Lehmbruch, *Proporzdemokratie*, pp. 33–7.
53. See G. Smith and P. Mair (eds.), *Understanding Party System Change in Western Europe* (London: Frank Cass, 1990).
54. Dachs, 'Grünalternative Parteien', esp. pp. 273f.
55. These and all subsequently cited electoral results derive from either (the source of) Appendix 1 of this volume, from *Österreichisches Jahrbuch für Politik* (1990), pp. 947–55, or, for most recent *Land* elections, from relevant issues of *Neue Freie Zeitung*.
56. Hölzl, *Propagandaschlachten*. On campaigning in the more recent period, see Gerlich and Müller, *Zwischen Koalition und Konkurrenz*; F. Plasser and P. Ulram, 'Wahlkampf und Wählerverhalten – Analyse der Nationalratswahl 1983', *Österreichisches Jahrbuch für Politik* (1983), pp. 19–43; ibid, 'Das Jahr der Wechselwähler – Wahlen und Neustrukturierung des österreichischen Parteiensystems 1986', in *Österreichisches Jahrbuch für Politik* (1986), pp. 31-80 and ibid, 'Eine Kanzler- und Protestwahl. Wählerverhalten und Wahlmotive bei der Nationalratswahl 1990', in *Österreichisches Jahrbuch für Politik* (1990), pp. 95–149, as well as K. R. Luther, 'Austria's Future and Waldheim's Past: The Significance of the 1986 Elections', *West European Politics*, Vol. 10, No. 3 (1987), pp. 376–99; W. C. Müller, 'Persönlichkeitswahl bei der Nationalratswahl 1990', *Österreichisches Jahrbuch für Politik* (1990), pp. 261–82; and W. C. Müller and F. Plasser, 'Austria: the 1990 Campaign', in D. Farrell and S. Bowler (eds.), *Electoral Strategies and Political Marketing* (London: Macmillan, 1992).
57. Indeed, in 1970 the SPÖ introduced a reform of the electoral system that further enhanced its fairness. See C. Haerpfer, 'Nationalratswahlen und Wahlverhalten 1945–1980', in Gerlich and Müller, *Zwischen Koalition und Konkurrenz*, pp. 111–49, here esp. 112–16.

58. See, e.g., H. Fischer 'Das Parlament', in H. Dachs *et al., Handbuch*, pp. 96–117; I. Kathrein, 'Der Bundesrat' and H. Widder, 'Der Nationalrat', both in H. Schambeck (ed.), *Österreichs Parlamentarismus. Werden und System* (Berlin: Duncker & Humblot, 1986), pp. 337–401 and 261–336 resp.; A. Nevalcsil, 'Regierung und Opposition im parlamentarischen Prozeß', *Österreichisches Jahrbuch für Politk* (1983), pp. 209–57; *idem*, 'Der Nationalrat in der XVI. GP', *Österreichisches Jahrbuch für Politik* (1986), pp. 465–94; *idem*, 'Der Nationalrat in der XVII. GP', *Österreichisches Jahrbuch für Politik* (1990), pp. 431–59.
59. Lijphart, *Democracy in Plural Societies*, p. 25. On the operation of the governmental arena during classic consociationalism see, e.g., H. P. Secher, 'Coalition Government: The Case of the Second Austrian Republic', *American Political Science Review*, Vol. 52 (1958), pp. 791–809; W. Rudzio, 'Entscheidungszentrum Koalitionsausschuß – Zur Realverfassung Österreichs unter der großen Koalition', *Politische Vierteljahresschrift*, Vol. 12 (1971), pp. 87–118 and J. Dreijmanis, 'Austria: The "Black"–"Red" Coalitions' in E. C. Browne and J. Dreijmanis (eds.), *Government Coalitions in Western Democracies* (NY: Longman, 1982), pp. 237–59. For analysis of recent developments, see W. C. Müller, 'Die neue große Koalition in Österreich', *Österreichische Zeitschrift für Politikwissenschaft*, Vol. 17, No. 3 (1988), pp. 321–47; *idem*, 'Regierung und Kabinettsystem', in Dachs *et al., Handbuch*, pp. 118–33.
60. By virtue of their very composition, the single party governments of 1966–83 and the SPÖ/FPÖ 'small coalition' were bound to operate differently from the grand coalitions up to 1966. For a cabinet composition in the Second Republic, see Appendix 4 to this volume. On the new grand coalition, see Müller, 'Die neue große Koalition in Österreich' and *idem*, 'Regierung und Kabinettsystem'.
61. For a detailed analysis of the development of Austrian economic policy, see Volkmar Lauber's contribution to this volume.
62. See Rudzio, 'Entscheidungszentrum Koalitionsausschuß'.
63. See the essay in this volume by Wolfgang Müller.
64. See also references in the relevant section of Appendix 5, Dachs *et al., Handbuch*, esp. pp. 333–415, as well as those listed under note 4 above.
65. Dachs *et al. Handbuch*, p. 373.
66. Gerlich, Grande, Müller (eds.), *Sozialpartnerschaft in der Krise*.
67. See, e.g., Secher, 'Coalition Government'; Engelmann, 'The Pooling of Opposition'; H. Neisser, 'Die Rolle der Bürokratie im Regierungsprozeß', in H. Fischer (ed.), *Das politische System Österreichs* (Vienna: Europaverlag, 1974), pp. 233–70; E. Gugler, 'Ergebnisse der 6. Bundespersonalvertretungswahl 1987', *Österreichisches Jahrbuch für Politik* (1987), pp. 621–32; G. Engelmayer (ed.), *Die Diener des Staates* (Vienna: Europaverlag, 1977); Müller, 'Party Patronage in Austria' and the section on administration in Wolfgang Müller's contribution to this volume.

Austrian Governmental Institutions: Do They Matter?

WOLFGANG C. MÜLLER

Political institutions are nowadays a much more fashionable subject in political science than they were one or two decades ago. Despite its expected demise, classical institutionalism has survived and gained new vitality from the incorporation of behavioural research methods. Rational choice theory has made institutional rules one of its major concerns; a wealth of studies has shown how different rules of decision-making affect the outcome of this process. More recently, new institutionalists of different traditions have argued that political institutions are 'more than simple mirrors of social forces'.[1] They view political institutions not as mere arenas, but also as political actors, and political actions as shaped by institutional environments and not merely by the values, norms and preferences of the political actors themselves.[2]

This article will focus on the relevance of the formal powers of Austrian governmental institutions. In examining the formal role which the constitution prescribes for them, as well as their actual role in the political process, the main focus will be the changes which have occurred during the Second Republic, namely since 1945. The traditional picture, that is the way these institutions were described in the 1950s, 1960s (i.e., in what this volume has termed the 'classic' phase of Austrian consociationalism), and also in the early 1970s will also be examined. A good deal of this literature is from American, British and German scholars, since at that time political science did not exist in Austria, or was only in its infancy. Interestingly enough, some of these publications hardly dealt with the Austrian institutional framework at all and political institutions do not play a great role in any of these analyses. In the 1950s the academic focus was dominated by a concern with political parties. They were seen as the key players in Austrian politics. According to the literature, their interaction was only marginally influenced by the configuration of political institutions and institutional rules.[3]

This of course reflects the permanent grand coalition government, one of the main features which made Austria an interesting case for the international academic community. Since grand coalition government meant the control of all political institutions by two very disciplined parties which were tied together by increasingly tight coalition contracts, there was not much room for institutional analyses. In the 1960s the focus began to change; the interest groups replaced parties as the key players and corporatism rather than party politics became the main feature of the publications;[4] this trend continued throughout the 1970s. This change in perspective reflected the growing immobilism of the old grand coalition and the rise of the 'social partnership'.[5] Within this picture, there was even less room for political institutions — the constitution seemed to be enormously malleable and thus of only little relevance for the conduct of politics.

This article has two main aims, which it will pursue by an examination of Austrian politics since the period of 'classic' consociationalism. The first is to challenge the view that formal governmental institutions are of little relevance for the conduct of politics by looking at subsequent developments. The second and related question to be addressed in this article is whether the Austrian governmental institutions are mere arenas or, as the new institutionalists claim, also actors.

THE INSTITUTIONAL FRAMEWORK

Austria's governmental institutions were established by its constitution, the main body of which dates back to 1920. In 1929 a major amendment was made in the anti-parliamentary and anti-party spirit prevailing at this time. Despite attempts by both the US and the Soviet occupation powers, as well as by Austrian communists, to create a new constitution, and despite the desire of the Socialist Party to go back to the constitution of 1920, the constitution as amended in 1929 was reintroduced in 1945 and thus brought to an end the short life of a provisional constitution. Since then, numerous amendments to the constitution and to constitutional laws and clauses[6] have somewhat modified, but not substantially changed, the formal framework in which politics take place.

Figure 1 provides an overview of the framework of governmental institutions in Austria. Popular sovereignty is one of the key principles of the Austrian constitution. Programmatically, it is laid down in Article 1, which states: 'Austria is a democratic republic. Its law emanates from the people.' According to this principle, the creation of all governmental institutions formally emanates at least indirectly from the people.

The people are involved in the creation of governmental institutions through three kinds of elections: they directly elect the federal president, the *Nationalrat* and the nine *Landtage* (the *Land* parliaments). The *Landtage* in turn elect the members of the second chamber of the Austrian parliament, the *Bundesrat*, by a proportional formula. These institutions

FIGURE 1

THE CREATION OF AUSTRIAN GOVERNMENTAL INSTITUTIONS

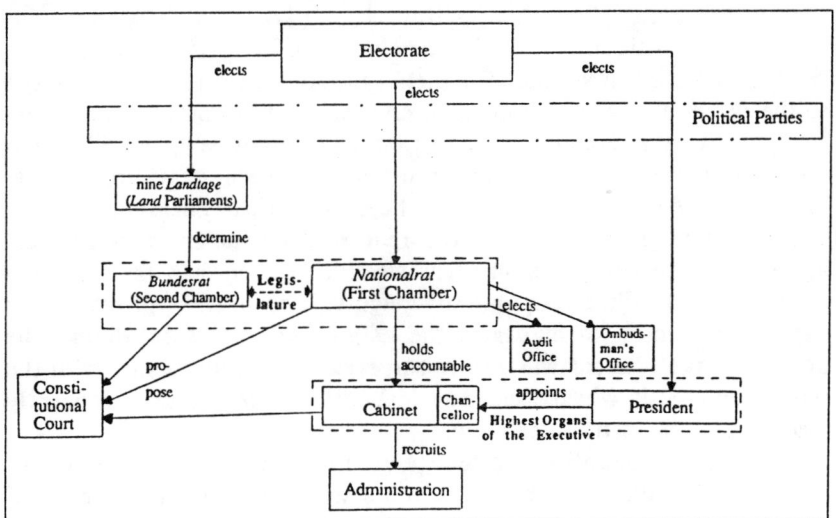

then create the other governmental institutions, in particular the cabinet (*Bundesregierung*) and the constitutional court (*Verfassungsgerichtshof*). The *Nationalrat* elects the president and the vice-president of the audit office (*Rechnungshof*) as well as the three ombudsmen (*Volksanwaltschaft*). The cabinet and individual cabinet ministers recruit the civil servants and direct the administration.

DIRECT DEMOCRACY

In addition to the elections, people can also become involved in the political process by three instruments of direct democracy: the referendum, the people's initiative and the consultative referendum.

A referendum (*Volksabstimmung*) is obligatory in the case of a 'total revision' of the constitution (Article 44) and in order to remote the federal president from office (Article 60). Both types of referendum have never been utilised, but Austria's accession to the EC would be held to imply a 'total revision' of the constitution and would thus require a referendum.[7] Other constitutional amendments have to be subjected to a referendum if this is demanded by a third of the members of one of the two chambers of parliament, though a referendum has never yet been demanded in this way. This is because throughout the Second Republic the two major parties, the Socialist Party of Austria (SPÖ) and the Austrian People's Party (ÖVP), have between them held more than two thirds of the *Nationalrat* seats; given their high levels of party discipline, there was never any realistic prospect of a members' coalition able to collect the requisite amount of support for such a motion. This applies even more to the *Bundesrat*, which has been even more clearly dominated by these two parties. A referendum can also be held on any law, provided that the *Nationalrat* demands it. This provision has been utilised only once: in 1978 the people were asked about the use of nuclear energy in Austria. This was done primarily in order to remove this issue from the political agenda for the 1979 parliamentary election, rather than because of a commitment to direct popular sovereignty. The strategy proved to be successful in terms of managing the 1979 electoral agenda, though the political establishment was rather surprised and disappointed with the referendum result, which decided against nuclear energy, and consequently did not use this instrument again.

The people's initiative (*Volksbegehren*) has been a constitutional instrument since 1920, but the ordinary law which established the required details and thus made this instrument available in practice was not enacted until 1963. The people's initiative is one means of initiating a law. It must be framed in terms of an actual bill and has to be supported by at least 100,000 voters (200,000 before 1981), or by half of the voters of each of three *Länder*. These supporters have to sign the initiative in the presence of the authorities and all the signatures must be collected within one week. The *Nationalrat* is then obliged to deal with this proposal, although there is no *legal* requirement beyond its mere treatment (thus, constitutional lawyers have argued that it is best regarded as a petition than as a people's initiative). *Politically*, however, a people's initiative clearly has more weight than other kinds of bills, though the chances for enactment are certainly higher for government proposals. From 1963 to 1990 ten people's initiatives were launched and succeeded in raising the requisite number of signatures.[8] Most of them were organised or supported by one of the opposition parties. The people's initiatives helped to lend weight to the opposition party's arguments, in particular when a high number of voters supported them. On the other hand, the party political origin of most people's initiatives has also made it easier for the parliamentary majority to reject them. Three of the people's initiatives were successful in leading to the enactment of a law which met their demands.

The consultative referendum (*Volksbefragung*) is the most recent addition to the instruments of direct democracy in Austria. It has been in force since 1989, but as of 1991 has not yet been used. In matters of principal importance which require regulation by law, the *Nationalrat* may decide to ask the people for their opinion. In contrast to the binding *Volksabstimmung*, the consultative referendum does not relate to popular acceptance or rejection of a statute already enacted by parliament. Although unlike the referendum, the parliament is not *legally* bound by the *Volksbefragung*, it certainly would be *politically*. This clause was introduced in order to maintain flexibility regarding the precise terms of legislation since the *Volksabstimmung* does not permit even a comma of the published text to be changed.

The Austrian constitution thus contains a variety of direct-democratic instruments. Nevertheless, the primacy of representative democracy and its institutions has been preserved. The parliamentary majority legally cannot be bypassed by direct democratic means. Notwithstanding these qualifications, a comparison of the 'classic' phase of Austrian consociationalism with the period after 1966 reveals that direct democracy has become much more important in the latter period, in terms of both the availability of institutions and of their actual use. It is particularly interesting to note in this context that the first ever people's initiative, launched towards the end of traditional grand coalition government in 1964, was directed against the *Proporz* broadcasting system,[9] thus already putting into question one of the cornerstones of consociationalism.

PARLIAMENT

Austria has a parliamentary system of government, with the cabinet obliged to resign after a parliamentary election. A new cabinet must present itself to the *Nationalrat* within one week after its appointment (Article 70) and relies on a majority in the *Nationalrat* to survive and to govern effectively. Since Austria is an extremely legalistic state, most relevant government decisions must have the form of a *law*, in which parliament must be involved. Thus the formal powers of parliament are very important.

The traditional picture of Austrian politics has, however, portrayed parliament quite differently.[10] Despite its formal powers, it was argued, parliament was merely a rubber-stamp for decisions previously made in the cabinet, the coalition committee, or within the institutions of the social partnership. It acted only as a 'public notary'. The coalition agreements between the ÖVP and SPÖ explicitly ruled out parliamentary amendments to government legislative proposals. Since the parties in parliament were highly disciplined and operated under tight control of the party leaders, parliamentary treatment of government bills was irrelevant for the outcome of the legislative process. Only few and short plenary meetings were held and little public attention was given to parliamentary debates. The opposition was powerless; it had no influence on the decisions and could hardly attract public attention for its arguments.

This picture changed somewhat when the old grand coalition was replaced by the ÖVP single-party government in 1966. Parliamentary activity tripled and more attention was given to the confrontation between government and opposition.[11] The opposition's opportunities to attract public attention and to control the government effectively were improved by two reforms of parliamentary procedure in 1975 and 1988. Since the opposition acted as a watchdog of the rights of parliament, formal parliamentary procedures became a greater constraint than hitherto. (From the government perspective, however, this was more than compensated for by the fact that the change to single-party government removed at a stroke the most severe problems of internal cabinet decision-making.) Despite increased confrontation in parliament, a basically consensual policy style prevailed and parliament became one arena in which negotiations between government and opposition took place. The various attempts at consensus-building between 1966 and 1986 resulted in about 80 per cent of the legislation being passed unanimously by the *Nationalrat*.

Parliamentary decision-making, however, remained very much a top-down process, in which the party leaders dominated and the MPs implemented their decisions. This held true in particular for governing parties' MPs whose *raison d'être* was to support their government and – to put it strongly – carry out the directives of the respective minister. Though the parties differed and there were differences over time, this was the pattern until 1987.[12] The introduction in that year of the new grand coalition reduced government willingness to negotiate and compromise with the opposition.

On one hand, a government in control of more than three quarters of the MPs does not need the votes of opposition members to achieve either a qualified majority, or to exclude items from the political agenda. On the other hand, government is now confronted with two quite different opposition parties, one on its right (FPÖ) and one on its left (Greens), making it nearly impossible for it to achieve unanimous acceptance of important bills. To compromise with just one of the opposition parties would intensify the criticism of the other and could lead to a public perception that the government was moving too far left or right as the case may be. Moreover, both opposition parties take more radical positions than used to be the case. Consequently, the proportion of legislation passed unanimously was reduced to 47 per cent in the 1986–90 parliament.

However, it would be wrong to equate the role of opposition with the impact of parliament.[13] The impact of the parliamentary groups of the governing parties also has to be considered. Here, a substantial increase in activity and influence can be seen. Many government proposals now only set the main principles of proposed legislation and leave it to parliament to work out the details. Moreover, the MPs of the governing parties have started to re-open discussions on government bills which had been regarded as finalised by the cabinet members. In addition, more MPs from the governing parties have been incorporated as experts and party representatives in cabinet-level negotiations. Thus the influence of parliament has increased substantially.[14]

The iron discipline of the parliamentary factions has also begun to disappear. In the 1986–90 parliament, there were more votes of dissent against, or abstentions from, the party line than had occurred in all other parliaments since 1945 put together. While violations of party discipline in previous parliaments were truly exceptional, in about 10 per cent of the legislation of the 1986–90 parliament several MPs voted against their party line. These are not merely 'parliamentary snipers' who vote against their party in closed lobbies, but MPs or intra-party groups who make their case publicly on the floor of the chamber. MPs now also table in part critical parliamentary questions to ministers of their own party. In three investigative committees of the 1986–90 parliament, which for the first time were held in public, the members tended to push their party affiliation into the background. The most spectacular events, however, were a motion of no-confidence by a group of People's Party MPs against their own minister of defence, and the rejection by a majority of MPs of the FPÖ candidate for the third president of parliament, on whose candidature the party leaders had previously agreed. This trend towards a loosening of parliamentary groups' cohesion is likely to continue, not least because a planned reform of the electoral system will strengthen the local ties of the MPs.

Comparing the parliament of the 'classic' phase of Austrian consociationalism with subsequent developments reveals substantial and important changes. What was a rather irrelevant institution at the end of the old grand coalition now has become a major political arena. Though we still live in an era of party politics, recent developments have clearly moved the Austrian parliament in the direction of again becoming a political actor. To that extent, parliament appears to be assuming the role which the new institutionalists would ascribe to it.

THE FEDERAL PRESIDENT

The Austrian president has a strong institutional position.[15] He is directly elected and thus has a legitimacy independent of other institutions. At six years with a maximum of two consecutive terms, his period of office is longer than any other elected organ of state. The president appoints the cabinet members and can dismiss them (Article 70) without being subject to any *legal* restriction in this respect. The strongest weapon in the hands of the president, however, is his right to dissolve parliament (Article 29). In the use of this weapon, the president is restricted only inasmuch as parliament can be dissolved just once for any one particular reason. Though it is in principle possible to dismiss the president from office, this would require a complex and risky procedure that could backfire on the parliamentarians by whom it is initiated.[16] Moreover, despite his nominal party-political independence, the president has always been a party nominee and it is thus highly unlikely that his sponsoring party would be prepared to countenance initiating dismissal procedures against him. Finally, the president's strong institutional position is combined with very little policy-making capacity, since in almost all cases he can act only on government proposals and also needs the government's approval for his decisions.

The federal president traditionally has had little impact on Austrian politics. He does not intervene in day-to-day politics and has never used his strongest institutional instruments. This is to some degree a heritage of the First Republic (the inter-war years) when presidents were powerless figure-heads. This remained so despite the 1929 constitutional reform, which considerably strengthened the presidency's legitimacy and formal powers. However, an important element of this reform, the introduction of direct presidential election, did not become effective until 1951. Moreover, from 1945 to 1986, socialist candidates always held the presidency. During the 1918–20 state-building process, the Social Democrats preferred a constitution without a president and opposed strengthening the presidency in later years.[17] Despite occupying the presidency for so long during the Second Republic, they maintained their general attitude that the president's considerable powers should not be used in day-to-day politics. Rather, the president should preserve his competences and authority for crisis situations. Such crises could be considered to have existed in 1953 and 1959, when Presidents Körner and Schärf responded by exercising influence designed to maintain grand coalition government. In 1960 Schärf also applied pressure on the parties to complete their exceptionally long coalition negotiations and in 1962–63 did the same to force them to come up with a definitive budget.[18]

The presidency was generally not regarded as a party-political office. The parties which participated in presidential elections normally did not nominate their most powerful leaders as candidates, but one of their 'elder statesmen'. The only exception was the candidacy of the Socialist Party's chairman Schärf in 1957. He was pushed and pulled by his younger party comrades, who wanted to take over his party and government positions and he stood for the presidency to postpone his retirement from politics by gaining presidential office.[19] Because of the system of direct election, and in view of their re-election ambitions, all presidents adopted a non-partisan image. The pattern of the passive, non-partisan president – or, to put it more positively, the authority-in-reserve president – soon became self-perpetuating, since all presidential candidates made reference in their campaigns to the role-interpretation and style of the former presidents and promised to follow this pattern if they should be elected.

The only exception to this electoral strategy was the campaign of the incumbent president, Kurt Waldheim. In contrast to his socialist opponent, Kurt Steyrer, Waldheim promised to be an 'active president' and to intervene in domestic politics. He was certainly not elected because of this promise but rather in spite of it;[20] had not other factors intervened it could well have given him the legitimation to be a significantly more active president than his predecessors had been. Waldheim has indeed made some public statements which constituted interventions in current domestic politics. For instance, he declared that the only result of the 1986–87 coalition negotiations that he would accept would be a grand coalition government. However, in stating this coalition preference, he was only subscribing to the most likely outcome of the negotiations. Moreover, when criticised for his statement by the Freedom Party, he tried to compensate for its exclusion from his stated coalition preference by announcing that the Freedom Party was of course also a party fit for government. Waldheim also stepped back in other cases where he had made public his opinion on certain aspects of domestic affairs. The most dramatic occasion arose after speculation in 1988 that Waldheim would resort to dissolving the government as a consequence of its acceptance of the critical report by an international commission of historians investigating Waldheim's activities during the Second World War. Since this speculation came to nothing, Waldheim has in effect been politically no more active a president than his immediate predecessor and, if one ignores the troubles with his past, has had less impact on domestic politics than the first three presidents of the Second Republic.

This is not to say that nothing has changed in respect of the presidency since Waldheim's election. Under previous office holders, the office of federal president was quasi-sacred; criticising the president violated established conventions. This was of course only possible on the basis of the president maintaining a restricted interpretation of his role. Though Waldheim has in this respect not been an exceptional president, he has been exposed to severe domestic public criticism from politicians and journalists. These have focused not only on his past, but also concerned his activities or lack of activities as president. Under Waldheim, the office of president has lost its quasi-sacred status.[21] This change is likely to be permanent, rather than restricted to this particular office holder.

Moreover, the acrimonious and extremely expensive electoral campaign of 1986 and the subsequent experience with an internationally isolated president are likely to have an impact on the future development of the presidency. Since the pay-offs of winning the presidency are small in party-political terms and none of the big parties was interested in repeating the 1986 experience, alternative scenarios were discussed. One was the nomination of a joint candidate of the big parties. So as to avoid an electoral campaign between the parties in government and having elected a joint candidate certainly would help maintain the grand coalition. In the event, the SPÖ, ÖVP, FPÖ and Greens have all fielded a candidate. Whatever the outcome of the election, which is due in May 1992, it is hard to see how this could lead to a change of the presidency's role in Austrian politics.

THE CABINET

The cabinet is the most important political institution and control of it is the main prize in the political game. This section discusses cabinet recruitment and cabinet decision-making.

The federal chancellor and, on his recommendation, the cabinet ministers, are appointed by the federal president. These constitutional provisions tell us little, however, about actual government formation and recruitment into cabinet. Government formation has always been the domain of party politics. The federal president has always given the leader (or 'chancellor candidate') of the strongest party in parliament the task of forming a government. If his party is not in command of an absolute parliamentary majority, cabinet formation is a matter of negotiation between the parties. While some presidents have had modest influence on government formation, the supremacy of political parties is undoubted. This is even more so with recruitment of cabinet members. The traditional pattern has been that the appointments were discussed and decided in the national party executives. One iron rule of traditional coalition government was that once the cabinet positions had been distributed among the parties, each party was free to nominate whomsoever it wished to be appointed to the cabinet. Within the SPÖ, a decisive influence in this process was exercised by the party leader. His influence was not unlimited, however, in particular when it came to reshuffles of existing government teams. Within the ÖVP, the factionalised party structure caused a more fragmented recruitment process, with the leagues (*Bünde*) and the *Land* party organisations playing a major role.

During the period of the various single-party governments (1966–83), the recruitment process to cabinet became less party-centred. The post-election chancellor candidates (Klaus in 1966 and Kreisky thereafter) benefited from the prestige of electoral victories and stressed their constitutional role as chancellors. Though decisions on cabinet membership were formally still taken in the party executives, both leaders had more leeway than their predecessors. Kreisky, in particular, managed in most cases to make the party's approval of his personnel decisions a pure formality.

The return to coalition governments since 1983 has not reversed this trend towards leader-centred cabinet recruitment. The current SPÖ leader, Vranitzky, constitutes the best example.[22] He has further stressed his constitutional role as chancellor *vis-à-vis* his party and has consequently not sought the detailed approval of the SPÖ party executive for his personal decisions, but has only reported them to it. Despite their recent poor electoral performances, ÖVP leaders have also managed to exercise greater influence on cabinet appointments than their electorally more successful predecessors in the old grand coalition. Moreover, since 1987 the cabinet post of minister of justice has been taken out of the party political realm altogether. This department has since been assigned to independent experts, who must be acceptable to both governing parties, a combination of qualities which proved difficult to find, however.

According to the constitution (Article 69), cabinet members are entrusted with the highest administrative business of the central state (*Bund*), insofar as this is not assigned to the federal president. Possibly an even more important factor is that the cabinet is in a unique position to initiate policy, since it has all the required resources at its disposal. Cabinet decision-making is not subject to detailed constitutional regulation.[23] All government decisions rest with the individual ministers concerned. The only exceptions concern functions explicitly mentioned in the constitution. The most significant are the power formally to propose legislation to parliament, the power to propose persons for appointment by the federal president and the power to submit appeals to the constitutional court. Those tasks which are assigned to the cabinet as such have to be decided unanimously. In respect of cabinet decision-making, the chancellor's constitutional role is that of chairman, not of chief. He is entitled to co-ordinate cabinet work, but not to issue instructions to ministers.

Notwithstanding the cabinet's constitutional importance, during most of the 'classic' phase of Austrian consociationalism, it was not the most powerful political body. That distinction was held by the 'coalition committee', made up of the ten or so most powerful members of the political elite from both *Lager*; only a few of them had a seat in the cabinet. The coalition committee not only dealt with the matters of high policy, but also negotiated and decided upon rather specialised policy questions, where these had become the subject of inter-party dispute. As may be imagined, there was hardly a political issue over which the parties did not at some stage have contradicting proposals. During 'classic' consociationalism the cabinet ministers' role was to a large extent thus one of policy initiation and implementation, while the intermediate phase of the policy process, namely, substantive decision-making, was beyond their capacity.[24]

While it is true that bodies outside the cabinet have also been relevant for cabinet decision-making since the end of the grand coalition in 1966, things have changed considerably.[25] First, all bodies established in the cabinet system since 1966 have been much more cabinet-centred in recruitment than the coalition committee of the 'classic' phase of Austrian consociationalism. Even the coalition committee of the new grand coalition comprises four cabinet members and only two 'externals', namely the leaders of the parties in parliament. Unlike in the old grand coalition, the two most powerful cabinet members − the chancellor and vice-chancellor − who are also the two party chairmen, are no longer members of this committee. Their involvement is restricted to the most tricky problems, which are referred to them for decision. Though it is clear that they do so on the basis of their party rather than cabinet positions, politicians from outside the cabinet do not take part in these decisions.

Second, the decision-making role of ministers has increased considerably since 1966. They enjoyed most autonomy in the single-party governments from 1966 to 1983. Being the trusted policy specialists of their respective party and benefiting from the principle of mutual non-interference within the politically homogeneous cabinet, they had considerable leeway in determining the policy of their departments. Little changed in the SPÖ-FPÖ government of 1983−86, which was based on mutual trust and the idea that each party should be permitted to use its government departments to appeal to its potential clientele. The incumbent new grand coalition has established a powerful coalition committee. However, its scope is much more limited than its predecessor's. It does not normally decide matters over the heads of the responsible cabinet ministes. Though ministers often have to compromise to get the cabinet's approval, their role in cabinet decision-making has remained almost as central as during the last two decades.

The chancellor's role in cabinet decision-making has never corresponded with the *primus inter pares* model outlined by the constitution. His power to determine the cabinet's composition and his role as party leader provide the chancellor with additional power and authority. However, both are effective only *vis-à-vis* his party colleagues. In coalition governments the second party's leader is usually appointed vice-chancellor and *de facto* also has these resources available in respect of his party's government team. He thus constitutes somewhat of a 'second chancellor'. Indeed, for most of the old grand coalition's duration, the vice-chancellor did not take over departmental responsibility, but was the co-ordinator of his party's government team. A kind of dual leadership of the chancellor and the vice-chancellor was thereby established *vis-à-vis* the public.

The powers of the chancellor were most extensive during single-party government. In this form of government the chancellor's capacity to dominate cabinet decision-making increased substantially and he could exercise at will a monopoly of representing the government *vis-à-vis* the public. This took place in particular through television, which since the late 1960s has become the most important medium of mass communication. Internally and externally directed chancellor dominance were mutually re-enforcing. It was during this period that academic observers recognised the establishment of 'chancellor government' or 'chancellor democracy'.[26]

In the coalition governments since 1983 and in particular in the grand coalition government in power since 1987, the chancellor's 'internal capacity', namely, his influence on cabinet decision-making, has been reduced. While continuing to be the cabinet's chairman, he is the chief only of his party's government team. However, the chancellor's 'external capacity', that is, his communication capability *vis-à-vis* the public, has not been likewise reduced, as one might have expected. It is still the chancellor who dominates the public's image of politics. Taking into account his limited 'internal capacity' and the public's weariness with old-style party politics, however, Vranitzky has changed the chancellor's public image: from that of a partisan actor towards that of a reasonable, non-partisan co-ordinator of cabinet work. This style, which of course requires a suitable personality, has proved successful. The 1986 and in particular 1990 general elections have more than ever been 'chancellor elections', with considerable dividends for Vranitzky's political position.[27]

Taken together, the changes the cabinet has undergone since the mid-1960s indicate that it has become less of a mirror of social forces. Though the cabinet has of course retained its party political underpinning, it has increasingly become a political force in its own right, assuming a political identity that is increasingly separate from the parties. This development had been fostered not only by the changed nature of coalition government in the post-1983, as opposed to the pre-1966 period, but also as a result of the personality of recent chancellors, as well as by the political requirement for a united external front placed upon the cabinet in recent years, as it has faced up to the need to introduce policies unpopular with the members of the two main subcultures.[28]

THE ADMINISTRATION[29]

According to the 'father' of the Austrian constitution, Hans Kelsen, the administration should be perfectly neutral, in the sense that it should implement the political directives of parliament. In principle, all activities of the administration should be governed by law, as stipulated in Article 18 of the constitution: 'The entire public administration shall be based on law.' It is to the law and not to the minister that civil servants' prime loyalty should be directed. A neutrality (or rather instrumentality) of the civil service is required only in *functional* terms, however; civil servants may still engage themselves in political activities in their capacity as citizens.

As elsewhere, the Austrian bureaucracy is in reality much more influential than the constitution outlines.[30] Its role in the making and implementation of laws is generally regarded as being very important, particularly because Austria is not accustomed to the practice of providing each government minister with a group of 'temporary civil servants', appointed on the basis of political criteria for the duration of the government's term of office as a sort of 'buffer' between ministers and their departments. Though the government departments have a monocratic structure and ministers can force through each particular policy decision, in general they depend on the co-operation of the bureaucracy. If it does not provide its expertise readily, if it 'overinforms' or 'underinforms' the minister, of if it follows a policy of deliberately limiting his alternatives in decision-making to the department's conventional wisdoms, the minister will have little policy impact and may run into political problems.

It is not necessarily the case, however, that the minister is faced with a single, monolithic bloc of bureaucracy. The common background of law studies of most civil servants and the socialisation within the bureaucracy certainly have an unifying effect, but as elsewhere, personal rivalries and career interests constitute limiting factors. The most important division within the bureaucracy since 1945 has, however, been political. The Austrian bureaucracy had traditionally been conservative, mainly Catholic-conservative but also German-national; social democrats were excluded. During the First Republic and in particular 1934–38, the civil service was further colonised and made more partisan by the Catholic-conservative *Lager*.

In the subsequent period of Nazi rule (1938–45), the bureaucracy was purged of Jews, of the partisans of the previous regime and of those who had remained highly loyal to the notion of an Austrian state. The remaining bureaucrats were either genuine Nazis, or were forced to join the Nazi Party in order to keep their job.[31] In 1945, 'denazification' removed some of them and brought some of the former civil servants back. However, the new government needed experts and the socialists suspected that, if denazification was carried out properly, the civil service would consist entirely of supporters of the Austro-fascist regime (1934–38) and ÖVP partisans. Thus both governing parties decided to give some of the former Nazis among the civil servants a second chance and absorbed them.[32] In order to recruit some SPÖ adherents for the higher ranks of the civil service, the *Proporz* system was established. This granted each of the two governing parties a proportion of public sector jobs roughly equal to their share of the vote in the last general election.

While this was made explicit for public sector firms in the coalition contracts, the *Proporz* was implicit in the civil service. Each party enjoyed personnel autonomy in the department under its control, which in turn were distributed according to electoral strength.[33] Due to the lack of qualified personnel in the socialist subculture and since the system of a tenured civil service does not permit large-scale adjustments of civil service personnel in the short term, *Proporz* was never fully established in the civil service.[34] Nevertheless, during the grand coalition government the bureaucracy became almost entirely party controlled. Both parties had their strongholds in those government departments which were under their respective permanent control but also had 'bridgeheads' in the other ministries. Both parties could rely on a number of top civil servants with extremely strong *Lager* ties and who were inclined to think instinctively along the same lines as politicians from the same party. This of course had consequences for the minister-civil-servant relationship and for the civil servants' role in general. Civil servants acted as *party* experts, and where a ministry was controlled by a party other than their own, even as party spies. Though all this violated the classical concept of a 'neutral', or 'non-partisan' bureaucracy, it led to a civil service and an army which for the first time in modern Austrian history incorporated both major political subcultures and were thus fully acceptable to the two main *Lager*.[35]

Since the end of the old grand coalition in 1966, the picture has become more complicated. The single-party governments (1966–83) felt obliged to announce a non-partisan approach in their civil service recruitment and promotion policy. Kreisky in particular was keen to appoint some 'blood group O' people (i.e., non party members) to top positions in the civil service and in the public sector more generally. On the other hand, electoral results to the personnel representation reveal that during the periods of their respective single-party governments, the ÖVP and SPÖ have maintained their traditional strongholds and have increased their respective support in the strongholds of the other party by roughly one per cent each year.[36] However, on this evidence, it would be wrong to conclude that nothing has changed in respect of civil servants' party loyalties. This author's interviews with about 50 post-war cabinet ministers point towards a diminishing of the importance of civil servants' party affiliation. In many cases, the desire for party patronage has replaced the conviction of earlier generations of partisan civil servants. As one long-serving minister put it: 'In terms of predicting loyalty to the minister's policies, the party book is nowadays often not worth the paper it is written on'. Indeed, many insiders assume that civil servants' party membership now primarily works the other way round, namely, to make it easier to convince the minister of the merits of the department's conventional wisdoms.

If civil servant loyalties can no longer be taken for granted on the basis of their party affiliation, cabinet ministers are called to engage in special activities in order to get the required administrative support. Two strategies have been applied, introducing ministerial cabinets and building up personal loyalties of civil servants by means of motivational techniques. Some ministers have succeeded with both strategies though they cannot easily be applied simultaneously.

The bureaucracy of the immediate post-war decades in many respects employed structures and behaviour patterns *vis-à-vis* the public which it has managed to maintain since the monarchy (up to 1918). Among other things, this meant little public accountability and little responsiveness. Since the mid-1960s attempts have been made to improve civil servants' training, to change the incentive structure in which they operate and to modernise the administration. These have included the setting up of a civil service training academy in 1975, the introduction in the 1980s of fixed-term appointments to a few top positions and the plan of the new grand coalition to carry out a comprehensive administrative reform. These internal reforms were accompanied by external changes. In short, the administration is nowadays exposed to more public scrutiny and criticism than ever before. The mutually re-enforcing activities of the media, the audit office, the ombudsman's office and, more recently, of parliamentary investigative committees and independent administrative review bodies have made life much more troublesome for bureaucrats. Moreover, citizens are no longer the docile, subject-orientated clients which they were during 'classic' consociationalism and for several years after.

Though changes in the bureaucracy are notoriously slow and are difficult to assess, it seems to be clear that significant changes have taken place since the 1960s. The power of *Lager* ties to determine bureaucratic structures and behaviour has shrunk as has their general significance in Austrian society. Other principles which for many decades guided the 'servants of the state' have also been eroded, albeit as yet without having been replaced by new examples.

THE CONSTITUTIONAL COURT

The Austrian constitutional court (*Verfassungsgerichtshof*) is constitutionally very powerful. It can settle disputes concerning competences between other federal institutions, as well as between them and the *Länder*, and also has numerous other tasks.[37] The most important function of the constitutional court, however, is that of being a 'negative legislator' (*negativer Gesetzgeber*), that is to say, it has to decide on the constitutionality of legislation (and of government decrees).[38] The constitutional court can only become active on a specific matter when a relevant appeal has been lodged with it. During the phase of 'classic consociationalism', only other courts, the cabinet and the *Land* governments had the right to appeal to the constitutional court. That right has subsequently been extended.

The judges are appointed by the federal president who can only act on the basis of proposals, however. The cabinet proposes the president and the vice-president of the court and six judges. Six judges are nominated by parliament, three by each of the two chambers. Once appointed, judges may maintain their position until the age of 70. The president of the constitutional court chairs its meetings, represents the court *vis-à-vis* the public and decides on the distribution of cases to individual judges who have to act as (usually very influential) *rapporteurs*; he does not, however, have voting rights. Decisions are made by a majority vote in plenary meetings.

The recruitment of the judges has always been party-controlled. In the intermediate post-war period, the two larger parties agreed to apply *Proporz* rules, that is, to have fixed proportions of socialist and conservative judges and not to exploit situations when they were in control of one of the nominating institutions at a time when a vacancy arose. In the first two post-war decades, the conservatives had an 8:6 majority in the constitutional court (a 7:6 majority among the voting members). In this period the court's political impact was limited. During the ten-year period of Allied occupation (1945–55) the court usually backed the government. It accepted ordinary legislation where constitutional laws were required by reference to a clause of the constitution (Article 10) which grants the central state the right to undertake 'whatever measures seem necessary by reason or in consequence of war to ensure the uniform conduct of economic affairs'. Since the government commanded a parliamentary majority of up to 97 per cent, it would in domestic politics not have been difficult to have made constitutional laws instead of ordinary legislation. This would, however, have allowed the occupation forces to intervene, since according to the Second Control Agreement of the Allied forces, constitutional legislation needed their unanimous approval, thus giving *each* of them an absolute veto power. Ordinary legislation, however, could only be influenced by the Allied forces if they acted jointly, which happened only seldom during this period. If the constitutional court did find government legislation unconstitutional up to 1966, the grand coalition government often decided to use its parliamentary majority (over two thirds) to re-introduce the same bill as a constitutional law which as such did not then fall under the jurisdiction of the constitutional court.[39] Alternatively, the parties anticipated problems with the constitutional court and introduced their bills as constitutional legislation at the outset.

In 1975 two constitutional amendments were made which facilitated access to the constitutional court. Since then, a parliamentary minority (at least one third of the MPs) in each chamber of parliament may now also lodge appeals with the court. The second amendment entitled all individuals to request the constitutional court to check the constitutionality of laws and government decrees which personally affect them. These new provisions have potentially increased the constitutional court's role by removing previous access restrictions. They have, however, also substantially increased its workload: appeals increased from under 200 in 1973 to almost 2,000 in 1987.[40]

A further change significantly affected the recruitment of judges. By 1973 the socialists had not only won an absolute parliamentary majority, but controlled all the institutions empowered to nominate judges to the constitutional court, namely, the cabinet and the two chambers of parliament. They decided to use their first opportunity to change the traditional power-distribution within the court so as to ensure that they could henceforth nominate seven of the 13 judges with voting rights, thus ensuring a 7:6 majority of judges nominated by the SPÖ. After initial protests this was accepted by the ÖVP and a new balance has thus been established.[41]

The various single-party governments of 1966–83 lacked the possibility of bypassing the constitutional court. Nevertheless, the number of decisions repealing laws passed by the parliament remained moderate and though in each case rejection was uncomfortable for the governing party, it did not substantially limit the scope of its politics. In a few cases which caused ideological debate during the mid-1970s, such as the legalisation of abortion and reforms of the broadcasting and the university systems, the political background of the judges was important.[42] In general, however, the court's limited impact was due to its judicial self-restraint. It practised a very formal interpretation of the constitution. The text of the constitution rather than certain constitutional principles (which could be re-interpreted) was the basis for the court's decisions.[43]

More recently, however, the constitutional court has assumed a more active role. It has switched from a formal to a more substantive interpretation of the constitution and has become less predictable in its verdicts. The constitutional court has in several cases changed its own earlier judgments. Examples of the new role of the constitutional court include verdicts which forced parliament to introduce a widowers' pension[44] and to change the electoral law in order to enfranchise Austrians living abroad. Moreover, important laws were in part declared unconstitutional. These included the law regulating shop opening hours. The court also declared unconstitutional a regulation which prevented shops from selling goods cheaper than they bought them, a measure which had been intended to protect grocers against multi-outlet firms and thus to maintain a localised system of food retailing. Another important case was the decision to declare unconstitutional a law which had prevented civil service pensioners from topping up their pension income with additional earnings. These restrictions were later deemed unconstitutional for all groups of the population. They had been introduced to reduce the workforce on the labour market and thus help younger people to find a job.

A further decision with an enormous impact concerned the invalidation of a law fixing different pension ages for men and women. This matter has not yet been resolved by new legislation, but the problem is a tricky one. Granting men the lower pension age that women already enjoy would lead to the financial collapse of the pension system, yet putting up the pension age of women is not seen as a politically viable alternative. Another case concerned a hard-fought three-party consensus about ethnic minority schools in the *Land* of Carinthia, which was undermined by the court declaring the relevant law unconstitutional because it violated the rights of the ethnic minority. The constitutional court has also engaged in detailed investigations to deal with individual complaints against police behaviour, an investigative role which only a few years ago nobody would have expected. Most recently the constitutional court has required that the costs of carers of dependent children or spouses be made tax deductible, which will place a serious burden on the budget.

It has to be mentioned, however, that the court's increased activity is only one side of the coin. Many of the cases just mentioned had been on the political agenda for years, but had not been tackled because they affected the vested interests of powerful groups and/or because they were extremely complex. Thus earlier political immobilism on the governmental and parliamentary levels had left unsolved a series of important issues to which a more self-confident constitutional court is now addressing itself.

What has caused this new behavioural pattern in the constitutional court? A prerequisite for this re-orientation has been the court's new power (since 1981) to reject consideration of individual complaints against administrative decisions when those complaints do not stand a reasonable chance of being successful, or (since 1984) where the decision would not help clarify constitutional issues. These amendments have reduced the workload of the constitutional court, thus increasing its capacity to engage in more 'useful' judgments.[45] Most observers argue that a generational change among the judges has also paved the way to the new interpretation of the constitution. The younger members of the court interpret constitutional law in a more substantive way and feel less duty-bound to the political party that nominated them for appointment to the court.[46]

Unlike in the times of the old grand coalition (1945–66), constitutional court verdicts are nowadays increasingly accepted as requirements to find solutions which fit into the existing constitution, rather than to enact the same bill again as a constitutional law and thus amend the constitution, though this still happens in a few cases. This changed attitude is in part due to differences within the coalition on the relevant subject matter. If one side – and it is usually the ÖVP – is perfectly happy with the court's decision, it has no incentive to agree to back the qualified parliamentary majority necessary to circumvent the verdict by means of a new constitutional law. However, it is not only the policy reward for one of the governing parties which prevent them doing so; another reason is that public opinion would interpret such a law as one more sign of party misbehaviour.

The consequences of the new role of the constitutional court are clear: the scope of the party system has been substantially reduced.

THE JUDICIARY

While the constitution deals with the constitutional and administrative courts under the heading of 'constitutional and administrative guarantees', the judiciary is dealt with under the heading 'federal execution' (*Vollziehung des Bundes*). All judges are guaranteed independence in exercising their judicial function and they also have constitutional guarantees against dismissal and transfer. There are, however, links between the judiciary and politics.[47] In their role as judicial administrators, judges are subordinate to the minister of justice. They are appointed by the federal president or the minister of justice on the basis of a cabinet proposal. In drawing up the cabinet proposal, proposals by the personnel committee of the respective court or, in the cases of the courts' president and vice-presidents, by the personnel committee of the next higher instance, have to be considered. Legally, the cabinet is not bound by these proposals from the courts. However, it is a constitutional convention that the cabinet restricts itself to considering the personnel proposed by the courts.[48] The judiciary is thus to a large extent in effect self-recruiting.

A second link between the judiciary and politics are the state prosecutors (*Staatsanwälte*). Unlike the judges, they are subject to instructions from their superiors. At the top of the command chain is the minister of justice. It was argued by Social Democrats and top bureaucrats that this right to give instructions is necessary to unify judicial decision-making, to promote a change in decision-making, to take into account new academic findings and to ensure the equal treatment of all citizens.[49] However, the justice minister's right to give instructions is clearly also potentially a highly effective means of influencing the outcome of cases brought before the judiciary: without an effective prosecution there is no real judge.

Traditionally, the judiciary has not played a great role in politics. Although for many socialists the judiciary still displayed a class bias, political controversy over court decisions seldom arose. There were a few politically relevant cases in the 1950s and 1960s, which basically concerned politicians in cases of corruption, but these mostly became judicial matters only *after* they had been decided politically. Politics was generally seen to be conducted by politicians, not judges. A transfer of issues from the political arena to the arena of the courts by one of the two big parties against the other would have violated unwritten consociational rules. Though both parties tried to make political capital out of corruption cases within the other *Lager*, in particular when elections were on the way, only a few politicians suffered from this.

In the late 1970s, and in particular during the 1980s, the picture began to change. The judiciary increasingly came to have a political impact by not only investigating cases involving politicians, but by also prosecuting them. Initially, the existing links between politics and the judiciary seems to have been used for delaying, or preventing prosecution, which in turn led to a decline in the population's trust in the judiciary. More recently, however, there have been quite a few important judicial cases with political implications. The list of politicians either accused of crimes, actually found guilty of serious offences by the courts – including for example tax evasion, acting as an accessory after the fact and perjury – reads like an extract from the 'Who's Who of Austrian Politics'. Verdicts against politicians have increased the population's trust in the judiciary,[50] whilst simultaneously confirming their increasing cynicism about the character and activities of the subcultural political elites.

Those parties whose politicians are implicated in such cases tend to criticise the judicial decisions whilst the others usually present themselves as the defenders of an independent judiciary (until of course their turn comes to have one of their politicians under fire). For some observers, the judiciary's increased political impact is not a sign of increased political corruption or rule-breaking, but of a more independent judiciary and greater professional ethics within it.[51] Such a development does indeed seem to have taken place. The wording of some verdicts, however, has clearly displayed an anti-party politics bias by making negative general statements about parties and politicians. While from a normative perspective this may be a step too far, from an analytical perspective, it clearly indicates that the judiciary has assumed the status of an actor in the political process.

CONTROL OF GOVERNMENT AND ADMINISTRATION: THE AUDIT OFFICE[52]

The audit office (*Rechnungshof*) is formally a parliamentary institution, since its president and vice-president are elected by the *Nationalrat* (formerly for an unlimited period, but since 1988 for a 12-year term). The other audit office personnel are appointed by its president. The audit office organisation is monocratic. Its tasks include the financial supervision of the federal and *Land* administrations, public sector firms and large towns. In doing so, the audit office has to check the legality, economy and expediency of management and policy. Its findings are reported to the *Nationalrat* and the *Land* parliaments and are subsequently published. In cases of maladministration the parliament may hold the respective member of the executive responsible.[53]

During 'classic' consociationalism, the presidency of the audit office was one of the many positions to be shared among the two governing parties according to *Proporz* rules. This office was considered to count almost as much as a ministerial post. The presidency was assigned to the coalition junior partner, the SPÖ. Consequently, audit office findings used to be seen within the context of coalition politics. While the media and the public did not normally pay much attention to the audit office's scrutiny, the ÖVP used to interpret criticism of its subculture's parts of the governmental and administrative system as party-political motivated. On the few occasions that the SPÖ's 'realm' was criticised by the audit office, the SPÖ also expressed its dissatisfaction with the audit office and its president in particular.

During a temporary flirtation with the FPÖ, the SPÖ in 1964 decided to nominate an FPÖ MP for the presidency of the audit office, from the control of which the SPÖ increasingly felt it was obtaining no real pay-offs. After the retirement of this FPÖ president in the 1980s, another FPÖ MP was elected and he still holds this position. The ÖVP has managed to hold the audit office's vice-president position throughout the Second Republic. Though rather powerless within the audit office, the vice-president is usually well-informed.

Since 1964 audit office impact has changed considerably. Though with a prominent opposition politician occupying its presidency it could still be argued that party politics influence audit office activities, the public has become more willing to accept it as a neutral institution. In 1975 new parliamentary rules of procedure granted parliamentary minorities of at least one third of MPs the right to instruct the audit office to scrutinise a particular branch of the executive. In 1988 the required number of MPs was reduced to 20. Thus the opposition is no longer obliged to wait to see what the audit office will, of its own accord, place under scrutiny. This means that the opposition can now select a branch of the executive which it believes to be a weak point of the government and seek the audit office to investigate further. The audit office's investigation normally not only provides the opposition with new facts and insights, but also makes its critique of the government more credible. Giving the opposition formal access to the audit office certainly has increased the latter's political relevance.

Moreover, in the 1970s, investigative journalism established itself as a main branch of the Austrian media. Popularising the findings of the audit office became one of its principal activities.[54] In doing so, usually the confidential draft versions of the audit office's reports, normally more critical than the final, are used. These draft versions are allegedly made available to investigative journalists by audit office representatives of those parties likely to benefit from its critique, or by audit office civil servants who want to see their criticism published in a form unrestricted by their superiors. Though the final version of audit office reports include the reaction of the criticised authorities or firms and only wording, but not their substantive conclusions may have been altered in that process, the publication of a confidential version that has not yet been toned-down is more 'newsworthy' and therefore politically effective.

The audit office's increased role in Austrian politics has provoked discussions about its reform. The governing parties' declared aim is to make the audit office more efficient by suggestions for general administrative reform rather than a detailed *post hoc* critique of administrative decisions. The formal subordination of the audit office to parliament should be made more effective and for the first time the question of who guards the guardians is also to be answered for the audit office by introducing external scrutiny. The crucial question, however, may be the pattern of recruitment to the presidency. While the FPÖ would like to maintain the current situation, the Greens claim to be the only true opposition party and that they should therefore be entitled to nominate the president. They have suitable candidates in the persons of Peter Pilz, an MP who was the star of two parliamentary committees of investigation, and Walter Geyer, a former MP and state prosecutor. The SPÖ and ÖVP have made proposals for an non-political presidency, either by appointing a business manager rather than a politician, or by creating a collective presidium with multi-party representation.

FEDERALISM

Austria is formally a federal state. Its two main levels are the central state (*Bund*) and the *Länder*. This article, however, does not intend to deal with the complex issue of relations between the *Bund* and the *Länder*, nor with the *Länder* themselves. Instead, the intention is to throw light on those federal elements that affect significantly political institutions at the national level.[55] There are three main federal elements in the Austrian constitution: the distribution of competences between the central state and the *Länder*; the second chamber of parliament, the *Bundesrat*; and indirect federal administration by the *Länder* and, in particular, the governor (*Landeshauptmann*).

The Distribution of Competences

In the first two decades of the Second Republic, a tendency to grant the central state more competences at the cost of the *Länder* prevailed.[56] The old grand coalition of course constituted a rather comfortable framework for the reshuffling of competences, the more so since the more 'federalist' party, the ÖVP, was for most of this time controlled by 'centralists' from Lower Austria, the *Land* surrounding Vienna. Since the old grand coalition ended, the reshuffling of competences, which still requires the consensus of both big parties, became much more complicated. The party in opposition at federal level tried to capitalise on its remaining positions at *Land* level and was unwilling to give up competences in favour of a central government under another party. The early 1960s also saw a more fundamental change begin.[57] Within the big parties, the *Land* party organisations gained power and thus reduced 'centralist' tendencies within their national leaderships. At the same time, the *Länder* also started to show more self-confidence *vis-à-vis* the central state. In 1964 they addressed a programme of demands — mainly for an extension of competences — to the central state, which in 1974 led to a constitutional amendment bringing some, albeit modest, reforms. Since then, the *Länder* have continued to push for more power. From the mid-1960s changes in competence distribution between the two levels has increasingly come from an agreement between the central state and the *Länder*, rather than of a unilateral decision by the former. There is more of a balance between the gains and losses of both sides.[58] The return to grand coalition government in 1987 has not reversed this pattern.

The Bundesrat

Traditionally, the prime role of a second chamber in a federal system is to permit the constituent units to take part in the decision-making process of the centre, and thus to represent the interests of the former. However, the Austrian *Bundesrat* has always been very weak both constitutionally and politically. For most matters it has only a suspensory veto and some matters, in particular the budget, are not referred to it at all (Article 42). Due to the developments described above, the *Bundesrat* has since 1984 been stronger in respect of constitutional legislation reducing the competences of the *Länder*. In contrast to other constitutional legislation, such changes now require a two-thirds majority in the *Bundesrat* (Article 44). Furthermore, in 1984 a reform of the *Bundesrat* rules of procedure included an hour's question time and has also given the governors, the most visible representatives of the *Länder* (see below), the right to speak in the *Bundesrat*.

In practice, however, the *Bundesrat* has not played the role of a warden for the *Länder*'s interests. Its party composition is similar to that of the *Nationalrat*; debates and voting have strictly followed party lines and have mirrored those in the first chamber. During the old grand coalition, the *Bundesrat*'s most significant function was to provide by its veto the chance for a second treatment of a *Nationalrat* bill which contained legal or textual errors. These vetos enjoyed the government's approval and were made to avoid the more time-consuming legislation of an amendment to the defective law.[59] *Bundesrat* activities have increased since the mid-1960s due to increased party competition and growing conflict between the parties.[60]

Having argued and voted against government legislation in the *Nationalrat*, the opposition wanted not to miss presenting its arguments again in the *Bundesrat* and, if possible, to delay its coming into force by using the suspensory veto of the second chamber. However, little public attention was given to the parliamentary battles in the *Bundesrat* and the government soon anticipated possible delays by an 'alien' majority in the second chamber. Only in exceptional cases did the *Bundesrat* have an impact on the conduct and outcome of the political process.[61] The new veto rights of the *Bundesrat* have not yet proved significant and the governors' speaking rights have been used only rarely and thus have not added much to its relevance as political arena for *Land* interests.

Summing up, it can be said that the *Bundesrat* had been transformed from an irrelevant addendum to the legislative process to an additional, though not significant, arena for inter-party duels. It has, however, not gained the status of an actor.

The Indirect Federal Administration

The institution of the *Bundesrat* is not significant for constituent units' participation in central decision-making and as the formal competences of the nine *Länder* are, when compared to other Western federal states (such as the United States, Germany and Switzerland) rather limited, the remaining formal institution through which significant affect takes place is the system of indirect federal administration by the *Länder* and, in particular, the governor (*Landeshauptmann*). In several important matters such as citizenship, agricultural interest organisations and traffic policing, legislation rests with the central state, but the *Land* administrations are entrusted with their execution.[62]

The governor has a double function in this system. On the one hand he is chairman of the *Land* government and responsible to the *Land* parliament (*Landtag*). On the other hand he is the top representative of the federal government in the *Land*. According to the constitution (Article 103), the governor in his role as indirect federal administrator has to follow federal ministers' directives and must use all his resources, including those of the *Land* government, to implement central state policies.[63] A governor who does not behave accordingly may be brought before the constitutional court, which has three kinds of sanctions at its disposal: to declare the behaviour of the governor unconstitutional; to deprive the governor of his office; to deprive the governor temporarily of his political rights.

Their double role made the governors extremely powerful and visible within their respective *Länder*. Since the distribution of competences between the central state and the *Länder* tends to assign the more popular tasks to the *Länder* (in particular, they only spend money, but do not tax the citizens), the governors are in a good position to become very popular. The local media, to which the governors have privileged access, have strengthened this tendency. On this basis, many governors have succeeded in gaining the image of the 'father of the *Land*'. Inasmuch as they were exposed to only very little political criticism, they have been similar to the federal president, but they differed by being the most powerful men in their respective *Länder*. All this has led to a very substantial incumbency bonus for the governor's party in *Land* elections and to governors who stayed in office for decades, clearly outranking the duration of national executive members.[64]

In the past, indirect federal administration did not lead to problems. Some governors may have implemented federal laws and directives from the Vienna ministries with more energy than others, but it seems that there were no attempts to reverse federal decisions and no governor openly violated the will of the central state. This may be to a large extent not attributed to the constitution's supremacy over conflicting political values the governors may have held. The smooth process of indirect federal administration may rather indicate that the central state's policies have been quite acceptable to the *Länder*, despite their interests' weak representation in the constitutional structure. Indeed, the formal constitutional structures with which this article is concerned are not the main way in which *Länder* interests are articulated and brought to bear in decision-making.[65] Most important are the political parties, which will not normally enact legislation at federal level against the will of their *Land* party organisations.

Moreover, a variety of extra-constitutional mechanisms exist in order to represent the *Länder* interests *vis-à-vis* the central state. The most significant of these are the governors' conference (*Landeshauptmännerkonferenz*) and the meetings of finance 'ministers' of the *Länder*. The governors' conference comprises all nine governors plus the cabinet minister responsible for constitutional affairs and specialist cabinet ministers on an *ad hoc* basis. Most major policy issues concerning central state–*Länder* relations, but also those pertaining to the national level are discussed at its biannual meetings. Though an in-depth political analysis of these extra-constitutional mechanisms has not yet been undertaken, it seems reasonable to assume that policies to be implemented by indirect federal administration stem from a negotiation between the two levels, rather than by a relationship in which the centre imposes its will.

Since the 1980s, however, the difficulties of constitutional regulation of indirect federal administration have become apparent. Two governors, both from opposition parties at national level at that time, openly refused to follow instructions from central government. Their political rationale was to take a position which was popular within the *Land* and then to define the conflict with the central state in terms of federalism, or rather anti-centralism (anti-Vienna), which substantially increases the support for the governor within his *Land*. The case could be brought before the constitutional court by the cabinet, as happened in the first case (1984). Yet whatever may be the verdict of the constitutional court, the governor would still benefit politically.

If the court were to accept his conduct, then he would be vindicated as a lawful defender of the rights of his *Land* (against Viennese interference). If the governor were punished, he would claim to be a martyr for his *Land*. If he commanded a majority in the *Land* parliament, he would likely dissolve the latter and hold elections. The governor's party would undoubtedly profit electorally and the party or parties which represented the government at the federal level would suffer. The *Land* parliament would then most likely re-elect the governor just deprived of his office by the constitutional court, which would be powerless to prevent this unless it had taken the highly unlikely step of suspending the governor's political rights. While this is as yet only a scenario, it clearly illustrates how the institutional framework is susceptible to abuse, in a manner that was never intended, or envisaged, and can be made into an arena for conducting party disputes.

Since 'classic' consociationalism the impact on Austrian national politics of *Land*-level political institutions has increased. As explained elsewhere in this article, the increased significance of formal institutions has had a twofold cause. First, the parties have increasingly used the formal institutions which they control not in a consensual manner but as a base from which to compete with each other. Second, the institutions have themselves become a greater significance in shaping the roles of political actors.

CONCLUSION

This article has surveyed Austrian governmental institutions and in particular their development since 'classic' consociationalism. It started from a situation in which the institutional framework seemed to be almost irrelevant and played little role either in politics, or in political science analyses. The elites of the two major *Lager* first enjoyed a duopoly of control of political institutions. Second, they tended to override constitutional norms by political norms, seeing themselves almost entirely as representatives of their respective *Lager* as well as agents of inter-*Lager* co-operation, which they often saw as not best served by a narrow interpretation of institutional rules. At that time, constitutional rules were thus to a large extent pushed into the background.

When in 1966 the major *Lager* elites opted for a more competitive approach by putting an end to grand coalition government, the institutional framework gained in importance. A strong opposition acted as a watchdog on governments' compliance with institutional rules and tried to use the institutional framework to contain governmental actions. From then on, that formal institutional framework may best be described as an arena, the rules of which were highly relevant for the political process. This development was further fostered by the reduced duopoly of the two major *Lager*. First, the 'Third *Lager*' became more acceptable and then gained in strength. Second, the Greens established themselves as a new and additional political force.

Moreover, there was a largely silent, though thorough, change of governmental institutions and of their role in the political process. The political 'core institutions' such as parliament and the cabinet are now less determined by the political subcultures than they used to be in the phase of 'classic' consociationalism. The behaviour of political officeholders is now shaped more than before by their respective institutions. Other institutions such as the constitutional court, the audit office and the judiciary, which in the period of 'classic' consociationalism were under the control of the elites, or practised 'self restraint', have gained in importance in recent years. In short, many of the political institutions have moved towards being political actors in their own right. Consequently, the political system now has many more relevant actors than in the immediate post-war period and the political process has become more complex and less predictable.

Both developments have been facilitated by institutional reforms, details of many of which have been covered. Most important, however, have been major changes of the political actors' environment, in particular the transformation of the political culture and the media.[66] These have encouraged the traditional *Lager* elites to engage in more competitive behaviour and the office-holders to stress their formal roles and to exercise more fully and more in keeping with the spirit of the constitution the powers which their respective institutions had been granted by it.

Since the 1970s, when a journalist argued that Austria had been transformed into a trade union state (*Gewerkschaftsstaat*),[67] it has become usual to use the term of the 'Third Republic', in order to characterise a fundamental transformation of the Austrian political system. In this author's view, this 'Third Republic' has not yet fully materialised, though Austria has moved close to a point where this label might be appropriate. However, Austria's membership of the EC, which now seems likely, will undoubtedly have significant consequences for her domestic politics. The outcome of changes which the EC membership will bring will mean that Austria will finally complete her transformation from consociationalism to a new type of polity, one which might well then justify the designation 'Third Republic'.

NOTES

1. J. March and J. P. Olsen, *Rediscovering Institutions* (NY: The Free Press, 1989), p. 18.
2. See O. K. Pedersen, 'Nine Questions to a Neo-institutional Theory in Political Science', *Scandinavian Political Studies*, Vol. 14, No. 2 (1991), pp. 125–48, here p. 126.

3. See, e.g., G. E. Kafka, 'Papierene Verfassung?' and 'Gelähmte Regierung', *Wort und Wahrheit*, Vol. 17 (1959), pp. 529–41 and 590–611; O. Kichheimer, 'The Waning of Opposition in Parliamentary Regimes', *Social Research*, Vol. 24 (1957), pp. 127–56; R. Preston, 'Austrian Parliamentary Democracy', *Parliamentary Affairs*, Vol. 10 (1957), pp. 344–52; H. P. Secher, 'Coalition Government: The Case of the Second Austrian Republic', *American Political Science Review*, Vol. 52 (1958), pp. 791–809.
4. See H. P. Secher, 'Representative Democracy or "Chamber State": The Ambiguous Role of Interest Groups in Austrian Politics', *Western Political Quarterly*, Vol. 13 (1960), pp. 890–909; G. Lehmbruch, *Proporzdemokratie* (Tübingen: Mohr, 1967); P. Pulzer, 'The Legitimizing Role of Political Parties: The Second Austrian Republic', *Government and Opposition*, Vol. 4 (1969), pp. 324–44.
5. Social Partnership (*Sozialpartnerschaft*) means the co-operation between the major interest groups and between them and the government in the areas of industrial relations, incomes and prices policy and social and economic policy-making. See the contributions to this volume by P. Gerlich and V. Lauber.
6. Besides the *Bundes-Verfassungsgesetz*, which is referred to as the constitution in this article, there are other constitutional laws and clauses with constitutional status within ordinary statute. There is no legal hierarchy between these three forms of constitutional legislation. They are all equally binding.
7. The constitution itself does not indicate what constitutes a 'total revision'. Constitutional lawyers and the constitutional court have interpreted this clause as referring to amendments which involve changes to one or more of the guiding principles of the 1920 constitution. These unquestionably include the principles of democracy, of federalism and of the rule of law, as well as of the separation of powers and of liberalism. See R. Walter, *Österreichisches Bundesverfassungsrecht* (Vienna: Manz, 1972), pp. 101–13. On the issue of Austria's potential EC membership see the contribution in this volume by D. M. Schultz.
8. There were also a few attempts at people's initiatives which failed to get the required support.
9. On the *Proporz* system see the section 'The Administration' in this article.
10. See Kirchheimer, 'The Waning of Opposition in Parliamentary Regimes'; F. C. Engelmann, 'Austria: The Pooling of Opposition', in R. A. Dahl (ed.), *Political Opposition in Western Democracies* (New Haven, CT: Yale UP, 1966), pp. 260–83; F. Koja, 'Der Parlamentarismus in Österreich', *Zeitschrift für Politik*, Vol. 14 (1967), pp. 333–51; A. Leclaire, 'Grosse Koalition als permanente Krisenregierung' (Ph.D., Univ. of Heidelberg, 1966); K.-H. Nassmacher, *Das österreichische Regierungssystem* (Cologne: Westdeutscher Verlag, 1968); A. Pelinka and M. Welan, *Demokratie und Verfassung in Österreich* (Vienna: Europa Verlag, 1971); K. Steiner, *Politics in Austria* (Boston, MA: Little, Brown & Co., 1972), pp. 355–70; H. Widder, *Parlamentarische Strukturen im politischen System* (Berlin: Duncker & Humblot, 1979).
11. See P. Gerlich, *Parlamentarische Kontrolle im politischen System* (Vienna: Springer, 1973).
12. Good descriptions of parliamentary activities are contained in H. Wittmann, 'Regierung und Opposition im parlamentarischen Prozess', *Österreichisches Jahrbuch für Politik* 1977, pp. 21–90; *idem*, 'Regierung und Opposition im parlamentarischen Prozess – Struktur und Arbeit des Parlaments in der XIV. Gesetzgebungsperiode 1975–1979', *Österreichisches Jahrbuch für Politik* 1979, pp. 39–68; A. Nevlacsil, 'Regierung und Opposition im parlamentarischen Prozess', *Österreichisches Jahrbuch für Politik* 1983, pp. 209–57; *idem*, 'Der Nationalrat in der XVI. GP', *Österreichisches Jahrbuch für Politik* 1986, pp. 465–94; *idem*, 'Der Nationalrat in ther XVII. GP', *Österreichisches Jahrbuch für Politik* 1990, pp. 431–59. For more general surveys of parliament, see H. Widder, 'Der Nationalrat', in H. Schambeck (ed.), *Österreichs Parlamentarismus. Werden und System* (Berlin: Duncker & Humblot, 1986), pp. 261–336 and H. Fischer, 'Das Parlament', in H. Dachs, P. Gerlich, H. Gottweis, F. Horner, H. Kramer, V. Lauber, W. C. Müller and E. Tálos (eds.), *Handbuch des politischen Systems Österreichs* (Vienna: Manz, 1991), pp. 88–109.

13. See Engelmann, 'The Pooling of Opposition' for the phase of 'classic consociationalism'.
14. See W. C. Müller, 'Die neue große Koalition in Österreich', *Österreichische Zeitschrift für Politikwissenschaft*, Vol. 17 (1988), pp. 321–47.
15. See K. Berchtold, *Der Bundespräsident* (Vienna: Springer, 1969); M. Welan, *Das österreichische Staatsoberhaupt* (Vienna: Verlag für Geschichte und Politik, 1986).
16. The dismissal procedure requires first a two-thirds majority of the *Nationalrat* in order to summon the *Bundesversammlung*, the joint meeting of the two parliamentary chambers. Second, the *Bundesversammlung* must vote (by simple majority) for a referendum in order to dismiss the president. The third requirement is a majority in the referendum itself. If, however, the referendum results in a majority against the dismissal, it is counted as the re-election of the president for another six-year term. (This clause may not, however, extend the length of his total term over 12 consecutive years.) A referendum which approves the president is also counted as a vote of no-confidence on the *Nationalrat*: it is automatically dissolved and a new parliamentary election has to be called.
17. See K. Ucakar, *Demokratie und Wahlrecht in Österreich* (Vienna: Verlag für Gesellschaftskritik, 1985).
18. See E. C. Kollmann, *Theodor Körner. Militär und Politik* (Vienna: Verlag für Geschichte und Politik, 1973), pp. 370–79; F. C. Engelmann, 'Haggling for the Equilibrium: The Renegotiation of the Austrian Coalition, 1959', *American Political Science Review*, Vol. 56 (1962), pp. 651–62; K. R. Stadler, *Adolf Schärf. Mensch – Politiker – Staatsmann* (Vienna: Europa Verlag, 1982), pp. 495–502. F. Weissensteiner (ed.), *Die österreichischen Bundespräsidenten* (Vienna: Österreichischer Bundesverlag, 1982).
19. See B. Kreisky, *Im Strom der Politik* (Vienna: Kremayr & Scheriau, 1988), pp. 258–61.
20. See K. R. Luther, 'Austria's Future and Waldheim's Past: The Significance of the 1986 Elections', *West European Politics*, Vol. 10, No. 3 (July 1987), pp. 376–99.
21. See H.-G. Heinrich and M. Welan, 'Der Bundespräsident', in Dachs *et al.* (eds.), *Handbuch des politischen Systems Österreichs*, pp. 126–31, here p. 131.
22. It is worth mentioning that Vranitzky's political career did not progress via party positions, but started in government. He became chancellor without having been a member of the party executive and only then succeeded to the party leadership.
23. See K. Berchtold, 'Die Regierung', in H. Fischer (ed.), *Das politische System Österreichs*, pp. 151–79, here pp. 157–60 and L. Adamovich, 'Die Koordinationskompetenz des Bundeskanzlers in verfassungsrechtlicher Sicht', *Juristische Blätter*, Vol. 95 (1973), pp. 234–42.
24. See W. Rudzio, 'Entscheidungszentrum Koalitionsausschuss – Zur Realverfassung Österreichs unter der grossen Koalition', *Politische Vierteljahresschrift*, Vol. 12 (1971), pp. 87–118.
25. See P. Gerlich and W. C. Müller, 'Austria: Routine and Ritual', in J. Blondel and F. Müller-Rommel (eds.), *Cabinets in Western Europe* (London: Macmillan, 1988), pp. 138–50; W. C. Müller, 'Die neue grosse Koalition in Österreich'; W. C. Müller, 'Regierung und Kabinettsystem', in Dachs *et al.* (eds.), *Handbuch des österreichischen politischen Systems*, pp. 110–25.
26. See M. Welan and H. Neisser, *Der Bundeskanzler im österreichischen Verfassungsgefüge* (Vienna: Hollinek, 1971); M. Welan, 'Die Kanzlerdemokratie in Österreich', in A. Khol, R. Prantner and A. Stirnemann (eds.), *Um Parlament und Partei* (Graz: Styria, 1976), pp. 169–80; P. Gerlich, W. C. Müller und W. Philipp, 'Potentials and Limitations of Executive Leadership: the Austrian Cabinet since 1945', *European Journal of Political Research*, Vol. 16 (1988), pp. 191–205.
27. See D. Meth-Cohn and W. C. Müller, 'Leaders Count: The Austrian Election of October 1990', *West European Politics*, Vol. 14, No. 2 (April 1991), pp. 183–88; W. C. Müller, 'Persönlichkeitswahl bei der Nationalratswahl 1990', *Österreichisches Jahrbuch für Politik* 1990, pp. 261–82.
28. See the contribution of V. Lauber in this volume.
29. This section is about bureaucratic, not governmental 'administration'.

30. See R. F. Kneucker, 'Austria: An Administrative State', *Österreichische Zeitschrift für Politikwissenschaft*, Vol. 2 (1973), pp. 95–127; H. Neisser, 'Die Rolle der Bürokratie', in Fischer (ed.), *Das politische System Österreichs*, pp. 233–270; Berchtold, 'Die Regierung'; H. Neisser, 'Die Verwaltung', in Dachs *et al.* (eds.), *Handbuch des politischen Systems Österreichs*, pp. 132–44.
31. See Steiner, *Politics in Austria*, pp. 375–83.
32. Initially also the Communists participated in the government. They advocated a more rigorous 'denazification' policy.
33. See Secher, 'Coalition Government', pp. 796–808 and Steiner, *Politics in Austria*, pp. 383–97.
34. See Engelmann, 'The Pooling of Opposition', p. 274.
35. Secher, 'Coalition Government', p. 809.
36. See W. C. Müller, 'Party Patronage in Austria', in A. Pelinka and F. Plasser (eds.), *The Austrian Party System* (Boulder, CO: Westview Press, 1989), pp. 327–56, here p. 337; cf. also K. R. Luther, 'Dimensions of Party System Change: The Case of Austria', *West European Politics*, Vol. 12, No. 1 (Jan. 1989), pp. 3–17, here pp. 16–18.
37. These include acting as an impeachment tribunal, i.e., to decide in cases where government members, e.g., have been impeached, as well as an electoral tribunal, i.e., to decide in cases in which elections had been challenged.
38. See M. Welan, 'Constitutional Review and Legislation in Austria', in C. Landfried (ed.), *Constitutional Review and Legislation* (Baden-Baden: Nomos, 1988), pp. 63–80.
39. Had these constitutional laws constituted a 'total revision' of the constitution, the intervention of the constitutional court would have been possible, however, since the constitution requires a referendum in such cases.
40. M. Michalitsch, 'Die geänderte, realverfassungsändernde Rechtsprechung des Verfassungsgerichtshofes', *Österreichisches Jahrbuch für Politik* 1989, pp. 197–207, here pp. 190–91.
41. See M. Welan, 'Der Verfassungsgerichtshof – eine Nebenregierung?', in Fischer (ed.), *Das politische System Österreichs*, pp. 271–315, here pp. 295–99.
42. Though *vis-à-vis* the public it is the constitutional court rather than the judges that acts (there is no institution of dissenting opinion) it was reported that in these cases the decisions were made along party lines, with a 7:6 majority, upholding the legislation of the Socialist parliamentary majority. Cf. F. Ermacora, 'Politische Aspekte der Verfassungsentwicklung in Österreich seit 1970', *Österreichisches Jahrbuch für Politik* 1978, pp. 59–84, here pp. 82–4.
43. See H. Schäffer, *Verfassungsinterpretation in Österreich* (Vienna: Springer, 1971).
44. See W. C. Müller, 'Vom Zusammenhang von politischen Entscheidungsmustern und Politikergebnissen am Beispiel der Witwerpension', *Österreichisches Jahrbuch für Politik* 1985, pp. 397–416.
45. See Michalitsch, 'Die geänderte, realverfassungsändernde Rechtsprechung des Verfassungsgerichtshofes', p. 190.
46. Some insiders argue that the second argument holds true only for the judges who were nominated by the Socialists. Those nominated by the ÖVP, have traditionally acted less cohesively in the court and are said to have displayed more party loyalty in recent years.
47. K. Steiner, *Politics in Austria*, pp. 398–48.
48. H. Keller, 'Die Justiz als Staat im Staate?', in Fischer (ed.), *Das politische System Österreichs*, pp. 317–36, here p. 328 and E. Markel, 'Sicherung der richterlichen Unabhängigkeit', *Österreichische Richterzeitung*, Vol. 62 (1984), No. 6–7, pp. 162–66.
49. See N. Leser, 'Recht und Gesellschaft', in J. Hannak (ed.), *Bestandaufnahme Österreich 1945–1963* (Wien: Forum Verlag, 1963), pp. 186–230, here pp. 221–24.
50. See *IMAS-report*, No. 12, May 1991.
51. H.-G. Heinrich and M. Welan, 'Gerichtsbarkeit, Verwaltungs- und Verfassungsgericht', in Dachs *et al.* (eds.), *Handbuch des politischen Systems Österreichs*, pp. 145–55, here p. 148.
52. Another institution for the control of administration is the ombudsman's office (*Volksanwaltschaft*). Its three members are elected by the *Nationalrat* for a six-year

term. The ombudsman's office can be appealed to by any individual who feels unfairly treated by the administration. Though the administration is formally obliged to respond to the audit office, the latter cannot oblige the administration to change unreasonable, albeit lawful, behaviour. It can, however, suggest legal reform to the *Nationalrat*. The main political significance of the ombudsman's office is thus restricted to exercising public, or moral pressure on the administration.

53. See J. Hengstschläger, *Der Rechnungshof* (Berlin: Duncker & Humblot, 1982), and H. Widder, 'Rechnungshof und Volksanwaltschaft', in Dachs *et al.* (eds.), *Handbuch des politischen Systems Österreichs*, pp. 156–65.
54. Cf. W. C. Müller and H. A. Bubendorfer, 'Rule-Breaking in the Austrian Cabinet: Its Management and Its Consequences', *Corruption and Reform*, Vol. 4 (1989), pp. 131–45.
55. For a review of a wider range of aspects see K. R. Luther, 'Bund-Länder Beziehungen: Formal- und Realverfassung', in Dachs *et al.* (eds.), *Handbuch des politischen Systems Österreichs*.
56. See J. Werndl, *Die Kompetenzverteilung zwischen Bund und Ländern* (Vienna: Braumüller, 1984), pp. 45–71.
57. See K. R. Luther, 'The Revitalization of Austrian Federalism', in M. Burgess (ed.), *Federalism and Federation in Western Europe* (London: Croom Helm, 1986), pp. 154–86.
58. See K. Berchtold, *Die Verhandlungen zum Forderungsprogramm der Bundesländer seit 1956* (Vienna: Braumüller, 1988).
59. See F. Koja, 'Die Vertretung der Länderinteressen im Bund' and R. Walter, 'Der Bundesrat', both in *Bundesstaat auf der Waage* (Salzburg: Pustet, 1969), pp. 9–31 and pp. 199–290.
60. See I. Kathrein, 'Der Bundesrat', in Schambeck (ed.), *Österreichs Parlamentarismus*, pp. 337–401, here pp. 377–85 and pp. 391–96.
61. The suspensory *Bundesrat* veto proved to be relevant only in those rare situations where the majority in the *Nationalrat* and/or the party composition of government changed during the time it was in force.
62. See K. Weber, *Die mittelbare Bundesverwaltung* (Vienna: Braumüller, 1987).
63. See W. Pesendorfer, *Der Landeshauptmann* (Vienna: Springer, 1986).
64. R. Nick, 'The States and the Austrian Party System', in Pelinka and Plasser (eds.), *The Austrian Party System*, pp. 309–26.
65. See K. R. Luther, 'Bund-Länder Beziehungen: Formal- und Realverfassung'.
66. See the contribution of Plasser *et al.* in this volume.
67. A. Vodopivec, *Die Dritte Republik* (Vienna: Molden, n.d.).

A Farewell to Corporatism

PETER GERLICH

'Es regiert der Regierer
bis er nicht mehr regiert'
Thomas Bernhard

TRADITIONS OF SOCIAL PARTNERSHIP

Austria has long been considered a prime case of corporatism. Using the term in its broadest sense, corporatism implies co-operative policy styles in various arenas of the political system. In Austria, consensual politics has been practised both in party politics, especially within grand coalition government, and in industrial relations and economic policy, within the system of social partnership.[1] Grand coalition government by Austria's two big parties, the SPÖ (Socialist Party of Austria) and the ÖVP (Austrian People's Party), began after the Second World War and lasted until 1966. This form of party cooperation is sometimes also referred to as consociationalism. After the 1966 elections, first the ÖVP and later the SPÖ formed one party governments. Grand coalition government between the SPÖ and ÖVP was not re-introduced until 1987, but this new coalition functions under changed conditions and according to different rules.[2] On the surface, less appears to have changed in the co-operation of Austria's large economic interest groups. Social partnership, regarded by many as the core element of Austrian corporatism, appears to be continuing as usual. But a closer examination reveals strains and stresses which call the whole system into question. Until recently, most observers would not have considered such a development possible.[3] But the winds of change have finally also reached the Alpine republic.

It is not easy to make clear to an outsider what social partnership is and how it has functioned up to now. Social partnership, a saying in Austria goes, 'cannot be explained to a foreigner, but need not be explained to a native'. Maybe it will be useful, for a first approach, to distinguish three institutional aspects: first, to characterise briefly who the social partners (the main interest groups) actually are and how they are organised; second, to describe the patterns of co-operation between them, and third to delineate how co-operation and co-ordination are implemented between the social partners on the one side, and the institutions of government and public administration on the other. In order to do this, the historical aspects of the gradual development of institutions and patterns of co-operation will be considered. Finally, on a somewhat more analytical level, an identification of the three sets of principles which have determined the practice and success of social partnership will be made.

Social partnership consists in the co-operation of five large economic interest groups, which in general represent all or all relevant individuals in their specific economic sectors. The two most important of these are, on the employer side, the Federal Chamber of Business (BWK) and, on the employee side, the Austrian Trade Union Federation (ÖGB). The Federal Chamber of Business is a statutory interest organisation, established by public law and with obligatory membership. All firms and those who are self-employed in business, be it in trade, manufacturing, tourism, or in a long list of other activities, are automatically considered a member of the Chamber of Business, and have to pay not inconsiderable membership dues, which are seen by those concerned as a form of tax.

In return, each member may make use of the range of services offered by the institution. For example, the Chamber of Business has a network of trade delegations throughout the world to service Austrian businessmen seeking to establish foreign contacts. Apart from the Chamber of Business there are also subsidiary business chambers in the nine states, or *Länder*. The character of these chambers at both state and federal level is to some extent ambivalent: on one hand, they are powerful and effective interest representations, and on the other they are also publicly established institutions, which assume some state functions.

The Austrian Trade Union Federation (ÖGB) is an interest group, based on voluntary membership, rather than a chamber. The decision to join or leave the ÖGB is a voluntary matter. Nevertheless, this organisation is also very powerful because, in practice if not legally, it has a virtual monopoly on workers' interest representation. Since there is just one Trade Union Federation in Austria, no rival exists. The organisation is considered to be unitary in two respects: first, it represents employees from all areas of the economy, and second, it comprises workers' representatives from all political parties. In Austria, the 15 branch unions have no independent legal status and are all clearly subordinated to the ÖGB. Although membership is in principle voluntary, membership figures and therefore the degree of organisation is very high. About two-thirds of potential members actually join the ÖGB.

In addition to these two main actors in the social partnership, three other organisations take part in corporatist co-operation. Two are statutory institutions, namely, the Chambers of Labour (AK) and the Chambers of Agriculture, and one is a voluntary organisation, the Federation of Austrian

Industrialists (VÖI). Like the Chamber of Business, the AK as an institution is incorporated into the social partnership primarily on the federal and only secondarily on the state level. It comprises, again by obligatory membership, all dependently employed persons, except for most public employees. A kind of co-operation, or rather division of labour, exists between the ÖGB and the AK; while the former usually plays the more important political role, both in general and within the framework of social partnership, the latter provides expertise to the ÖGB and services to individual workers.

The Chambers of Agriculture represent the farmers of Austria. Again, membership is obligatory. However, since the regulation of agricultural interest groups is reserved by the Austrian constitution to the states, chambers of agriculture as such exist only at the state level. Nevertheless, the presidents of the state chambers of agriculture are informally organised at federal level and there jointly represent agrarian interests, especially within the social partnership. The Federation of Austrian Industrialists is a voluntary interest group, representing the vast majority of industrialists. It is a very influential organisation, although it usually refrains from direct participation in social partnership negotiations, since the industry's interests are also represented by one section of the Chamber of Business. This more detached position allows the VÖI at times to take a more explicit stand without consulting the other social partners.

The historical development of social partnership institutions can be traced back to the failed bourgeois revolution of 1848. One of the few surviving achievements of that year was the creation of Chambers of Business. The Chambers of Labour were established at the beginning of the First Republic in the early 1920s as were the Chambers of Agriculture. The trade unions, at first very splintered, were created during the 1870s and 1880s as a consequence of industrialisation. At the same time, partly as a countermeasure, the industrialists also began to organise. The history of these economic interest groups can be described as one of gradual integration and centralisation.

The idea of creating comprehensive and centralised interest group organisations was particularly stressed and implemented during the 1934–38 period of Austrian fascism, which involved authoritarian corporate rule. After the democratic republic was re-established in 1945, these principles were re-introduced, if in a somewhat modified form. Of particular importance was a comprehensive trade union federation founded right at the end of the war, uniting the differentiated trade union organisations split along party lines during the First Republic. The chambers also established strong central organisations during the first years of the Second Republic.

Since 1957 these organisations have co-operated within the Joint

Commission (*Paritätische Kommission*).[4] This institution, which some consider a kind of second cabinet, consists of two representatives from each of the three chamber organisations, as well as two from the Trade Union Federation. It has three main functions, represented by three working subcommittees: wage negotiations, price setting and, in the case of the influential Advisory Council for Economic and Social Affairs, formulation of recommendations to the government or to individual ministers. These may be on a variety of policy areas. As far as wage negotiations are concerned, the Joint Commission, or the subcommittee decide on whether it should permit negotiations to start between certain groups of employers and the respective groups of employees. The subcommittee on prices engages directly in price setting and in a substantially unbureaucratic way. The Joint Commission grew from several wage and price pacts concluded between the ÖGB and the Chamber of Business during the immediate post-war years to facilitate economic reconstruction. Such arrangements had also emerged in earlier periods, particularly during and shortly after the First World War. However, these earlier forms of formalised business/labour co-operation served a narrower purpose than the Second Republic social partnership. Although institutionalisation of consensus and co-operation developed gradually, the process was often threatened and could easily have broken down.[5]

General observers and the social partners themselves often stress the autonomy of the co-operation, namely, its independence from the government. Closer scrutiny, however, reveals a close relationship, with various forms of intensive interaction. First, the chambers originally were and still are based on public legislation. Second, a number of cabinet ministers usually take part in the meetings of the Joint Commission. Traditionally, sittings of the Joint Commission are presided over by the federal chancellor, the chairman of the cabinet. Finally and more importantly, the economic interest groups are intensively involved in public policy-making and policy-implementation. Draft legislation is as a rule sent to them during the preparatory stage in order to receive comments, usually incorporated into the final draft before the bill is sent to parliament.

In parliament the interest groups are traditionally strongly represented: more than 50 per cent of the deputies have close interest group ties.[6] The social partners also take part in legislative programmes, through their membership in hundreds of advisory committees, which civil servants have to consult before applying legislation to concrete cases.[7] The close relationship between the social partners and government also has a long tradition: it was the government which introduced chambers and from the very beginning strove to co-operate closely with them. Of course there are also policy areas in which co-operation between the social partners is more autonomous and less influenced by the government, notably in the determination of wages and prices.

The fundamental principles by which Austrian corporatism, or social partnership, functions can be differentiated into three categories: first, the organisation of the participating bodies; second, the style and patterns of interaction; and third, the basis for the stability of the whole arrangement. All of these principles, after having long been generally accepted and considered quite legitimate, are now either being called into question or even actively changed or undermined, or both. For several reasons the political system is being substantially transformed and the structures and mechanisms of social partnership are also being affected by the change.[8]

But before going into the details of these changes, let us look at the three sets of principles. The first refers to the organisations taking part in the corporatist arrangement. These can be characterised by the principles of monopoly representation, of organisational centralisation and of hierarchy.[9] All five organisations have a virtual monopoly of representation; they represent more or less everybody in their respective fields. This is achieved in the chambers by obligatory membership, and in the voluntary organisations by the fact that no alternative, competing organisation exists. In addition, all five institutions are organised in a way which gives the bulk of the power and authority to the central structures.

One result of this has been that social partnership was for a long time identified as the co-operation of the presidents of the two most important bodies, namely, the Chamber of Business and the Austrian Trade Union Federation. These two men – Rudolf Sallinger and Anton Benya – stayed in office for almost 25 years and both recently retired. They outlasted many governments, and, in the Austrian public's eyes, embodied interest group co-operation. It was not just that they seemed to exercise the power, they actually did so. To some extent, their power rested on the hierarchical nature of their organisations. Although political party factions are represented within them, the majority group always exercised such dominance that, since party discipline is very strong in Austria, these leaders, unlike party leaders who sooner or later lose a general election, are practically irremovable.

The effect of the principles of monopoly, centralisation and hierarchy is that the interest groups' main representatives have the opportunity and inclination to negotiate compromises by mutual accommodation. Afterwards they can make these agreements stick; their mutual arrangements will be respected by all the functionaries and members and there are no relevant groups outside which could effectively challenge their decisions.

The procedural principles of social partnership might be defined as informality, intimacy and introversion.[10] Informality refers to the fact that, in contrast to the political system which is generally characterised by legalism and bureaucratic formality,[11] social partnership is only based on a kind of gentlemen's agreement. The Joint Commission has no basis in the Austrian constitution, or in a parliamentary statute. It has no office or building of its own, no publicised agenda, or published minutes. Representatives of the system stress that this informality constitutes a necessary condition for its successful operation. Intimacy refers to the fact that, unlike in parliament, the public is pretty much kept in the dark as to what is happening. Only a few functionaries, who know each other rather well, attend the meetings in which the compromises are negotiated. This creates a climate of great mutual respect and understanding, providing the necessary lubrication for the consensus mechanism.

One consequence of this is what could be termed 'introversion': the social partners divert their attention from numerous alternatives and concentrate only on those positions which are mutually acceptable. Other alternatives, for example those that would be unpleasant for one of the partners, are not even raised. The same applies to the range of issues recognised. The participants tend to limit their attention only to those activities which fall into the framework of their common philosophy. New developments challenging the system from the outside are easily ignored, or in true Austrian manner — after all this is the country of Freud — repressed. The limited openness of the social partnership though active in international trade, managed to seclude itself rather effectively from outside influences. This, however, appears to be no longer the case or even possible.[12]

Finally, the legitimising principles of social partnership could be identified as acceptance, success and political linkage. Social partnership seemed for a long time to be legitimate because it was generally accepted and appeared to operate quite successfully. Its connections to government and politics through mutual linkages and dependencies tended to provide 'ultra-stability'.[13] Acceptance was based on compatibility with general patterns of political culture in Austria, which put a high premium on consensus and co-operation.[14] Moreover, the system worked smoothly for such a long time, that everybody became used to it and accepted it as a quasi-natural fact of life. Finally, the success of the system, or at least the perceived successes, naturally also contributed to the acceptance of interest group co-operation.

This success has been perceived both on a general economic level — Austria's relatively quite successful macro-economic development being attributed to the workings of the social partnership — and on the specific levels of representing the common interests of the groups and servicing the concrete needs of member individuals.[15] One basic and generally accepted assumption in this context has been the effectiveness of a kind of generalised exchange, or of the existence of a comprehensive contract between the groups. Exchanges between the social partners are not necessarily on a quid pro quo basis, but concessions here and now might be compensated by gratifications in another field, or at a later date.

The third and final stabilising principle is political linkage.[16] As has already been hinted at above, the two areas overlap in many ways. The first is through personnel; representatives of the social partners are to be found within parties, parliament and the cabinet and, vice versa, parties and cabinet ministers are influential within the interest groups, or in respect of their co-operation. The social partners also have considerable political influence. They take part in preparing legislation, legislative decision-making and – by way of a great number of special committees within the bureaucracy – also in the implementation of legislation. The third way in which political linkage stabilises the social partnership is through co-operation. Interest groups perform tasks for the state, but are also given support by state authorities in performing their autonomous tasks as when, for example, the state lends its authority to get decisions of interest group functionaries accepted by their members.[17]

WINDS OF CHANGE

As already mentioned, practically all these principles are now being questioned and discussed. A number have even been actively undermined. Several factors which seem to have contributed to this climactic change within Austrian politics can be identified. Some are connected with the changing international environment; developments within the EC and Austria's attempts to become a member have only underlined the increasing openness of the system. To this has now been added the fundamental changes in Austria's eastern neighbours. *Perestroika* elsewhere has led people here to question long-established atrophied authorities.

Independently of these external changes, the domestic political environment has likewise changed. In particular the rising level of education has made critical citizens out of formerly docile subjects. In addition, newer issues, particularly environmental problems and other aspects of the limits to growth, have become salient.[18]

A consequence of all this has been a much more competitive climate between the political parties. The two governing parties, SPÖ and ÖVP, are being challenged very effectively by the two main opposition parties: the now populist Freedom Party of Austria (FPÖ) and the relatively new United Green Party of Austria. One could even say that these developments have revitalised some formerly rather paralysed institutions of the liberal Austrian Constitution. Citizens have become more active, some sections of the media less deferential, parliament less dependent and more lively, and even the courts no longer display deference for political authorities if legal or constitutional rules appear to have been violated. Of course there are also powerful forces of continuity: the large parties, the huge public bureaucracy and the larger economic interest groups.[19] All, however, have lost much of their earlier unquestioned legitimacy and are now rather on the defensive. The social partnership, although still functioning, has been deeply affected by these developments.

To a degree quite inconceivable only a few years ago, the organising principles of large economic interest groups are now up for debate.[20] The seriousness of these discussions is shown by the fact that the chambers, for years regarded as above reproach, are now themselves offering to reform and change their organisations. Since each interest group is dominated by internal factions that assert either a socialist, or a conservative identity, it is relatively easy for the opposition parties to make political capital out of any perceived interest group excesses by seeking to hold the respective government party responsible for 'its' interest group's activities.

One main theme in these debates is the question – and now one being publicly discussed – of obligatory membership in chambers. The Freedom Party in particular has been pushing this issue and it appears that it has tapped a substantial source of dissatisfaction. This became indirectly obvious in the declining turn-out rate at chamber elections: at the last elections in 1990, only 61 per cent of Chamber of Business members and only 48 per cent from the Chamber of Labour chose to vote. Likewise, surveys show that the popularity of all interest groups, including the voluntary groups, is continuously on the decline.[21]

The chambers are now promising to improve their services and are frantically trying to improve the effectiveness of their public relations. The Styrian Chamber of Agriculture even chose the desperate option of putting obligatory membership to a membership referendum vote. The farmers, dependent on their chamber for distribution of most government subsidies, responded by showing a high degree of support (83 per cent) for obligatory membership. But the other chambers are far less confident of their members' support for its continuation and do not dare to follow this example.[22]

If the Freedom Party should become part of a government in the future – a prospect not completely out of the question – it will certainly be obliged to press the point. After all, obligatory membership can be abolished by a simple majority vote in parliament, even though the chambers of course insist that this should not happen.[23] The principle of hierarchy, or conversely the lack of democracy within the economic interest groups, is taken even more seriously both in intellectual circles and in general public opinion.

New chamber electoral procedures, giving members more choice and influence, are being demanded and also offered as part of reform schemes. The lack of interest among compulsory members and the actual 'exit' of, for example, trade union members, lend a special urgency to these proposals.[24]

Similarly, even long-established functioning principles of the social partnership, and in particular the very style of its co-operative interactions, have become controversial. Informality is no longer considered to be an unmitigated blessing. A debate which has its origins in the very early years of the social partners' co-operation has now been revived by several prominent jurists. These lawyers point out that it is one of the basic foundations of constitutional government that all exercise of power should be controlled by law and that persons obliged by decisions of authorities should have the greater opportunity to apply for judicial review. The very informality of social partnership, the lack of formal decisions, makes such appeals impossible.

The Joint Commission in effect constitutes a kind of second cabinet, making decisions which might be even more relevant for many Austrians than acts of government or parliament, but which could nevertheless not be legally controlled. It was proof of the success of the corporatist arrangements that these criticisms had for some time disappeared; possibly the social partners had also found ways to placate the legal experts. But now the debate is on again. In this connection it is likewise remarkable that the Constitutional Court has discontinued its long-term practice of more or less accepting even questionable legislation as constitutional, as long as the social partners had agreed on the benefits for general welfare. In a number of recent cases, the court has declared such legislation unconstitutional.[25]

Intimacy as a principle of social partnership interaction is increasingly felt to contradict the basic democratic requirement that public matters should indeed be public. In a number of recent parliamentary inquiries this became especially clear when the public, or rather the media, were admitted and clever questioning by members of parliament threw the full glare of publicity on rather doubtful conduct, usually practised under the shield of intimacy. One of these cases concerned economic interest groups taking part in government regulation and caused considerable controversy, not least between interest group functionaries and members of parliament of the same political persuasion. For some insiders, this incident marked a kind of *Götterdämmerung* for the social partners.[26]

The problem of introversion is also increasingly under discussion. Social partnership limits the possibility of the political system to be open, to learn and to adapt to an ever changing international and national environment. This is increasingly seen as a potential danger, even by some representatives of the social partners themselves. Nevertheless, the social partnership has always contained both aspects: mere narrow interest representation by political functionaries who tended to have a very conservative outlook, and also discussions orientated by consideration of general welfare by an open-minded group of experts. This is particularly the case within the Advisory Council for Economic and Social Questions, one of the Joint Commission subcommittees. These experts continually point out new developments and suggest new avenues, particularly in the area of economic policy.

Had this group not existed, the social partnership would not have been able to function so well for such a long time. Nevertheless, the problem of excluding unpleasant issues or alternatives from political discussion still exists. It is particularly evident in the area of electronic and print media in Austria, which have reached a very high degree of concentration, are to some extent under the influence of the social partners and often appear to refrain from publicising non-established viewpoints.[27]

The specific conditions on which the durability of Austrian corporatism rests, its stabilising principles, also seem to be eroding. As has already become quite clear, the acceptance of big interest group co-operation is declining. While it is true that survey research shows continued approval of consensual arrangements, the legitimacy of the big interest groups has declined in the eyes of general public opinion. Public debate among experts, journalists and intellectuals has become much more critical. In addition to traditional legal, democratic, left-wing or environmentalist criticism, a new dimension has emerged: the liberal belief in the greater efficiency of competition in the market place.

From these perspectives, the success of corporatism is no longer taken for granted. While Austria's overall economic performance has been quite good in comparison with the rest of Western Europe, the question is now being raised as to whether less co-ordination and more competition could not have led to even better performance – speculation which can of course neither be proved or disproved! That social partnership has successfully been practised for such a long time is decreasingly seen as an argument in favour of its legitimacy. In fact, the criticism is often raised that the corporatist arrangements have become mere routine and lack innovative spirit.[28] Political culture is also changing. Co-operation, authority and clientelism are still generally accepted, but in certain groups, especially among young people, the better educated or the economically more active, these practices are increasingly being questioned, affecting the acceptance of corporatist patterns of co-operation.

The success of social partnership can be evaluated on different levels. While the overall performance of the Austrian economy continues to be satisfactory, and thus does not add to the decline in esteem for corporatism, the question as to what extent different groups or individuals profit from these developments is increasingly considered open. Relatively large groups of business people and workers feel themselves no longer effectively represented. The reorganisation of the nationalised industries and the increasing unemployment figures threaten labour; European integration causes concern for smaller businesses and agriculture. The fact that in the past the state often footed the bill of mutual arrangements between the social partners at the cost of high budget deficits has also led to criticism.[29] Finally, many members, especially of the chambers, do not feel that sufficient attention is given to providing services. Many members feel that in some ways the chambers have tended to decay into self-service organisations for the benefit of functionaries and the internal chamber bureaucracies. The justification of much of this criticism may indirectly be deduced from the alacrity with which chamber representatives declare their willingness to reform, to change and to improve.

Finally, the close linkage between parties, government and the social partners is becoming less and less intense. This has been particularly obvious with respect to personnel linkage, traditionally considered to be the key to the ultra-stability of Austrian corporatism. Parties have responded to pressures to decouple. Increasingly, for example, it is no longer considered legitimate to nominate interest group functionaries for seats in the legislature. Some *Land* parties, such as the ÖVP in Styria and in Salzburg, have explicitly pledged themselves to discontinue this practice. Given the increasingly negative public attitude towards economic interest groups, when drawing up legislation the governing parties have more and more disregarded such groups both procedurally and substantively. In this way, they hoped to appear more effective in the eyes of the electorally critical segments of an increasingly volatile electorate and thus to be able to safeguard their position in a political system characterised by heightened party competition and vulnerability.[30] The interest groups are often no longer consulted in the policy-initiation and policy-formulation process, or their positions are no longer acted upon.

The controversies over the construction of two large power plants of Zwentendorf and Hainburg, one nuclear and one hydro-electric, in which the government ultimately had to accept the position of the anti-corporatist opposition, were the beginnings of a development in which similar positions have been taken on less prominent controversies. It is, however, true that on certain occasions the government has also asked the social partners to try to act as a 'fire-brigade' and work out a solution for a particularly pressing problem. The influence of the corporatist interest groups is not only being pushed back in the preparation of legislation and legislative decision-making, but also in the area of implementation. Again the involvement of the social partners in countless advisory commissions, where they were supposed to assist civil servants in the execution of laws, is considered less and less justified by many commentators. Even the social partners themselves are beginning to view such activity as taking them beyond the realms of what can reasonably be considered central to their prime role. Likewise, government-interest group co-operation of the type that involves the latter in assuming what are essentially government functions, or involve them in distributing government resources, is increasingly being questioned. More and more the chambers are insisting on their autonomy. This was especially obvious in the controversy as to whether the Auditing Office should be given the task of investigating the finances of the chambers, an idea that the chambers energetically reject.

FUTURE PERSPECTIVES

When social scientists have in the past tried to speculate on the future of corporatism in Austria, they have usually sketched different possible future scenarios of development.[31] It was usually taken for granted that social partnership as such would continue; it was only the means by which the social partners would co-operate that seemed a topic of speculation: would corporatism continue as usual, would it open up to become more democratic, or would it turn more authoritarian? Theoretically, it sometimes seemed conceivable that interest group co-operation would end as a consequence of economic difficulties, but experience tended to disprove such considerations.

At present, a somewhat different spectrum of possible future developments seems appropriate. On the basis of the eroding principles described above, there are three possibilities. Social partnership could continue, albeit in a changed, reformed and reduced way; it could more or less fade away; or, it could simply be abolished, a possibility that is no longer impossible to conceive. A continuation seems rather probable. But equally probable, not least because both the social partners and the political parties themselves declare quite officially that this will be the case, is a reform in which the corporatist spheres of influence will be reduced. Social partners will in future no longer concern themselves with almost all fields of politics, legislation and policy implementation, concentrating instead on industrial relations, economic policy and European integration. The joint representation of Austrian economic interests in Brussels will certainly constitute an important future task along these lines.[32] In any case, the close linkage between interest groups, political parties and the government will certainly be reduced in intensity. At the same time, there are likely to be numerous institutional reforms in the chambers, with the goals of increasing the intra-chamber influence of members and of enhancing the services which they are offered. One option increasingly coming to the fore, especially in academic circles, is that of formally institutionalising the corporatist consultation process on the model of The Netherlands.[33] A second perspective is that of a slow fading-out of corporatism. If Austria participates in the single European market, this will happen in any case. However, regardless of whether or when Austria formally joins the EC, market forces will of necessity reduce corporatist arrangements. This is already obvious with respect to price regulation. Price-setting by the Joint Commission has lost most of its former importance, since an increasing number of prices are determined by imports and simply cannot be set independently by referring only to Austrian standards. It can be assumed that the same will happen with wages if the freedom of labour within the single European market becomes a reality. The social partners will, according to this second scenario, still go through the motions of consultation and co-operation, but the area of leeway open to them will become increasingly restricted.

Dissolution of the social partnership could become a reality if, under the influence of former opposition parties in a new government, compulsory chamber membership is indeed abolished, or if the monopoly principle is otherwise threatened. Traditionally, such far-reaching reforms would seem unlikely in a country known for its tendency to conduct politics by slow adaptation and muddling through. But with major transformation elsewhere and under the pressure of changing circumstances, such fundamental changes no longer seem impossible. The dynamics of re-organisation and privatisation within the nationalised industry sector prove that even politically costly change is no longer impossible.

CONCLUSION

Even if these scenarios tend to make the decline of corporatism appear self-evident, it is important, in retrospect, not to underestimate its earlier merits. From its establishment in the aftermath of the First World War, the small Republic of Austria was confronted by many problems which only exacerbated political tensions within a socially deeply divided society. The experiences of civil war, of the authoritarian state, of Nazism, of the Second World War and of foreign power occupation, forced political parties and interest groups together. Slowly they built up mutual confidence and a foundation was created on which later a competitive market economy would be able to function. This stage has now been reached and, consequently, corporatist arrangements seem no longer necessary.

This development proves the point of consociational theory, which maintains that co-operative patterns of politics may constitute something like a missing link between dictatorship and democracy, a stepping-stone on the way from a traditional to a modern form of politics and social life.[34] But this perspective also implies that the main guiding principles for the conduct both of political and of economic activity now have to change. In politics, the new pattern implies conflictual interest articulation, open decision-making and clear responsibilities for the implementation of decisions. These principles replace the earlier consensual, confidential and (because of joint responsibility) ultimately irresponsible style. Within the economy, there would likewise have to be change, with competitiveness and efficiency as the new standards, deregulation and privatisation as the means to better achieve them.[35] The concomitant change in priorities can indeed already be observed within Austrian politics and society.

As a consequence of these changes, Austria will become a country similar to many others within the new Europe. It looks today as if the small Alpine republic will no longer travel a road of 'exceptionality', but is about to take its position alongside the other European nations, giving up its specific practices and becoming similar in its political system to the other liberal democracies.

NOTES

1. For general introductions to Austrian corporatism see P. Gerlich, E. Grande and W. C. Müller (eds.), *Sozialpartnerschaft in der Krise. Leistungen und Grenzen des Neokorporatismus in Österreich* (Vienna: Böhlau, 1985); P. Gerlich, E. Grande and W. C. Müller, 'Corporatism in Crisis: Stability and Change of Social Partnership in Austria', *Political Studies*, Vol. 36, No. 2 (1988), pp. 209–23 and A. Pelinka, *Modellfall Österreich? Möglichkeiten und Grenzen der Sozialpartnerschaft* (Vienna: Braumüller, 1981).
2. See W. C. Müller, 'Die neue grosse Koalition in Österreich', *Österreichische Zeitschrift für Politikwissenschaft*, Vol. 17, No. 4 (1988), pp. 321–47.
3. See, e.g. some of our own evaluations in Gerlich, Grande and Müller (eds.), *Sozialpartnerschaft*, pp. 364–66.
4. See J. Farnleitner, *Die Paritätische Kommission: Institution und Verfahren* (Eisenstadt: Prugg, 1974).
5. See E. Tálos, 'Sozialpartnerschaft: Zur Entwicklung und Entwicklungsdynamik kooperativ – konzentrierter Politik in Österreich', in Gerlich, Grande and Müller (eds.), *Sozialpartnerschaft*, pp. 41–83.
6. See P. Gerlich, 'Sozialpartnerschaft und Regierungssystem', in Gerlich, Grande and Müller (eds.), *Sozialpartnerschaft*, p. 121.
7. See I. Bulda, M. Hengl and W.C. Müller, 'Das österreichische Beiratssystem in den siebziger und achtziger Jahren', *Österreichisches Jahrbuch für Politik* 1989, pp. 763–87.
8. See more generally E. Damgaard, P. Gerlich and J. Richardson (eds.), *The Politics of Economic Crisis. Lessons from Western Europe* (Aldershot: Avebury, 1989).
9. See E. Grande, 'Konfliktsteuerung zwischen Recht und Konsens. Zur Herrschaftslogik korporatistischer Systeme', in Gerlich, Grande and Müller (eds.), *Sozialpartnerschaft*, pp. 225–54.
10. See Grande, 'Konfliktsteuerung zwischen Recht und Konsens', pp. 227–33.

11. See P. Gerlich, 'Politik in Österreich', in H. G. Wehling (ed.), *Österreich* (Stuttgart: Kohlhammer, 1988), pp. 40–53.
12. See the contribution of D. M. Schulz to this volume.
13. See G. Lehmbruch, 'Sozialpartnerschaft in der vergleichenden Politikforschung', in Gerlich, Grande and Müller (eds.), *Sozialpartnerschaft*, pp. 85–108.
14. See Gerlich, 'Politik in Österreich', pp. 45–47.
15. See G. Winckler, 'Sozialpartnerschaft und ökonomische Effizienz', in Gerlich, Grande and Müller (eds.), *Sozialpartnerschaft*, pp 109–34.
16. Gerlich, 'Sozialpartnerschaft und Regierungssystem', pp. 109–34.
17. See Grande, 'Konfliktsteuerung zwischen Recht und Konsens', pp. 233–43.
18. See P. A. Ulram, *Hegemonie und Erosion. Politische Kultur und politischer Wandel in Österreich* (Vienna: Böhlau, 1990), pp. 247ff.
19. See P. Gerlich, 'Österreichische Politik im Übergang', *SWS-Rundschau*, Vol. 30, No. 1 (1990), pp. 3–13.
20. See, e.g. the discussion about the reform of the Chamber of Business in *Wirtschaftspolitische Blätter*, Vol. 38, No. 1 (1991), or more generally a series of background articles published by the highly regarded daily newspaper, *Salzburger Nachrichten*, in April and May 1991 under, for Austrian circumstances, the almost revolutionary title 'Ende des Kammernstaates' (End of the Chamber State).
21. See P. Ulram, 'Die Handelskammerorganisation aus der Sicht ihrer Mitglieder – Die Ergebnisse der Meinungsumfragen', *Wirtschaftspolitische Blätter*, Vol. 38, No. 1 (1991), pp. 29–40.
22. See Ulram, 'Handelskammerorganisation'.
23. A similar referendum was held by the Österreichische Hochschülerschaft (Austrian Students' Organisation), an institution established by law for university students, also involving compulsory membership. This kind of membership was approved by the student electorate with a majority of more than 80 per cent in May 1991.
24. See, e.g. K. Kehrer, 'Interessenvertretung durch die Kammerorganisation in den achtziger Jahren und die Pflichtmitgliedschaft', *Wirtschaftspolitische Blätter*, Vol. 38, No. 1 (1991), pp. 5–18.
25. See J. Farnleitner, 'Die Zukunft der Sozialpartnerschaft', *Wirtschaftspolitische Blätter*, Vol. 38, No. 1 (1991), pp. 96–105.
26. For experiences with parliamentary inquiries see F. Ermacora, 'Der Lucona-Ausschuss im Lichte staatswissenschaftlicher Erfahrungen', *Österreichisches Jahrbuch für Politik* (1989), pp. 225–41.
27. See H.-H. Fabris, 'Zwischen Politik und Politikinszenierung: Mediendiskurse der achtziger Jahre', *Österreichische Zeitschrift für Politikwissenschaft*, Vol. 18, No. 2 (1989), pp. 119–28.
28. See A. Guger, *Corporatism: Success or Failure? Austrian Experiences* (Vienna: WIFO Working Papers, No. 36, 1990).
29. See Winckler, 'Sozialpartnerschaft und ökonomische Effizienz', p. 311.
30. See now especially E. Tálos, K. Leichsenring and E. Zeiner, *Veränderungstendenzen des gesellschaftlichen Politikmusters?* (Vienna: Research report, 1991). On the electoral and party political changes that have increased party vulnerability see, e.g. the contributions to this volume by F. Plasser *et al.* and K. R. Luther.
31. See for example, E. Matzner, 'Sozialpartnerschaft', in H. Fischer (ed.), *Das politische System Österreichs* (Vienna: Europaverlag, 1974), pp. 446–48, and Gerlich, Grande and Müller (eds.), *Sozialpartnerschaft*, pp. 364–66.
32. See Farnleitner, 'Die Zukunft der Sozialpartnerschaft', p. 104. See also the contribution of D. M. Schulz to this volume.
33. See J. W. Pichler and T. Quené (eds.), *Sozialpartnerschaft und Rechtspolitik* (Vienna: Böhlau, 1990).
33. See A. Lijphart, *Democracy im Plural Societies* (New Haven, CT: Yale UP, 1977), p. 238.
34. See P. Gerlich, 'Deregulation in Austria', *European Journal of Political Research*, Vol. 17 (1989), pp. 209–22.
35. See P. Gerlich and W. C. Müller, 'Austria: a crisis resolved or a crisis postponed?', in Damgaard, Gerlich and Richardson (eds.), *The Politics of Economic Crisis* pp. 146–62.

Changing Priorities in Austrian Economic Policy

VOLKMAR LAUBER

During the 1950s Austria developed a set of principles of economic policy which it continued to apply for about two decades, until the economic crisis which followed the first oil crisis. Under the impact of these crises actual policy was considerably adjusted. However, this change was usually explained by new and different circumstances and not by a change of principle. Even in the late 1970s this policy, together with the practice of social partnership, was highly successful in providing Austria with record rates of economic growth (the highest in OECD Europe), low rates of inflation and an exceptionally low rate of unemployment. It is at this time that 'Austrokeynesianism' attracted particular attention, partly because it stood out against the neo-conservative (monetarist and supply-side) developments that began to spread in an increasing number of countries, partly because of Austria's quite impressive economic results.

But in the early 1980s, doubts as to the viability of 'Austrokeynesianism' began to emerge. For a few years there were signs of crisis and retreat, until an important reorientation of economic policy in 1985–86 which drew substantial inspiration from neo-conservative economic thinking. In some respects, however, this was simply a return to what was normal before 1974. According to most economists, 'Austrokeynesianism' is now dead, though it could be argued that some of its principles re-emerged only recently, or even that in order to correspond to basic principles policy simply had again to be adjusted to circumstances. In any case, there was substantial change regarding the conditions, instruments and even actors of economic policy since 1985–86.

THE ESTABLISHMENT OF 'AUSTROKEYNESIANISM'

Most of this policy's principles emerged during the 1950s as a highly pragmatic response to the problems and opportunities of that time. The larger background was the economic disaster and class strife of the interwar period, plus the renewed catastrophe of the Second World War. After the *Anschluss*, Nazi Germany built up a substantial industrial base in Austria, the lack of which had been painfully evident between 1918 and

1938. Many of these industries were nationalised after the war, in part for ideological reasons but primarily for lack of private capital capable and willing to invest the required amounts, and finally to protect these industries against Soviet reparations claims. As a result, Austria found itself with one of the largest nationalised industrial sectors of any Western country, with attendant potential for political intervention in the management of those firms.

The large public sector had another important consequence: it greatly strengthened the position of organised labour. Labour is particularly well organised in the nationalised industries, and its representatives enjoy (or at least enjoyed) direct access to the government.[1] This state of affairs lasted roughly until the mid-1980s. If a strong public sector used to be considered as one of the preconditions of 'Austrokeynesianism', such a characterisation applies even more forcefully to the co-operation between the country's largest interest groups in settling differences by elite accommodation. This requires much depoliticisation of the rank and file, an effective centralised organisation and high membership ratios. The membership problem was resolved in a unique way: all workers and employees, all businessmen and all farmers are by law members of the Chamber of Labour, the Chamber of Business and the Chamber of Agriculture respectively. (The fourth large corporatist interest group is the Trade Union Federation, which enrols about 60 per cent of its potential membership; only Sweden seems to have higher membership levels.) The first steps towards interest group co-operation were taken in several wage and price agreements negotiated between 1947 and 1951 by the peak associations of business and labour. In one case, those associations managed to impose their will against a very large mobilisation of labour from below, the only case of such a mobilisation in post-war Austria.[2] It is true that this cooperative interest group behaviour lapsed again during the early 1950s, but it was revived in 1956 as will be shown below.

After a period of substantial state control over the economy which could not, however, contain inflationary pressures, currency and budget stabilisation were undertaken in 1952. Inflation was stopped quite suddenly, leading to the highest unemployment figure of the post-war period, at one point almost nine per cent. But the stabilisation was successful, and the hard currency policy has remained a central tenet of Austrian economic policy ever since, with only two brief deviations in later decades and even these were rapidly corrected by political decisions. After the stabilisation success, the promotion of supply-side measures (as they later came to be called) was given priority.

The stimulation of economic growth by acting on the supply side took two main forms. These were first, a reduction of business and income taxes by about one third (which reduced the share of taxes in the GDP by more than 10 per cent between 1953 and 1955), and second, tax promotion of savings and investments (most importantly an accelerated write-off of 50 per cent for investments). It was argued that the growth and employment effects of reduced taxes would together increase the sum total of tax revenues, and this expectation was confirmed by subsequent developments.[3] Austria quickly became one of the economically most successful OECD countries. Exports increased rapidly, investment ratios rose too and remained at very high level. If the commitment to a strong currency was the first cornerstone of 'Austrokeynesianism', the promotion of investment and savings was the second.

Its third cornerstone was the depoliticisation of incomes (and to some extent of business cycle), which followed a few years after stabilisation. As unemployment receded and the economy began to boom, inflationary pressures grew stronger again. The need for an incomes policy became more and more urgent, but as in most countries, the logic of competition between the major political parties did not facilitate matters. In Austria this competition intensified after independence was achieved in 1955, while the basic reason for co-operation between the two large parties was thereby removed.

In this situation, the government decided to revitalise the institutions of interest group co-operation. It decided that the four large interest groups (Trade Union Federation, the Chamber of Labour, the Chamber of Business and the Chamber of Agriculture) would combine with government officials to form the *Paritätische Kommission*, which would decide upon wage and (to a lesser extent) price increases. The commitment by the Trade Union Federation to act as a strongly moderating influence on wage increases was decisive in creating this institution in 1957, and again later in making it permanent. For decades afterwards, incomes policy did not give rise to significant political conflict in Austria; the basic principle was one of symmetric increases for the different income groups. As a result, an important source of inflationary tensions was effectively brought under control. This proved to be a very valuable asset in the days – and years – of stagflation.

In the early 1960s the functions of the *Paritätische Kommission* were expanded. It was henceforth to discuss all important questions pertaining to the national economy and to make recommendations to the government. This meant that the management of the economy – in particular with regard to the business cycle – was *de facto* transferred from the government to the *Paritätische Kommission* and the newly created *Beirat für Wirtschafts- und Sozialfragen* (Advisory Council for Economic and Social Affairs) set up in 1963. In the first decade or two, the chief experts on economic policy were concentrated in the *Paritätische Kommission* and the *Beirat* and these organisations clearly outmanned the government and its bureaucracy. The culture of expertise prevailing in these organisations proved to be another factor that insulated these institutions of economic policy-making from the daily political battle, and further promoted stability.

Stability was also enhanced because the institutions of social partnership not only survived the end of the grand coalition government in 1966; in fact their role in resolving economic conflict became even more important.[4] In order not to disturb the politically symmetric power relationships within the *Paritätische Kommission*, the government officials represented in it (who now came from the People's Party only) renounced their right to vote, though this was in effect a largely symbolic act, since the institution functioned on the principle of unanimity both before and after this change. This renunciation was, however, meant to demonstrate that the government had relinquished the very possibility of modifying the practice of unanimous decision-making.

The fourth cornerstone of 'Austrokeynesianism' is the one that is most commonly understood as properly Keynesian in character and comprises the stabilisation of demand by deficit spending. The international recession of 1957–58 affected Austria as it did other countries, but under the Austrian People's Party (ÖVP) Finance Minister Reinhard Kamitz, who had been in office since 1952, the country adopted a response that was quite innovative in non-Scandinavian mainland Europe. In order to stabilise the business cycle he accepted a rapid increase of the budget deficit, which in 1958 reached the substantial level of about four per cent of GDP. An important role in this was played by the automatic stabilisers, namely by the automatic shortfall in revenue produced in particular by the declining receipts of taxes on business profits. The use of the deficit was purposefully anti-cyclical and the return to a nearly balanced budget was achieved within three years. Anti-cyclical budget deficits came to be an accepted element of 'Austrokeynesianism'. The policy was based on the assumption that deficits in recession years should be reduced quickly and be offset by surpluses in boom years, in such a way as to maintain the public debt at a constant level in absolute figures and even to reduce it in terms of a percentage of the GDP.[5] Surpluses were not achieved, but in good years the budget was nearly in perfect balance (see Figure 1).

Thus Austrian economic policy from the mid-1950s to the mid-1970s combined measures to stimulate economic growth with an arrangement to contain inflationary pressures. The incentives to investment (and the more modest incentives to savings) served to contain increases in consumption. The hard currency policy, by limiting the profits made by export-orientated

FIGURE 1
ECONOMIC GROWTH RATES AND BUDGET DEFICITS 1957–1985
(in per cent)

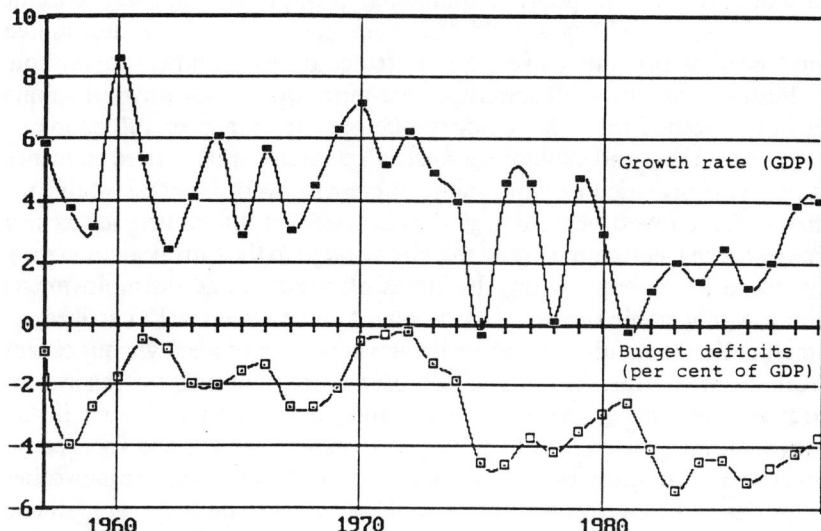

Source: Manfred Hellrigl, 'Paradigmen und Wirtschaftspolitik' (Salzburg (1991), p. 102, as updated by Hellrigl. Calculations based on data from the Austrian Statistical Office (real prices for GDP growth, current prices for budget deficits).

firms, also served to keep wage demands in this sector to what was economically acceptable. Even the budget deficit was repeatedly used for anti-inflationary purposes. Faced by the 1967–68 recession (the most serious since 1958) and at the same time by the threat of stagflation, the government anticipated the lowering of income tax rates scheduled for a later date and stepped up social welfare spending (thereby increasing the budget deficit) in exchange for a commitment by organised labour to moderate wage demands. This 'big bargain' procedure was applied repeatedly thereafter.[6]

With the exception of deficit spending, what was Keynesian about early 'Austrokeynesianism'? Those Austrian economists who consider that this was an appropriate designation, argue that Keynes' main concern was with the destabilising effects inherent to a market economy. Financial markets tend to be erratic; decisions to spend, save or invest are based on expectations strongly influenced by collective moods. The results are alternating cycles which destabilise the economy and subject it to shocks at irregular intervals. Many of these shocks initiate sudden downward spirals that tend to be self-reinforcing. Thus expectations and investments are rapidly adjusted downward, in turn multiplying the negative effects throughout the economy. Under these circumstances productive capacities cannot develop to the point of optimality, or be put to their most efficient use.[7] Economic policy should therefore counteract those destructive tendencies by providing a stable and predictable environment favourable to business, as this will encourage long-term growth. Downward spirals must be avoided, or at least stopped before they run their full course.

Based on this understanding, Austrian economic policy tried to secure stability. It provided low and stable interest rates for business; stable indirect aids to investment through the tax system; a stable currency closely linked to the Deutschmark (and thereby *de facto* to the European monetary system in more recent years); low rates of inflation and unemployment; and a highly stable incomes policy, plus a record low level of strikes. In emergencies demand-side management was used to prevent vicious circles from going too far. Automatic stabilisers were built into the tax system to make sure that it reacted strongly and promptly to variations in the business cycle. Discretionary budget deficits were added and focused on investment programmes, not as much on social transfers as in many other countries.[8] The large public sector could be relied upon to be sympathetic to government policy. In short, Austria tried to become an investor's paradise while at the same time making sure that labour would benefit symmetrically from the resulting economic growth.

APOTHEOSIS AND DECLINE (1974–85)

From 1970, there were some modifications in the network of actors that formulated economic policy. Over the preceding 15 years the large corporatist interest groups had built up their role in economic policy-making. When the socialists came to power in 1970, they made an effort to reduce their dependence both on the expertise furnished by 'their own' corporatist interest groups and also by the upper-level finance ministry civil servants who often sympathised with the People's Party. Within the People's Party there was a similar development, although it took place with a delay of nearly a decade and only after the party had first become 'colonised' by its business wing and associated business organisations. Because of its internal disagreements the advisory council of the *Paritätische Kommission* also declined in importance in the early 1970s. However, in the field of wages and prices corporatist influence was undiminished.[9]

During the first years of socialist rule Austria benefited from the international boom and also from its reorientation to the European Economic Community (EEC). At the level of the industrial structure this was achieved around 1970; in 1972 an agreement was concluded with the EEC to lower customs barriers substantially by 1977. In retrospect, Austria's membership of EFTA (European Free Trade Association) proved to be a handicap for trade with its most important partners, the Federal Republic of Germany (whose share of Austrian exports and imports stands today at roughly 40 per cent) and Italy, and resulted in weak industrial growth and balance of payments deficits by the mid-1960s. The 1972 agreement gave important new impulses; thanks to the successful operation of the corporatist (social partnership) system, an inflationary spiral could be contained despite the boom in 1973.

A Policy to Outlast the Recession?

The big challenge came, of course, with the oil crisis and the resulting recession. To make up for the shortfall of demand, the 1975 budget deficit was set at four and one half per cent of the GDP. In 1976 it reached almost five per cent. At that time it was still expected that the crisis would be brief and that an international business upturn would soon materialise. The deficit served its purpose; while German investments dropped sharply in 1976, the evolution in Austria was quite smooth.[10] When it became clear that the international recession was to last for some time, the budget deficit was reduced regularly, but only moderately; in the five years to 1981 it was scaled down to slightly below three per cent (see Figure 1). It was the first time during the Second Republic that deficit spending at such levels was continued for such a long time.

The central goal of public policy at that time was to outlast the recession (*Durchtauchen*) by maintaining full (or at least maximum feasible) employment; this was financed by a substantial increase in the public debt (see Table 1). Remarkably however, most of the deficit spending went into investment, much of it for infrastructure. Because of the wage moderation practised by the labour unions, the policy of full employment was quite successful.

Public sector industry contributed to this by maintaining a high level of employment until 1980, whereas private industry reduced its manpower from 1973 onwards (see Figure 3). The overall employment situation did not deteriorate until 1980, partly due to tertiary sector expansion. In that year, the unemployment figure of two per cent contrasted very impressively with an average of about seven per cent for the European member-countries of the OECD (see Figure 3). This was probably 'Austrokeynesianism's' moment of greatest prestige.

Even the conservative opposition, which had begun to object to the succession of budget deficits and the resulting increase in indebtedness, was muted in its criticism. The success of governmental policy was too

TABLE 1

PUBLIC DEBT: AN INTERNATIONAL COMPARISON
(per cent of GDP/GNP)

	1974	1975	1979	1980	1981	1982	1983	1984	1985[1]
Central government									
Germany[2]	7.3	10.5	14.9	15.9	18.0	19.6	20.8	21.4	21.8
France	15.7	16.1	15.1	15.0	15.9	17.2	19.6	21.4	23.2
United Kingdom	49.2	44.1	43.7	40.9	44.3	44.1	44.4	47.3	47.8
Japan	11.7	15.4	30.2	34.5	38.6	40.5	45.2	49.7	49.7
Netherlands	25.5	25.6	27.2	29.5	33.6	39.3	46.4	51.9	–
Sweden	27.2	27.4	37.9	43.7	51.6	60.1	65.3	68.2	–
United States[2]	35.2	36.8	35.4	35.5	34.8	37.7	43.0	44.1	47.6
Austria[2]	10.0	15.3	25.1	26.3	28.0	30.0	34.5	36.4	38.5
General government									
Germany	19.6	25.0	30.7	32.5	36.3	39.4	41.0	41.9	42.0
France	24.7	25.8	26.2	25.0	25.9	28.3	29.8	31.8	33.6
United Kingdom	69.5	65.2	55.6	54.9	54.9	53.5	53.9	54.8	54.2
Japan	18.0	22.5	47.6	52.9	58.1	62.7	68.7	69.4	69.3
Netherlands	41.3	41.3	42.7	45.9	50.3	55.6	62.3	66.3	66.8
Sweden	30.5	29.6	39.6	44.8	52.9	62.6	65.9	67.1	68.6
United States	40.1	43.3	37.8	38.0	37.1	41.0	43.7	44.4	46.5
Austria	17.6	23.9	36.0	37.2	39.2	41.3	45.7	45.1	44.7

Notes: 1. Preliminary estimates
2. Federal government.

Sources: Finanzschuldenbericht 1985 der Österreichischen Postsparkasse: OECD estimates. *OECD Economic Surveys 1985/1986. Austria* (July 1986), p. 26.

CHANGING PRIORITIES IN ECONOMIC POLICY 155

FIGURE 2
UNEMPLOYMENT IN AUSTRIA AND IN EUROPE (per cent)

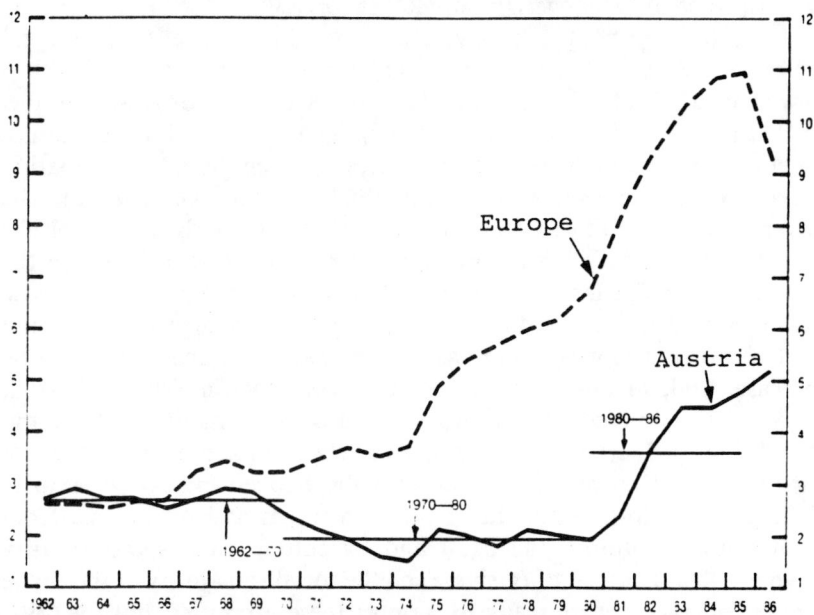

Source: OECD *Wirtschaftsberichte 1987/88, Österreich* (December 1987), p. 15.

FIGURE 3
EVOLUTION OF EMPLOYMENT IN NATIONALISED AND PRIVATE INDUSTRIES
(Index 1970 = 100)

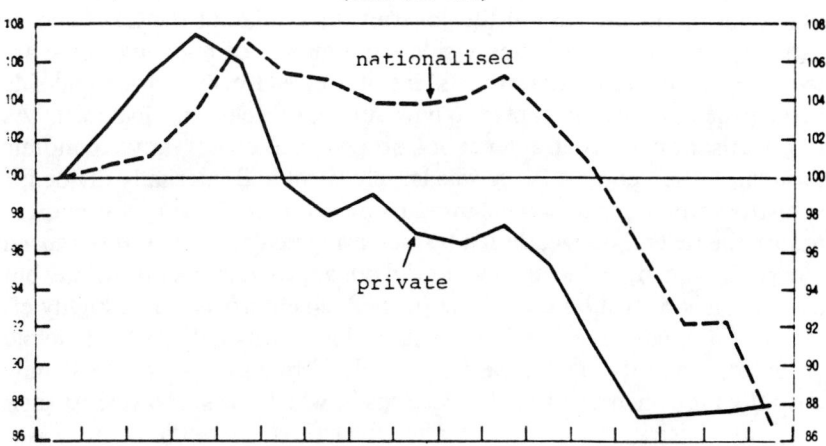

Source: OECD *Wirtschaftsberichte 1987/88. Österreich* (Dec. 1987), p. 55.

impressive; Austria's economy and society simply did not present the symptoms of disturbance that could give credibility to the neo-conservative prescriptions of 'Thatcherism' or 'Reaganomics'.

After the apotheosis, however, came decline and fall. The second oil crisis deepened the recession everywhere. Industry reacted with a new wave of dismissals; this time the public sector response was parallel to that of private industry (see Figure 2). The resulting shock could not be absorbed; unemployment went up steeply, even though the situation still compared quite favourably with OECD Europe (see Figure 2). The government reacted by stepping up subsidies (particularly to large public sector firms) and by promoting early retirement, thus transferring the problem from the labour market to the social security system, whose deficit promptly increased.[11] The hopes that the budget deficit would in due course disappear were dashed. Instead, 1982 brought on a new increase, and, at about five and a half per cent, in 1983 the deficit exceeded even the record level of 1976. Indebtedness made another jump (see Table 1). During the campaign for the 1983 elections, chancellor Bruno Kreisky proposed to deal with the budget and social security deficits by instituting new taxes both on wages and on income from capital (the 'Mallorca package') and by cutting back social security payouts. The Chamber of Business and the socialist majority of the Trade Union Federation were ready to support these proposals, but the ÖVP (in opposition since 1970) decided to make this a populist issue in the electoral campaign.

The ÖVP was increasingly frustrated by its opposition status. It also lacked a clear profile that contrasted with that of the socialists. Like them, it also argued for a full employment policy. In 1981 it came out in favour of stabilising the increase of the government's 'take' of the GDP and – in a very mild variant of supply-side economics – of reducing this share over the medium term. Even in 1983 it still stressed Keynesian demand-side management, though it wanted to have supply-side elements included.[12] As to privatisation – a central tenet of European neo-conservative economic thought – the People's Party was largely silent and internally divided;[13] similarly with regard to deregulation. Its objections to Kreisky's attempt to reduce the federal budget deficit by increasing taxes and that of the social security system by reducing payouts did not appeal to higher principle, but used slogans of 'robbing the little people' which proved to be highly effective.[14] The government withdrew its social security deficit plan to avoid criticism, while its tax increase proposals were also cut back and only partially implemented after the elections in which the socialists lost their majority. Kreisky retired and for the next three years the country was governed by a coalition between the Socialists and the small FPÖ

(*Freiheitliche Partei Österreichs* – Freedom Party of Austria), which under Steger had a markedly liberal orientation.

Downward Adjustment of Expectations and Ambitions: the Small Coalition Government of 1983–86

The new coalition government realised the need for budget stabilisation but shied away from paying its political cost, particularly in the face of the ÖVP's criticism. The budget deficit was slightly reduced; in addition to the new taxes there were also cuts in expenditure. In 1984 Franz Vranitzky became finance minister, and in 1985 he set new accents by declaring that public sector industry should in the future only receive subsidies for new and promising ventures. (In the preceding decade by contrast, nationalised industrial firms had been the main recipients of subsidies, and these had predominantly gone to declining firms, even when their declared purpose was otherwise. This outcome was assured by the political mechanisms of allocating the subventions.)[15] At the end of 1985 Public Sector Minister Ferdinand Lacina dismissed all the chief managers of Austria's largest nationalised firm (VOEST, engaged mainly in steel production) because of its financial debacle. The new management was entrusted with putting the firm back on a course of profitability (the firm had operated quite profitably until the mid-1970s, but subsequently gave priority to maintaining employment and accepted contracts even when they produced losses).[16] Vranitzky also declared as early as 1985 that partial privatisations of public sector firms were quite acceptable to the Socialist Party and by no means a matter of ideology, but simply of practical management.

In mid-1986 Vranitzky became chancellor. When the FPÖ elected Haider as its new leader he declared that the Freedom Party was no longer an acceptable coalition partner for the Socialists and called a snap election. Even before that election Vranitzky very clearly presented his economic plans for the future, namely a reduction of the budget deficit (which in 1986 had widened again to about five per cent; see Figure 1) to 2.8 per cent by 1991, mostly by cutting back expenditure. He set the Socialist Party on this new course with amazing rapidity. Despite the fact that it was mostly of neo-conservative origin, the SPÖ under Vranitzky integrated the new economic thinking even quicker (albeit sometimes reluctantly) than the conservative ÖVP. It now emphasised budget consolidation, profitability and privatisation for the public sector. The strategy of budget consolidation and of structural reform of the supply-side called for another grand coalition and Vranitzky was clearly preparing such a course.[17]

The Policy Reorientation of 1986–87

After the election, negotiations were conducted for this grand coalition. The main argument for such a coalition was the recognised need to consolidate the rising deficits in public finance and to improve the structure of production by acting on the supply-side (including privatisation). Only a government backed by a grand coalition, it was argued, would be able to take the drastic steps required by the emergency and even then it would probably need two legislatures (i.e. eight years) to achieve this goal. The probable results of continuing the previous policy were explored during the negotiations and estimates made of its likely consequences. The resulting study concluded that the deficit would rise to nine per cent of GDP by 1992, with the public debt increasing from 45 per cent to 70 per cent of GDP. Interest payments on the debt would be about double and crowd out other parts of the budget, and debt amortisation would amount to 25 per cent of government expenditure, as opposed to seven per cent in 1987.[18] Thus there was no alternative to consolidation. The other main problem to be faced by the coalition concerned structural policy. In the 1980s Austrian competitiveness – which had held up quite well until then – had been declining and economic growth had fallen below the average of OECD Europe even though unemployment was considerably lower in Austria (see Figure 4). This decline in economic growth was explained by deficiencies in the adjustment of Austria's economic structure to changing world markets and thus a need to encourage structural change in different ways was identified.

The budgetary policy announced by the new government in 1987 was to reduce the deficit gradually, to two and a half per cent of GDP in 1992 and to stabilise the gross debt to GDP ratio at around 50 per cent. This goal was to be reached by expenditure cuts, privatisations and a reform of the tax system. The cuts in public expenditure were decided rather quickly and extended over a broad range: civil service employment; employment programmes; government construction programmes; and subsidies for agriculture and the nationalised industry. The sale of federal assets (stock shares in the country's two largest banks, the national airline, the national oil corporation, the federal electric utility etc., but also real estate holdings) produced about 40 billion Schillings by the end of the 1990 legislative period.

The tax reform of 1988–89 was meant to correct the increasing failure of the automatic stabilisers (increases in tax revenues had of late no longer kept up with GDP growth) and to stop the erosion of the tax base by closing the increasing tax loopholes and exceptions. In the short run, however, the tax reform reduced revenue, since it lowered income tax

FIGURE 4
ECONOMIC GROWTH AND UNEMPLOYMENT IN AUSTRIA AND IN EUROPE 1962–87
(in per cent)

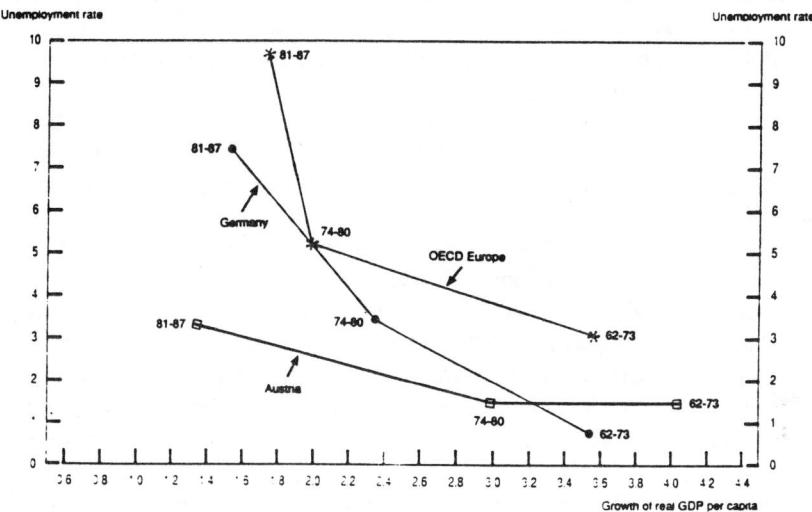

Source: OECD Economic Surveys 1989/1990, Austria, p. 36.

brackets and the rate of corporation tax. This last measure was meant to act on the supply side and is dealt with under the heading of structural reforms.

The consolidation goals seemed so ambitious in 1986–87 that only a grand coalition government, it was widely thought, would be able to apply such austerity. In fact the austerity lasted only for two years. The unexpected boom that emerged in 1988 made it possible for some time to achieve without much pain the goals set in 1986. The opportunity was not used, however, to accelerate the consolidation; in fact the opposite happened, and in 1990–91 a budget deficit target amounting to two and a half per cent of GDP was postponed by at least two years, from 1992 to 1994, or even 1995. The 1991 budget would in fact have shown a new deficit increase if certain items had not been taken out of the budget and accounted for separately. This was euphemistically referred to as a 'pause for breath' in austerity. In fact the budget of 1991 no longer fitted the austerity course. One reason was that the boom that began in 1988 was expected to continue well into the 1990s. Despite a general slow-down of economic growth in most OECD countries, it was widely assumed that Austria would continue its high growth rate due to its close connection with the German economy, which in turn (except for the region of the former East Germany) was expected to grow rapidly as a result of the re-unification process. For the medium term additional impulses were anticipated from trade with eastern European countries. Under these circumstances, the original rationale of the grand coalition – to spread the political burden of austerity over time and over both large parties – seemed less pressing.

The second reason for the 'pause for breath' of 1991 and the gradual abandonment of austerity in the preceding years resulted from the political weight of the grand coalition – and thus its capacity to contain demands on the budget – not living up to the expectations of 1986–87. This was mostly due to the political weakness of the People's Party, which suffered both from internal divisions and even more from its set-backs in the confrontation with the FPÖ. From 1986 the ÖVP's political fortunes were on the decline, whilst those of the FPÖ were by contrast rising. The ÖVP was thus afraid of alienating voters by consenting to hold down increases in civil service pay or retirement pensions, the hard core of the federal deficit; in other areas there were similar hesitations. The lingering spectre of a small ÖVP-FPÖ coalition to replace the grand coalition, viewed in some ÖVP circles as necessary to remedy the party's declining fortunes, further undermined the grand coalition's ability to implement a course of austerity. For the weakening of the ÖVP had its impact on the corresponding determination prevailing within the Socialist Party.

The policy outline of the grand coalition government presented in early 1987 also included a structural policy to act on the supply side, in order to strengthen competitiveness (not only of industry). The idea of a structural weakness of the Austrian economy had been of some importance in the mid-1960s, but had barely surfaced again until the poor growth performance of the early 1980s. Continued economic integration in Europe and in particular potential Austrian membership of the European Community (an application for EC membership had been presented in 1989) gave added urgency to such considerations. The problem arose, it was most commonly argued, from insufficient dynamism in the adaptation of Austrian firms to rapidly changing international conditions. The reasons for this were seen in the system of direct and indirect subsidies to business as well as in protective regulations. The great majority of direct subsidies ended up supporting obsolescent productions and declining firms, especially in the public sector, to which they were directed by mechanisms of political patronage and in which management responsibility had generally been lax for some time.

The guarantee that the state would eventually cover losses removed the main incentive to strive for greater profitability by adaptation and innovation. Indirect subsidies operated through the tax system; they were instituted by the mid-1950s and made it possible within a given firm to deduct investments from its profits. This arrangement benefited existing, established firms and handicapped new ventures. Tax write-off schemes which permitted deducting investments from taxable income were also criticised for their perverse effects; they encouraged investments that would have been unattractive without the tax bonus and systematically diverted resources into low-yield ventures. A number of regulations supposedly protecting the public against unfair competition completed the picture. All these factors, it was argued, were responsible for the relatively large share of semi-finished goods in the Austrian economy, and the yet unsatisfactory share of high-tech finished goods.

The first structural reform concerned the revitalisation of public sector industry. Steps taken stressed managerial qualities rather than the political affiliation of executives; the firms were also reorganised to stress clear lines of command and of responsibility; and profitability was stressed (as indeed already in 1985) as a basic goal also for public sector firms, the only alternative being closure.[19] Actual or upcoming privatisations created a constituency of shareholders that had a strong interest in high returns and which counterbalanced the power of labour unions. The latter's decline was further promoted by reorganisation of nationalised industries, including the depoliticisation of management, as well as by massive reduction of the work force (20 per cent between 1985 and 1987).

The success of restructuring showed within a few years. Even VOEST – the nationalised steelmaker – returned to profitability. In 1990 Austrian Industries (which includes several other nationalised firms, but in which the VOEST is the single largest firm) prepared a partial privatisation for 1992. In 1990 the province that had suffered most heavily from the steel firm's decline, Styria, showed one of the highest growth rates of the country. In some cases new private ventures had converted loss-making VOEST subdivisions into successful businesses.

The 1988 tax reform is another important supply-side measure. It was one of the most sweeping tax reforms in the history of the Second Republic. Its character as a supply-side measure results from the considerable lowering of income and corporate tax rates, the suppression of incentives to low-risk/low-yield investments and the creation of a new capital income tax to make low-risk savings books and bonds comparatively less attractive. The reform was designed to reorientate business investments towards new ventures (also by new firms, not only those well-established) that stood out by their promise of high profits, rather than by their potential for tax avoidance.

Financial resources for business, the finance minister declared in 1990, should in the future be provided by an effective capital market (including a functioning stock exchange) and no longer by government by means of special tax incentives or subsidies. While the traditional tax deductions and investment premiums were abolished, the corporate tax rate was lowered to only 30 per cent (among the lowest in Europe), in the hope of encouraging profitability and of attracting new firms to Austria. (The corresponding rate in the Federal Republic of Germany was 50 per cent at the time, although a lowering of the rate there was expected before the new financial demands resulting from the accession of the new *Länder* and the Gulf War of 1990–91 increased the drain on government resources.) Since the 1988 tax reform greatly restricted or abolished group privileges (except in agriculture), the broad basis of a grand coalition was certainly helpful for its realisation.[20] An additional tax reform was planned for the early 1990s, if only to adapt the Austrian tax structure to that of the EC.

Direct subsidies had been on the increase since the mid-1970s and had reached a level of about three per cent of GDP, not particularly high by international standards. Since 1986, only modest reductions have been achieved; however there was a shift from a primarily defensive approach to more targeted programmes in favour of research and development, innovation and environmental protection.[21] On the other hand, even the new subsidy programmes ended up under political control, which means allocation by political criteria rather than those of economic efficiency.[22]

Deregulation was another area which the grand coalition promised to tackle. At the end of the 1980s about half of Austria's GDP was produced in sectors sheltered from competition. This concerned above all the large number of small and medium-sized firms (mostly outside the secondary sector) which pervade the Austrian economy and which are subject to the Trade Regulations Law (*Gewerbeordnung*) and similar legislation that supposedly ensure the quality of goods and services by a tight control of competition and of market access. The legal protection against 'unfair competition' was long the major concern of corporatist chamber organisations who, as the OECD noted in a recent report on Austria, tended to be quite successful in promoting the interests of their membership by 'agreements between powerful interest groups, with the government often as a third party' and usually 'at the expense of non-organised customers'.[23]

Apart from the regulated trades already referred to, the protected sector includes the liberal professions, transportation, the postal service, telecommunications and the marketing of agricultural commodities. In banking and insurance, competition was stepped up only in recent years, and a wave of mergers seems to be underway to prepare that branch for EC membership. It is widely agreed among the top leadership of the political parties and the large interest groups that a major productivity reserve is at stake here, but because of the expected electoral costs there is great reluctance to take concrete steps to tackle this problem. Many measures to step up competition were actually initiated by constitutional court decisions which deemed unconstitutional particular restrictive laws or regulations. It seems as though the large parties were counting on EC membership and the resulting intensification of competition to solve this particular problem for them, hoping that most of the restrictive practices would quickly give way once they would be challenged on the basis of EC law.

THE SIGNIFICANCE OF THE POLICY REORIENTATION FOR 'AUSTROKEYNESIANISM'

The foundations of 'Austrokeynesianism' were laid in the 1950s and according to Austrian economists, it started to expire in the early 1980s. The extent of the change that occurred by the early 1990s will now be reviewed by focusing on the main elements of 'Austrokeynesianism': its overall goals, its central assumptions, its social and organisational preconditions, and its main instruments.

The overall goal of 'Austrokeynesianism' was to achieve a growth rate higher than the average of OECD Europe by the optimal use of Austria's productive resources; for the labour market this implied full employment. Its central assumptions were Keynesian in that it did not expect such optimal use to occur spontaneously from market forces, but only as a result of a public policy designed to stabilise expectations and to encourage investment. This policy benefited from the stabilising influence of strong corporatist institutions of business, labour and (less importantly) agriculture that were prepared to evolve a co-operative relationship above and beyond the daily political and economic battles. These were capable not only of representing, but also if need be of controlling, their respective constituencies. As to the main instruments of 'Austrokeynesianism', they were (in order of appearance) a hard currency policy, promotion of investment by tax incentives and cheap credit, an effective incomes policy, and judicious use of the deficit in the budget, public sector industry and the social security system.

At the outset of the 1990s, the original goals (outstanding growth rate, optimal use of resources) were still valid. However, there was a considerably greater reliance on market forces to achieve that purpose. On the other hand, the institutions of corporatist co-operation were still in place and to some extent their moderating influence was still taken for granted. The hard currency policy had survived two brief attempts to suspend it and now enjoyed very broad acceptance. The promotion of investments had been greatly modified. The policy of low interest rates for business credits had been given up some time ago and the tax reform of 1988 did away with most tax incentives to investment.

The biggest motivation for business investment after the reform was simply profitability. Corporatist incomes policy still worked quite well, though it may have been declining in effectiveness. In any case, since the inception of 'Austrokeynesianism' the country experienced almost none of the bitterness that in many other countries regularly recurs over wage conflicts or austerity policies and this record represented a valuable heritage that could be drawn on for some time to come. As for the budget deficit, there were substantial variations. Deficit expansion under Bruno Kreisky from 1975 onwards and its continuation during the socialist-liberal coalition (1983–86) contrasted with the consolidation policy of 1987–88, when the deficit was reduced despite the expectation of a continued recession. But the slow progress of consolidation despite the high boom that began in 1988 no longer fitted the new course of austerity, given the expectation that this phase of expansion would continue over the medium term.

The change of course concerning the nationalised industries seemed clearer, both with regard to reducing of government influence (by privatisation, de-politicisation and the weakening of union influence) and in the stress on profitability, rather than on the security (and sometimes the comfort) of employment stability.

It can be said that government influence on the economy (i.e., on the decisions of business managers) diminished as a result of the 1986–87 reorientation. There was greater reliance on the market in taking investment and employment decisions, particularly in the public sector. Added to this, the private sector's relative size was increased. The long continued growth of the state's share in the GDP was slowed down, or even reversed. This certainly amounted to a departure from Keynesian practices and assumptions, which in the main stress the need for governmental management to prevent an erratic performance of the economy within a market framework. As to business cycle policies, it could not simply be said (as some did) that the consolidation course implied a rejection of Keynesian ideas; particularly in the Austrian context, the need to counterbalance deficits had always be stressed. It was simply never specified just how long deficit spending could be continued if the economic situation remained stubbornly difficult and at what point a reversal should occur. The strong 1987–88 efforts at consolidation were certainly unusual, but so was the 1991 'pause for breath' in austerity. The course of policy in those years seemed to be dictated more by electoral considerations than by economic principle.

CAUSES OF THE 1985-86 REORIENTATION

In retrospect, it is quite clear that the main reorientation occurred between 1985 (when nationalised industry was told to make profits) and the turn of 1986–87 (when the agreement on policy priorities of the newly-formed grand coalition government was concluded). So far mainly economic reasons for this reorientation have been considered: the financial disaster of the nationalised industries, the dragging on of a high budget deficit, the steady increase of government indebtedness, and the low growth rate of the economy. Those were certainly the reversal's immediate causes. However, general social change such as a gradual emergence of new attitudes, values, and priorities also constitutes a cause. Yet another set of factors is that relating to party tactics and strategy.

The change in values and attitudes can perhaps best be summed up by the notion of the 'crisis of the social democratic consensus'.[24] This crisis, much discussed since around 1980, came to Austria with a certain delay. The term social-democratic consensus is not meant to apply exclusively to parties of that name, but rather to a particular vision of social evolution and of economic policy and includes several elements: the notion of a collective advance through a generalised increase in living standards (including rising personal incomes, expanding social security, improved public services and amenities); the idea that a strong and cohesive labour movement can and will decisively contribute to such a collective advance; and parallel with this the granting of power and prestige to those social forces and organisations (particularly but not exclusively social democratic parties, labour unions and related institutions) that embody these notions and aspirations.

In many countries several of these elements began to weaken in the 1970s. The rising integration of the world market and its intensification of competition meant that the different branches within the national economies experienced quite different evolutions. The important differences in productivity gains (often due to differences in the capital intensity of production) also brought divergent fates for firms within the same branch and of course for the wage-earners employed by them. Increasing unemployment further contributed to differentiate the living standards of wage-earners. New aspirations (for part-time, flexible working hours and the like) compounded the problem.

All this brought strong centrifugal pressures to bear on labour unions, and sometimes resulted in a free-for-all among the different groups. As inflation intensified in many countries, labour unions not only found it ever more difficult to deliver on the promise of a steady collective advance but often also became the target of criticism for their purportedly excessive power. The decline of traditional industries, the difficulty of recruiting union members in the expanding service sector and the increase of unemployment reduced union membership often drastically. Other elements of the social democratic model also suffered a set-back. Thus the consensus on the need to improve public services and amenities gave way to a rising concern over increasing tax burdens to finance governments' rising share of GDP.

It has been shown that all these changes do not inevitably mean the end of social democratic policies.[25] In Austria the social-democratic consensus was probably most dominant during the first decade of Kreisky's government, at a time when its fortunes were already declining in several other countries. The success of economic policy in the later 1970s delayed many of the problems experienced elsewhere. The economic divergence of different groups of wage earners, centrifugal tendencies among labour unions and the decline of union membership were successfully contained. Labour officials actually increased their political power and prestige, as Kreisky was eager to enhance their role in order to protect the social fabric from the destructive effects of what he viewed as narrow business rationality.

During the 1980s the 'crisis of the social democratic consensus' seems to have reached Austria. Labour solidarity was exposed to strains as unemployment went up, with great variations according to regions and branches. Labour union officials came under attack as they were seen to impede the return to profitability. The defence of employment security was no longer beyond controversy. In many public sector firms in which they had a particularly strong status, the chief labour officials were now pejoratively referred to as *Betriebskaiser* (roughly: little emperors) who opposed economic logic by political intervention at the level of state and party bureaucracy, or even in parliament, of which some of them were members. They were disciplined, often by persons at the highest levels of the SPÖ backed by the president of the Trade Union Federation himself.

This development coincided with another broad change, namely the weakening of political party affiliation and rising public aversion to the political patronage system practised for decades by the two large political parties. The expansion of state intervention and even its maintenance were criticised not only because of demands on public resources, but also because state control was increasingly perceived as a cover for control by one of the big parties, a form of control viewed as inspired by partisanship and lacking functional expertise.

Collective and traditional authorities such as parties and unions lost in legitimacy and strength. By 1990 the obligatory membership in the corporatist chambers, well established for decades although unique among Western countries, had become the subject of intense political controversy and individual chamber presidents were heavily attacked for what came to be considered as unjustified privileges, misuse of public funds and abuses of power. Individualist strategies gained in attractiveness. In business, the social prestige of entrepreneurs seemed to be on the increase. In another economic sphere the new individualism could be seen in the behaviour of savers. Less and less money came to be put in the traditional individual savings accounts, for decades the main form of savings in Austria. Instead, even before the 1988 tax reform, savers turned to investments with higher yields and/or higher risks (such as the stock market, whose index and transactions literally multiplied in the second half of the 1980s after a long period of stagnation at a low level).

Apart from these social changes, more immediate political reasons lay behind the reorientation of economic policy and in particular its timing. Social-democratic economic assumptions were shaken, although this hardly became apparent under Kreisky and his immediate successor, Sinowatz. If a rethinking was on the way, it took place rather quietly. For some time there was no coherent set of ideas that openly replaced the socialist visions of the 1970s. At governmental level, the new line was first formulated in 1985 by Vranitzky and Lacina. The erosion of the Socialist Party's electoral support reinforced this development. Hand in hand with the shrinking employment in the traditional industries went the decline of traditional socialist constituencies; new voters had to be recruited more from the centre, and with different appeals.[26]

Finally, the loss of a majority in parliament and the difficulty of conducting an austerity policy with the 'small' coalition's narrow majority made it highly necessary for the socialists to come up with a policy that could be agreed upon in a grand coalition with the ÖVP. That party in turn had its own interest in such an arrangement: unable to achieve a majority in 1986, or even to become the strongest party after 16 increasingly frustrating opposition years, the People's Party had a strong motivation to join forces with the Socialist Party, with which it now found itself in considerable policy agreement. It would have found it difficult to explain to its voters a 'small' coalition with the Freedom Party and possibly more difficult still to live up to the demands that a coalition partner led by Jörg Haider might have made.

REORIENTATION AND POLITICAL COMPETITION

Since the early days of 'Austrokeynesianism', economic policy was to a large extent taken out from the realm of political controversy. This applied most strongly to incomes policy, and to a somewhat lesser extent to business-cycle policy. These policy areas were largely turned over to corporatist co-operation. During the last two decades first the Socialist Party and later the People's Party took steps to reverse this trend and to regain the initiative in this field of policy making. Did this mean intensified political competition?

During Kreisky's years of triumph in the second half of the 1970s, the People's Party had not offered much of an alternative programme to what seemed in any case an eminently successful policy. This changed in the first half of the 1980s with increasing calls for reducing budget deficits by cuts in spending large enough to overcompensate the tax cuts that were also proposed. This was one side of the People's Party's criticism, but at the same time it also proposed new state expenditure (e.g. for families) and opposed the socialists' consolidation efforts of 1983 (new taxes, reduced social security benefits). Thus its criticism of governmental policy was to some extent contradictory,[27] reflecting perhaps the party's different groups for which the leadership may have been unable or perhaps even unwilling to find a common denominator, preferring instead to follow a populist strategy. On privatisation there was no great competition between the two big parties, since they discovered the theme at about the same time. However, the People's Party was first to criticise state subsidies to nationalised industry (traditionally a socialist stronghold). The popularity of this criticism contributed to the reversal of the socialist policy position by Franz Vranitzky and Lacina from 1985 onwards. In fact both large parties had misgivings about selling state-owned assets in whose management they actively took part at various levels, federal and provincial. As to deregulation, it was verbally supported by both parties, but mostly for traditional constituencies of the other party.

Thus political competition played but a modest role in the policy reorientation; it was in order to avoid its pitfalls that the two large parties joined forces. In the main, economic policy was a matter of consensus between them just as it had been in the past, with a brief and partial exception of the first half of the 1980s. The most important difference between those two periods of consensus was probably in the amount of power and initiative exercised by parliamentary actors versus corporatist institutions, with the former showing clear gains at the latter's expense in the second period.

By the end of the 1980s, however, populist competition resurfaced, initiated by another actor. The FPÖ's electoral fortunes were on the upturn since Jörge Haider's takeover in 1986; its prime target was the electorate of the ÖVP, a party with deep internal divisions and with increasing reservations regarding the grand coalition, the alternative being a 'small' ÖVP-FPÖ coalition. With every election and in particular at the

1990 parliamentary election, ÖVP decline was accentuated. This restricted its reliability as a partner in austerity. Thus even the grand coalition proved only a temporary safeguard against populist competition. Given the circumstances, it seemed likely in 1991 that fiscal stabilisation would be postponed, at least until the problem would re-emerge with greater urgency – and perhaps until a 'small' ÖVP-FPÖ coalition would preside over a different distribution of its costs, one that would break the pattern of symmetry in Austrian incomes policy. Some changes in this pattern had already occurred in the 1980s (increasing the share of income from property at the expense of work income). A further increase of this divergence would doubtless strain the Austrian pattern of labour relations and eventually social partnership itself.

THE POWER OF GOVERNMENTAL AND OF CORPORATIST INSTITUTIONS[28]

The reorientation of economic policy also affected the power of economic policy-makers, both in government and in the large interest groups. Part of this power was renounced altogether by both groups and replaced by a greater reliance on the market (which may be regulated at a different level, as by the European Commission in the EC case). Within Austria, the balance between corporatist institutions and the government shifted in favour of the latter. This shift had begun in the early 1970s and continued during the 1980s, when serious setbacks were suffered particularly by labour organisations. Deregulation also meant the reduction of corporatist power, not only of labour unions but also of business and its various chamber organisations.

The reorientation of 1985–86 did not change the basic goal of Austrian economic policy (i.e., rapid modernisation of the economy by a policy of record growth). However, it changed the strategy and many of the instruments. An important part of this strategy was the granting of power to corporatist institutions to represent key groups in society and to protect the legitimate interest of their membership. By getting these interest groups to co-operate a kind of cartel was set up. Whatever this cartel agreed upon was almost by definition considered to be in the national interest. The agreement of the corporatist interest groups included, for labour, the protection of employment (in exchange for moderate wage increases), and for business a favourable business environment (again in exchange for some moderation in price increases). This corporatist agreement could become 'dysfunctional' for the economy as a whole if the protection of employment or the protection of business against competition came to impede adjustment and structural change, a central part of modernisation.

The perception underlying the 1985–86 reorientation seems to have been that corporatist institutions inevitably end up impeding such adjustments, particularly when they serve their individual constituencies. Many reorientation reform measures were intended to end practices which had come to be considered as abuses, or in any case as conflicting with the public interest, even though they were the outcome of corporatist efforts. This applies to protecting employment against the effects of structural adjustment; to directing subsidies destined for innovation to declining sectors and firms in order to ease the transition; and to protecting a large part of the Austrian economy, producing about one half of the country's GDP, against competition that was judged 'unfair' or otherwise undesirable. In all those cases corporatist institutions had been able to secure protection. From 1986 market competition was brought in (though only incompletely by 1991, especially as far as the protected sector was concerned) to displace protection of different kinds.

Of course, corporatist politics in Austria could long claim to take a far-sighted view of economic policy. Although the protective measures considered all served to enhance the welfare of particular groups (only employment protection could, within the Keynesian understanding, claim to serve a wider public interest), a good part of corporatist policy consisted by contrast in restraining interests, primarily to achieve national goals, in the second place also for the interests' own sake. This was the case of wage, and to a lesser extent price, moderation. For the reasons mentioned above it seems likely that in these cases too, corporatist influence will decline along with union power. Here too, the market, in the form of enhanced competition within the EC and/or the European Economic Space, will take over at least some corporatist functions. As the market increases, the power to regulate and manage the economy will diminish in scope, and with it the function and power of both state and corporatist institutions.

In the 1950s the desire to achieve a record growth rate plus a measure of security for labour and also for business led to the granting of power to institutions of corporatist co-operation, as well as to the 'Austrokeynesian' instruments enumerated above; a market framework alone was not viewed as sufficient. In 1986, the same goal (record growth rate) was reaffirmed. However, considerations of security played a lesser role. As a result of this and of other changes (both domestic and external), the market was viewed as the chief instrument of growth. With the function of corporatism thus diminished, its further decline seemed plausible at the outset of the 1990s. At the present time there certainly appear to be no new attempts to legitimate that power.

NOTES

The author thanks the Jubiläumsfonds of the Austrian National Bank for supporting the research project on Austrian economic policy (Project No. 3551), and Manfred Hellrigl for carrying it out under his direction.

1. H. Ostleitner, 'Die Zukunft der Beschäftigungspolitik in Österreich', in K. Vak and H. Zilk (eds.), *Europas Aufstieg* (Vienna: Europa Verlag, 1989), pp. 337–52.
2. H. Prader, 'Ziele und Resultate kooperativer Gewerkschaftspolitik im Wiederaufbau nach 1945', *Österreichische Zeitschrift für Politikwissenschaft*, Vol. 3, No. 3 (1974), pp. 347–66.
3. K. Aiginger, 'Die wirtschaftsprogrammatischen Vorstellungen der ÖVP 1945–1985', in *Schwarz-bunter Vogel* (Vienna: Junius, 1985), pp. 98–100.
4. W. C. Müller, 'Die Rolle der Parteien bei Entstehung und Entwicklung der Sozialpartnerschaft', in P. Gerlich, E. Grande and W. C. Müller (eds.), *Sozialpartnerschaft in der Krise* (Vienna: Böhlau, 1985), pp. 162–75; E. Talos, 'Sozialpartnerschaft: Zur Entwicklung und Entwicklungsdynamik kooperativ-konzertierter Politik in Österreich', in Gerlich, Grande and Müller (eds.), *Sozialpartnerschaft*, pp. 67–81.
5. S. Koren, 'Monetary and Budget Policy', in K. Steiner (ed.), *Modern Austria* (Palo Alto, CA: SPOSS, 1981), p. 180.
6. E. Nowotny, 'Wirtschafts- und Sozialpartnerschaft und Finanzpolitik', in Gerlich, Grande and Müller (eds.), *Sozialpartnerschaft*, pp. 326–7.
7. G. Tichy, 'Austro-Keynesianismus gibt's den? Angewandte Psychologie als Konjunkturpolitik', in *Wirtschaftspolitische Blätter*, Vol. 29, No. 3 (1982), pp. 50–64, here pp. 57–60.
8. E. Streissler, 'Die Fiktion des Austro-Keynesianismus. Zum real existierenden "Keynesianismus" im Schrifttum von Hans Seidel', *Wirtschaftspolitische Blätter*, Vol. 34, No. 5–6 (1987), pp. 714–25, here p. 720.
9. W. C. Müller, 'Die Rolle der Parteien', pp. 180–93; Nowotny, 'Wirtschaft-...', p. 323.
10. W. Hankel, *Prosperity Amidst Crisis* (Boulder, CO: Westview 1981), p. 182.
11. E. Nowotny, 'Prozesse und Institutionen der finanzpolitischen Willensbildung', in W. Weigel, E. Leitner and R. Windisch (eds.), *Handbuch der österreichischen Finanzpolitik* (Vienna: Manz, 1986), pp. 226–9; E. Tálos, 'Arbeitslosigkeit und beschäftigungspolitische Steuerung', in idem and M. Wiederschwinger (eds.), *Arbeitslosigkeit. Österreichs Vollbeschäftigung am Ende?* (Vienna: Verlag für Gesellschaftskritik, 1987), pp. 91–166.
12. K. Aiginger, 'Die wirtschaftsprogrammatischen Vorstellungen der ÖVP', p. 110.
13. W. C. Müller, 'Privatising in a Corporatist Economy: the Politics of Privatisation in Austria', *West European Politics*, Vol. 11, No. 4 (1988), pp. 101–16.
14. W. C. Müller, 'Die Rolle der Parteien', pp. 203–4 and pp. 219–24.
15. K. Aiginger, 'Ausmass und Wirksamkeit der Subventionen', in *Handbuch der österreichischen Finanzpolitik*, pp. 489–98.
16. F. Summer, *Das VOEST-Debakel* (Vienna: Orac, 1987).
17. M. Hellrigl, 'Paradigmen und Wirtschaftspolitik. Die Rolle von Policy-Paradigmen in der Wirtschaftspolitik der Zweiten Republik'. Research project supported by the Jubiläumsfonds of the Austrian National Bank, Project No. 3551 (Salzburg: mimeo, 1990).
18. OECD Wirtschaftsberichte 1987/88. *Österreich* (Paris: OECD 1987) p. 19.
19. K. Aiginger, 'Industriepolitik', in H. Dachs, P. Gerlich, H. Gottweis, F. Horner, H. Kramer, V. Lauber, W. C. Müller and E. Tálos (eds.), *Handbuch des politischen Systems Österreichs* (Vienna: Manz, 1991).
20. G. Lehner, 'Ökonomische und steuerpolitische Auswirkungen der Steuerreform 1988', *Österreichisches Jahrbuch für Politik*, 1988, pp. 591–613; E. Nowotny, 'Die grosse Steuerreform 1988 – Analyse und Bewertung', *Österreichisches Jahrbuch für Politik*, 1988, pp. 571–89.
21. OECD Economic Surveys 1988/89. *Austria* (Paris: OECD 1989) p. 29.

22. K. Aiginger, 'Industriepolitik'; *idem*, 'Ausmass und Wirksamkeit der Subventionen'.
23. OECD Economic Surveys 1989/90. *Austria* (Paris: OECD 1990), p. 59.
24. For a sceptical overview see W. Merkel, 'Niedergang der Sozialdemokratie?', *Leviathan*, Vol. 18, No. 1 (1990), pp. 106–33.
25. W. Merkel, 'Niedergang der Sozialdemokratie'.
26. Many middle-class voters had strongly sympathised with the Socialist Party in the 1970s but turned away from it in the 1980s. C. Haerpfer, 'Die Sozialstruktur der SPÖ', *Österreichische Zeitschrift für Politikwissenschaft*, Vol. 18, No. 4 (1989), pp. 373–94.
27. G. Chaloupek, 'The Austrian Parties and the Economic Crisis', *West European Politics*, Vol. 8, No. 1 (Jan. 1985), pp. 71–81.
28. On this topic see the contributions to this volume by W. C. Müller and P. Gerlich respectively.

Austria in the International Arena: Neutrality, European Integration and Consociationalism

D. MARK SCHULTZ

Austria's distinctive political system is the product not only of a balance between powerful domestic interests and political parties, but also a balance between Austria and its international environment. This article examines the inter-relationship by looking at two of the dominant themes on Austria's post-Second World War foreign policy agenda: neutrality and integration with the European Community.[1] In both these areas external factors play a vital role in moving opposing forces in Austrian politics towards co-operation, and this co-operation has greatly influenced the conduct of Austrian foreign policy. One also sees that the balance between internal and external forces in the determination of Austrian foreign policy is tilted towards the latter, as one would expect for a small state. Austria's domestic structures and foreign policies do not create the external environment so much as adapt to externally-imposed constraints. This interplay is also dynamic, as this look at almost 40 years of policy shows. The article concludes, therefore, with some hypotheses regarding how recent changes in Europe may impact on both Austria's foreign policy and weaken the foundations of consociationalism.

NEUTRALITY

Much work, particularly by Peter Katzenstein on small European states, has traced the relationship between Austria's dependence on trade and the development of its consociational political system.[2] These studies suggest that small states adopt liberal trade policies to compensate for the limitations of their domestic markets. Integration with the international economy, in turn, promotes consociationalism in order to protect the economy's competitiveness and to ensure that powerful social groups – especially organised labour – are compensated for the dislocations that trade imposes. The premises for this system are highly organised and balanced interest groups, centralised decision-making, low public participation in decision-making, and a willingness to compromise in pursuit of national goals. This discussion of integration policy confirms these conclusions, but in Austria's case there is another connection between consociationalism and the international context, namely, the political situation after the Second World War.

The war was a watershed event in the development of Austria's consociationalism because it revolutionised the premises of Austrian politics. By marginalising pan-Germanism and strengthening the nationalists,[3] the war destroyed one of the dominant themes of Austrian politics in the interwar period: the idea that Austria was a transitional arrangement until integration with Germany could be achieved.[4] This change was critical because it united the two sides of Austria's ideological-confessional divide in pursuit of an over-arching goal: that of reconstituting the country. The challenge was not just to re-establish civil authority and reconstruct the economy, but, on the foreign policy side, the Austrians also faced the critical task of reasserting the boundaries between Austria and the international environment by wresting control of Austria from the occupation forces and the Allied Control Council.

Karl Renner of the *Sozialistische Partei Österreichs* (SPÖ), the chancellor of the interim government, and the other architects of Austrian reconstruction (Leopold Figl of the *Österreichische Volkspartei* (ÖVP) and Adolf Schärf (SPÖ)) worked from the premise that only a coalition government of the main political groups (including initially the *Kommunistische Partei Österreichs* (KPÖ) when the Soviet Union's sponsorship made this indispensable) would ensure unity and effective policy-making and implementation. Only a coalition could deprive the occupying powers of reasons for interfering in Austria's domestic affairs, and thus preserve the state's integrity against prolonged occupation or, with the onset of the Cold War, partition.[5] The parties demonstrated their willingness both to compromise between themselves and to ensure their constituents' support for government policy in several vital areas: the gradual extension of the government's authority in domestic and foreign policy; the apolitical approach to price-wage agreements, currency reform, and nationalisation policies; and the common front against the communist-led 1950 general strike. The Austrian government's performance during the occupation thus demonstrated a central tenet of consociationalism: controlled conflict over the orientation of domestic and foreign policies.

The coalition government established its control over foreign and domestic policy until the last outstanding issue was a State Treaty that would reinstate Austria's full sovereignty. Cold War politics delayed the process, and there were only sporadic negotiations from 1947 to 1954. As outstanding issues were resolved, the Soviet Union demanded as its final price for a State Treaty financial compensation from Austria and, more importantly, a treaty that would recognise the Soviet Union's security interests by prohibiting Austria's integration with Germany.[6] To achieve this, the Soviets initially requested a broad neutrality commitment in the State Treaty.[7] The Austrians resisted this, but indicated at the April 1955 Moscow Conference that they were prepared to adopt permanent neutrality outside of the Treaty. In the end, the Soviets consented to this approach and so the State Treaty contains no reference to neutrality, but rather a stipulation that Austria must protect its independence, and specifically that it must forego political or economic union with Germany as well as agreements that could jeopardise Austria's economic or political independence from Germany (Article 4). The Austrian parliament completed the arrangement by passing the Neutrality Act on 26 October 1955, with only the right-wing *Verband der Unabhängigen* (predecessor of the Freedom Party, or FPÖ) opposed, on the grounds that Austria was not freely adopting neutrality.

It is not surprising that there was little public discussion in Austria of the neutrality option before it was offered to the Soviets as a solution to the treaty problem. With both major parties in coalition, public debate was superfluous. This consensus is reflected in the central role that protection of neutrality took in Austria's foreign policy. The political parties shared the understanding that neutrality, as derived from the developed legal conventions, defined Austria's military options (no alliance involvement, and sufficient military forces to deter aggression against Austria). There was also general agreement that neutrality does not commit Austria to neutralism, namely cultural or moral equidistance between the two sides of the Cold War. However, as the following discussion of integration policy shows, ambiguity and disagreement between the parties had arisen over the details of neutrality, particularly what domestic, military, and foreign policies a neutral state must pursue in peacetime in order to ensure that its neutrality commitment is credible. Even in disagreement, though, the parties contained their differences carefully, on the principle that Austria's foreign policy must be predictable and constant so that Austria is a stabilising force in Europe, and to ensure that neutrality policy attracts as little attention and interference as possible from third parties, particularly the Soviet Union.

AUSTRIA AND THE EUROPEAN COMMUNITY, 1958–72

The Trade Parameter

Neutrality re-established Austria's sovereignty and preserved its unity, but the costs that this solution imposed became clear in the country's policy regarding European economic integration. As a state dependent on trade, Austria's interests were directly affected by the movement towards

Western European economic integration that began in the 1950s, and particularly the formation of the European Community (EC), which in 1958 took almost 50 per cent of Austria's total exports (see Table 1). The challenge to Austria's trading interests was clear: not only did the EC include Austria's two largest trading partners – West Germany and Italy – its proposed common external tariff was generally higher than West Germany's tariffs at the time. Business, government, and labour agreed that remaining outside the EC's tariff barriers would place Austrian companies at a competitive disadvantage *vis-à-vis* firms in the Community and cost Austria exports. Over the long-term, it was argued, Austria would also lose investment, as firms invested behind the tariffs instead of investing in Austria. The need for a trade agreement of some sort with the EC that would avert this dislocation was broadly accepted.

A dominant theme in the integration debate became the idea that if Austria did not come to an arrangement with the EC the future of the Austrian economy and state would be jeopardised.[8] It would perhaps be easy to discount these comments as scare tactics by proponents of an arrangement were it not for Austria's disastrous economic and political performance in the inter-war period. This was widely attributed to Austria's

TABLE 1
AUSTRIA'S EXPORTS AND IMPORTS BY AREA (1955–88)[1]

Year	European Community[2]		Federal Republic of Germany		European Free Trade Association[3]	
	Exports	Imports	Exports	Imports	Exports	Imports
1955	51.1	52.5	25.1	35.4	12.1	12.0
1958	49.6	54.3	25.1	38.9	10.9	11.4
1961	49.5	59.5	27.5	42.9	15.1	12.8
1964	47.5	58.8	27.9	41.7	19.2	14.6
1967	40.7	58.5	22.2	41.7	19.2	14.6
1970	39.4	56.0	23.4	41.2	26.6	19.6
1973	49.2	64.5	21.8	41.7	18.2	12.0
1976	46.6	63.4	23.4	41.1	14.4	9.7
1979	53.5	64.8	30.3	42.3	12.2	8.4
1982	53.1	61.2	29.3	40.6	11.7	7.7
1985	54.2	61.6	30.1	40.9	10.8	8.0
1988	63.9	66.6	35.0	43.6	10.8	7.3

Sources: 1955–85, Österreichisches Statistisches Zentralamt, *Statistisches Handbuch für die Republik Österreich*, various years. 1988 from International Monetary Fund, *Direction of Trade Statistics Yearbook*, 1990. Author's calculation.

Notes: 1. Calculated as percentage of total exports and imports.
2. 1955–71, EC=EC6; 1973–82, EC9; 1985, EC10; 1988, EC12.
3. EFTA includes Finland; from 1973, minus UK and Denmark, plus Iceland; 1988, minus Portugal.

loss of exports when the Habsburg Empire broke up and the succession states attempted to develop their own industries behind high tariff barriers designed to shut out imports from Austria. Most of the participants in the EC-integration debate had experienced this personally, and they drew parallels between the trade problems then and Austria's developing separation from the EC market. The historical experience undoubtedly helps explain why business, agricultural, and labour interests supported the position that Austria needed urgently to achieve an agreement with the Community. It also became a powerful argument in favour of trade liberalisation, since the proponents could dismiss concerns for the costs that trade liberalisation might impose by arguing that the alternative would be collapse.

The Parties and Integration

Both the SPÖ and ÖVP accepted the need to preserve Austria's access to the EC market, but there were important differences between and within the parties. Although ÖVP spokespersons most often cited the economic costs of Austrian isolation and were more aggressive advocates of an agreement with the EC, they were also sensitive to Austrian business' vulnerability to increased competition from the EC, and the social disruption that this might imply.[9] The SPÖ was more sceptical of the economic arguments used to promote a trade agreement with the EC, but leading SPÖ politicians such as Bruno Kreisky (Foreign Minister), Karl Czernetz (spokesperson on integration and West European affairs), and even Bruno Pittermann (party leader and Vice-Chancellor) at various times acknowledged that Austria would pay a high price if trade barriers between it and the EC increased.[10] The interests represented in the groups constituting the parties' bases accounted for these inconsistencies. The ÖVP had to balance internationally-orientated business with protectionist small firms and agricultural producers. The SPÖ had to accommodate the interests of protectionist workers in the nationalised industries, while not wishing to prejudice employment prospects in general, or protect conservative small agriculture or industry. Thus, while the parties advocated a trade arrangement with the Community they also hoped to accomplish this while protecting their constituents.

Conversely, both sides also saw potentially advantageous political benefits from trade liberalisation. In the early 1960s Austrian industry and agriculture were insulated from import competition by relatively high trade barriers, which would have had to have been dismantled through integration with the EC.[11] Some proponents of a trade agreement maintained that Austria would benefit from the increased discipline that a 'cold shower' of competition from the EC would provide for industries such as forest products, textiles, and iron and steel that by the late 1950s had started to reveal structural weaknesses through slow growth and declining exports. Conservatives therefore pointed to the need to expose protected industry to international competition; socialists hoped to discipline the (conservative) agricultural community.[12] Some conservatives also hoped that integration with the EC would discipline Austrian policy makers who, they felt, were prejudicing the country's performance by sheltering the economy from international competition. Predictably those interests in business and labour that would lose from the prescribed 'cold shower' of competition and restraint on government involvement in the economy played down this aspect of trade-liberalisation, and emphasised instead the need for EC policies and concessions to prepare business for a new trade environment.

The focal point and decisive consideration in Austria's formulation of an integration policy was not the economic implications, but the relationship between integration and neutrality. It has already been noted that the parties divided on their understanding of neutrality's scope, and this was reflected in their positions on European integration.[13] The FPÖ and KPÖ espoused the fringe positions on the right and left. The FPÖ maintained that neutrality was not inconsistent with membership in the EC because neutrality applied only to war and could be dissociated from integration policy, while the KPÖ represented the Soviet Union's holistic interpretation of neutrality and advocated strict distance from the EC, which it considered the economic arm of NATO. The SPÖ and ÖVP occupied the ground between these extremes, with the ÖVP generally taking a permissive view of neutrality and the SPÖ a stricter view.

Here too the SPÖ's and ÖVP's positions were neither rigidly defined nor internally consistent.[14] The SPÖ is most often criticised for introducing neutrality into the EC debate, and indeed Pittermann and Kreisky first invoked neutrality as an argument against membership in the EC. It is important to remember, though, that there were also those in the SPÖ, such as Czernetz, who attempted to confine neutrality to the military sphere.[15] Bruno Kreisky also distinguished between integration and neutrality policy, writing, for example, that 'some think of the EC as an economic correlate of NATO. But it would be a serious error of judgement to view the economic integration of Europe – which in one form or another is a necessary stage in the development of a modern economy – only in connection with alliance policy'.[16] It is also significant that Pittermann and Kreisky used the neutrality argument first in 1959, that is to say, after the government had decided against immediate membership in the Community. For its part, the ÖVP was not insensitive to the political issues that neutrality raised. In 1964 Fritz Bock, who was Minister for

Trade and Reconstruction in the 1960s and responsible for integration policy, argued that EC membership was not an option, saying: '... it is quite obvious, and not disputed by anyone in Austria who is able to think responsibly, that strict obedience to our neutrality obligations and the obligations of the State Treaty is the first and paramount precept to which all other decisions must be subordinate'.[17]

The major parties' inconsistent positions on the question of EC membership undoubtedly reflected the divided interests of their constituents, but domestic considerations were not the only factor. The Soviet Union repeatedly voiced its opinion that EC membership would implicate Austria in economic and political relations that were incompatible both with the State Treaty's prohibitions on integration with Germany and with neutrality.[18] The neutrality argument was not merely an invention of the domestic opponents to membership in the EC to impede Austria joining the Community.

Whatever the discrepancies in the parties' rhetoric, the decisive fact for Austria's integration policy was ultimately that both parties adopted the position that a trade agreement with the EC was necessary, but neutrality foreclosed the easiest option: membership in the EC. Specifically, the Austrian government's position was that neutrality would be compromised by:

(1) The precedence of EC law over national law.
(2) Majority voting in Community decision-making.
(3) Harmonisation of agricultural policies, with the resulting implications for national self-sufficiency in the event of conflict.
(4) Harmonisation of economic policies, including social, transport, and competition policy.
(5) EC trade policy, which would inhibit Austria's ability to pursue an independent policy *vis-à-vis* its trade partners in Eastern Europe.
(6) After 1975, the EC's fiscal autonomy.[19]

There was also uncertainty about how the Community's goal of political and military integration would be embodied institutionally, namely, if this would be incorporated into the EC itself or other institutions. As a neutral, Austria of course could not participate in joint defence efforts, and so the institutional questions were vital. There was also a strong feeling that even if EC membership did not require participation in military co-operation, it could involve Austria in policies that would either compromise its ability to pursue the peacetime policies necessary to preserve neutrality, or damage the credibility of Austria's neutrality. These shared perceptions[20] – and not party differences – led the government to pursue an arrangement with the EC that would preserve Austria's access to the Community market but stop short of full membership.

Austria's First Approach

Austria's first choice for a trade arrangement with the EC was a European free-trade zone including the EC and the other members of the Organization for European Economic Cooperation (OEEC), but when negotiations towards this collapsed in 1958, the government chose not to pursue a trade agreement with the EC independently, but opted instead to continue multilateral efforts. Power politics played an important role in this decision. The government feared that the unbalanced stake in the relationship, and the resulting unequal interests in arriving at an agreement, would make negotiations on a bilateral basis with the EC difficult.[21] Thus, to strengthen its negotiating position, Austria took a leading role in creating the European Free Trade Association (EFTA) from the OEEC members remaining outside the Community: Austria, United Kingdom, Portugal, Switzerland, Sweden, Denmark, and Norway, with Finland associating in 1961. Austria's first applied to the EC for an association agreement in tandem with Switzerland and Sweden, and the UK's first membership application. Though this approach was ultimately unsuccessful, it warrants comment since it was the first formulation of both Austria's and the Community's positions on association, which later negotiations – the 1963–67 Independent Approach (*Alleingang*), the 1969–72 negotiations, and EC-EFTA negotiations for a European Economic Area (EEA) – extended.

The EC's position. The EC responded positively to formulate a comprehensive position relating to the EFTA-states, which appeared as the Birkelbach report from the political committee of the European Parliament.[22] Despite the explicit provision in the Treaty of Rome for association with the Community, the Birkelbach report was sceptical and uncompromising. It stated firmly that the EC had little sympathy for outside states' desires for preferential agreements that stopped short of membership, citing several reasons. First, the report suggested that association would be an inequitable relationship, insofar as associates would benefit from integration with the Community without paying the costs that the members bore in order to produce those benefits. The report also suggested that associates could abuse their policy-making freedom to their exporters' advantage. The report concluded that association would have to be as near as possible to full membership in order to ensure that the relationship was balanced. This position was captured neatly in a phrase that has recurred often in EC-Austrian relations: 'entry into association with the Community does not mean that a state gets an opportunity to pick the raisins out of the cake'.

However, at the same time as the report demanded that associates would have to assume many of the Community's policies, the report also insisted that the EC would not concede decision-making power to its associates. It argued that if the associates were granted decision-making rights, the Community would become entangled in a web of agreements with third states and lose its ability to act autonomously. These considerations led the Birkelbach Report to conclude that the Community desired association agreements only with states that had the intention of applying for full membership, but which required a transitional status to allow their economies to develop to the point where membership was possible. Other states were pointed towards the General Agreement on Tariffs and Trade (GATT).

The Austrian association policy. The Birkelbach report placed the onus on Austria to justify its application and ensure that the Community's demands were satisfied. Thus, when Bruno Kreisky outlined Austria's position to the EC Council of Ministers at the beginning of negotiations, his statement focused on the two points raised in the Birkelbach Report. Kreisky declared that Austria supported the principles of the Treaty of Rome and was prepared to harmonise trade and economic policies with the EC's insofar as this was consistent with neutrality. Kreisky also contrasted Austria's economic history after the First World War with Austria's economic success and political stability after the Second World War, and warned that if an agreement was not achieved the failure would not only be detrimental to Austria, but would also threaten 'the stability and peace of central Europe'.[23]

Kreisky outlined the list of reservations that the Austrian government felt would be necessary to make an agreement consistent with neutrality. These were: exemptions for civil and military air transportation; exemptions for war material; control over trade relations with third states; a suspension clause, to be invoked in the event of conflict or the threat of conflict; protection for certain areas of the economy integral to maintaining neutrality; agreements with the European Coal and Steel Community and Euratom; transition measures (including advanced tariff reductions by the EC) and protection for vulnerable sectors to minimise the adjustment costs for Austria; and an independent committee to implement and supervise the agreement.

At this juncture, a fundamental weakness in the Austrian strategy emerged. Austria's strategy of affiliating with EFTA to increase its leverage *vis-à-vis* the EC also ensured that Austria's concerns were subordinated to the broader question of EC relations with the other EFTA-states, and particularly the UK. Austria could exert little influence in this larger context, and thus when France announced in January 1963 that it was unwilling to proceed further with negotiations with the UK, Austria's initiative also stalled. Although the Stockholm Treaty committed Austria to solidarity with EFTA, its incentives to reach an agreement were no less compelling. Furthermore, the government, and particularly Bock and the ÖVP, had always been sensitive to the limitations of the EFTA strategy, and had repeatedly insisted that solidarity with EFTA could not take precedence over Austria's interests.[24] Accordingly, the government affirmed its commitment to EFTA's goals, but continued negotiations with the Community on its own.

This Independent Approach took place from 1963 to 1967 and reached agreement on:

- tariff reductions;
- Austria's adoption of the Community's Common External Tariff, while retaining control of trade promotion with third states;
- economic policy harmonisation to avoid trade distortions;
- provisions for suspending or cancelling the agreement;
- supervisory and dispute resolution committees;
- the EC's right to compensation from Austria for insufficient harmonisation.[25]

Despite this far-reaching accord, intractable problems remained involving mainly harmonisation and institutional arrangements – the two difficult areas identified by the Birkelbach report.[26] Although the EC conceded that Austria required a degree of autonomy to protect its neutrality, the problem was how to concede this without releasing Austria from its obligation to harmonise its policies with the Community. Although Austria expressed its willingness to undertake far-reaching harmonisation, it insisted on retaining the right to judge which measures might conflict with neutrality. To the EC, this suggested that Austria could 'pick the raisins from the cake'. In the end, external political events intervened again and disrupted Austria's efforts before these questions could be resolved. In December 1966 the EC had decided that before concluding an arrangement with Austria, it would reconsider the whole association question. Then in June 1967 Italy linked the trade negotiations to South Tyrol and terrorist activities there on the part of those fighting for greater autonomy for the German-speaking population of this formerly Austrian region, and vowed to obstruct Austria's efforts until this problem had been resolved. Third, the Soviet Union stepped up its campaign against Austria's association plans. As a result of these factors, no agreement was reached.

The 1972 Austrian Free Trade Agreements

Between 1967 and 1969, the political context changed dramatically and dissolved the impediments to a trade agreement between Austria and the EC. In 1967, in response to the membership applications from the United Kingdom, Ireland, Denmark and Norway, the EC stated that it would consider association agreements with the other EFTA states for whom membership in the EC was not an option.[27] In 1969 France relaxed its opposition to membership negotiations with the UK, and after Italy and Austria reached an agreement settling their dispute over South Tyrol, Italy rescinded its veto against further negotiations with Austria. A third significant development was the relaxation of the Soviet Union's attitude towards the EC after West Germany concluded its treaties with Eastern Europe.

In the interval between the end of the Independent Approach and the start of new negotiations, neither Austria's nor the EC's position had changed dramatically. The EC reaffirmed its position that association would have to balance benefits and obligations, and could not impede the Community's development. In Austria, despite the changes of government – from grand coalition to ÖVP majority in 1966, and then to SPÖ government in 1970 – Austria maintained its neutrality reservations, and again impressed upon the Community that its commercial and political interests were best served by a prosperous and stable Austria, which could only be guaranteed through a trade agreement with the EC. One significant change was Austria's move away from its insistence on policy-making independence to a desire for expanded policy co-operation in other areas of economic policy in addition to trade. This new approach was based on the recognition that the EC was already playing the central role in European industrial and economic policies going well beyond trade.

Negotiations between the EC and Austria took place during 1971–72, making rapid progress on the basis laid through the talks over the preceding decade. The free trade agreements (FTAs)[28] that resulted were consistent with Austria's neutrality commitment and the State Treaty. Indeed, the preamble to the Global Agreement with the EC stated specifically that the FTA could not prejudice the signatories' existing international legal commitments. To protect Austria's neutrality further, special provisions were included to govern armaments; the agreement could be suspended in the event of international tension or conflict; Austria was freed from joining the Community's politically-motivated trade actions against third states; the Joint Committee established to adjudicate disputes and make changes to the agreement was formed on the basis of parity; termination would be possible with 12 months notice; and, most importantly, Austria was not committed to any political association to achieve this.

With regard to the commercial provisions of the agreements, the FTAs provided for the removal of quotas and tariff on most manufactured goods from October 1972 (under the Interim Agreement) to January 1977. Certain 'sensitive products' — metal and paper products that the EC had insisted on protecting through slower tariff reductions — and a small number of products based on agricultural commodities were put on an extended tariff-reduction schedule. Agricultural produce had been exempted from the FTA at the Community's insistence, and instead quotas were increased in separate agreements and the two sides pledged to liberalise trade in agricultural products. Ostensibly, agriculture had been kept out of the FTA because of difficulties that would have arisen in attempting to have free trade with the EC's Common Agricultural Policy, but another factor was that the Community did not anticipate many benefits from including agriculture. To ensure fair competition, the FTA included origin rules, a cumulation system,[29] some enforced harmonisation, and protection clauses, which could be invoked if free-trade produced adjustment problems or balance of payments difficulties — especially if the EC felt that the negative effects were attributable to the lack of policy harmonisation.

Austrian business welcomed the agreements, but agriculture and the metal industries criticised the provisions for these industries. In the parliamentary debate on the FTA,[30] the opposition parties affirmed their support for the agreement with the EC, and the ÖVP claimed a share in the credit for the preparatory work it had done during its 1966–70 government. The opposition did, though, criticise what they maintained were the FTA's unequal terms. For example, the ÖVP's leader, K. Schleinzer, referred to the regime for sensitive products, the fact that the EC was not reducing its tariffs before Austria, and the exemption of agricultural products from the arrangement, and accused the government of not bargaining strongly enough. The FPÖ's criticism was that the agreement did not go far enough.

The government rejected the opposition's claims that it had inadequately pursued Austria's interests. Chancellor Kreisky, Foreign Affairs Minister Rudolf Kirchschläger and Minister for Trade, Commerce and Industry Josef Staribacher, all emphasised that Austria had successfully negotiated an agreement that was consistent with the country's neutrality and that secured access to the EC market. Staribacher emphasised how much better the final terms were than the EC's original offer, pointing out that:

- Austria had resisted the EC's demands for unilateral concessions in agricultural trade;
- 'sensitive products' were included in tariff reductions from the start;
- the protection clauses were less rigid, and included the requirement for prior consultation.

As for the criticism that Austria had conceded too much to achieve these gains, SPÖ spokespersons had a simple explanation: the power imbalance between the two parties left no other possible outcome. Responding to Schleinzer's criticisms, Erwin Lanc (SPÖ) explained candidly that Austria was the weaker party and it was naïve to expect that its interests would prevail against the EC. In a revealing comment on Austria's position, Lanc reminded the critics that Austria would have gained nothing had it not accepted the deal, even with the somewhat unbalanced terms.

Austria's Integration Policy Post-FTA

With the 1972 FTA, the government – reflecting the position of the SPÖ – believed that Austria's integration policy-goal had been attained, and that the outstanding questions in Austria's relationship with the Community were resolved.[31] By reducing the discrimination that had impeded Austria's exports to the EC after 1958, the FTA provided the framework for the reintegration of Austria's exports into the Community markets, and this was reflected rapidly in the shift of Austria's exports and imports from third markets – including EFTA – to the EC (Table 1). Moreover, a rapid growth in direct investment in both directions accompanied the redirection of trade. The Community's expansion from six to 12 members reinforced the effects of the tariff reductions to increase Austria's dependence on EC markets.

From 1972 to the mid-1980s fundamental change in Austria's relationship with the EC was not on the agenda, and further development was anticipated through *ad hoc* co-operation within the FTA, or through multilateral bodies such as GATT and the Council of Europe.[32] In a 1978 lecture on Austrian foreign policy, for example, then-Minister for Foreign Affairs Willibald Pahr emphasised that 'in the current phase of Austrian foreign policy, sensational events or decisions are not to be expected...'. There would be continuity based on the 1955 State Treaty and the 'primacy' of security policy.[33] Indeed, through the 1970s and early 1980s under Chancellors Bruno Kreisky and Fred Sinowatz much of Austria's attention to foreign and trade policy turned from the EC to focus on other issues and areas such as disarmament and *détente*, trade liberalisation through GATT, and expanding trade with Eastern Europe and the Middle East.

As for trade with the EC, the Austrian government worked on fine-tuning the FTA. In conjunction with EFTA, Austria strove to rectify the shortcomings in the administration procedures by simplifying the documentation and relaxing the rigid cumulation system, which made it difficult for companies in EFTA countries to import goods from other EFTA states and, after additional processing, meet the minimum local value-added criteria that qualified goods for duty-free export to the EC. Austria also sought to redress the rapid and serious degeneration in its trade-balance with the EC in agricultural products by expanding Austria's quotas for wine, beef, and cheese exports to the Community. Third, Austria sought to alleviate the growing financial and environmental burden of transit traffic between West Germany and Italy by promoting its strategy to shift freight passing through Tyrol from road to rail. Austria pursued these goals through multiple avenues. It approached the Community itself, and worked through the member states; it acted independently, and in conjunction with EFTA; and it circumvented the EC altogether by using direct bilateral contacts with Community members.

At the same time as the SPÖ had closed the book on integration policy, the ÖVP and FPÖ were arguing that the agreements were only a 'partial solution'[34] to Austria's integration problem. The opposition critics were echoing legal experts who looked at the FTA's implications for neutrality policy.[35] These commentators pointed out that by confining itself to free trade manufactured goods the FTA governed only a fraction of the Austria-EC relationship and left out large areas where the Community already formulated policy or intended to, such as agriculture, public procurement, taxation, competition, services, capital mobility, and labour. These critics also argued that the FTA left Austria with no voice in formulating EC policies that would directly affect Austria. They suggested that unless Austria rectified this apparent inconsistency, the FTA would enhance economic integration, but with the result that over the long-term the Austrian state would be progressively 'hollowed out'.[36]

The government, however, viewed these concerns with comparative indifference. Responding to Alois Mock's (ÖVP) question of how Austria would take part in the next stage of European integration without decision-making rights in the Community, Staribacher simply restated the EC's position on the question, namely, that Austria could not have decision-making rights in the EC when it was not a full member.[37] Instead of striving for complete participation in the EC, the SPÖ government was comfortable with two levels of European integration. In 1975, for example, Foreign Minister E. Bielka described the EC as a 'core' striving towards 'as dense and comprehensive an integration as possible', while around this core were 'in a somewhat looser form, those member states who are able to participate in the integration process, but who for good reasons are not – or not yet – in a position to accept an all-embracing integration into the future Europe'.[38]

Through the 1970s and early 1980s, the government's strategy for managing relations with the EC was tenable. Even though the *ad hoc* approach did not resolve the outstanding issues in Austrian-EC relations, it appeared that the relationship was manageable using the existing institutions. This apparently disproved the critics' arguments that the FTA was incomplete or unstable. Indeed, the stability reflected itself in that from 1972 Austria's EC-policy entered into a period of quiescence that lasted to the mid-1980s. However, as the Community showed renewed dynamism in pursuit of the Single Market ('1992') it became apparent that the government's approach was viable only as long as the EC stagnated. That is to say, as long as the Community was not developing, Austria was not forced to confront the tensions between economic integration without decision-making rights that was inherent in the FTA. So '1992' shook the government's complacency by showing that integration with the Community implicated Austria in developments with a logic and a timetable that it could not control without input into the EC's decision-making processes. A fundamental debate in Austria ensued on the scope and structure of the relationship, which echoed strongly in both tone and vocabulary the pre-1972 debate.

AUSTRIA'S INTEGRATION POLICY, 1986–91

'1992' and Austria

From an economic perspective, given the existing trade and investment links, any improvement in the EC's economic performance as a result of '1992' would have benefits for Austria. Austrian firms operating in the Community or exporting to it would benefit from a unified market if, as the EC expects, consumer purchasing power increases and firms' operating costs decline as companies organise their business activities on a continental basis. But the Austrian government and business community alike viewed the EC moves less as a business opportunity than as a cause for anxiety. The concern in Austria was that the creation of the Single Market would have as its corollary increased discrimination against outsiders, which would jeopardise the integration Austria had already achieved and distort the evolution of future trade and investment flows unless Austria's firms had equal access to the proposed Single Market.

Austrians saw several challenges in the Single Market plan. One threat was the automatic discrimination against outsiders that the reduction of the EC's internal barriers implies. Companies outside the Community would be at a competitive disadvantage if they faced administrative impediments — for example, licensing or testing requirements — that their competitors inside the Community did not. Austrians were also concerned that post-'1992' the EC could be more protectionist if it adopted a more aggressive common anti-dumping policy to protect EC producers against imports. A third, non-economic consideration, was the widespread apprehension that Austrians would be cast as outsiders and second-class citizens in the new European social and cultural community that was developing in conjunction with the Single Market. Plans for a 'European' passport for EC nationals and a common immigration policy, Bavaria's proposals for AIDS tests for non-EC workers, and France's visa requirements for non-EC visitors in 1986 were provocative indications of what a future outside the EC could mean for Austrians personally.

These considerations were, of course, most important for Austrian business who, after adjusting to the opportunities and increased competition post-FTA, had the most to gain – and lose – from '1992'. Many industrialists also felt that while they had adjusted to European competition after 1972 they were still forced to rely on protected and often uncompetitive Austrian services, especially financial services, and so wanted integration with the EC extended beyond goods. Private industry also hoped that the nationalised industries – in the mid-1980s a significant burden on the state's finances and the private sector's competitiveness – would not survive further integration with the EC without major restructuring. The prospect of larger markets outside Austria, and liberalisation and deregulation at home, moved many business people, led by the Austrian Association of Industrialists (VÖI), to advocate further integration with the EC. Though the Chamber of Business concurred, its rhetoric was more restrained, most likely because its members include the full range of Austrian businesses, including many who would face difficult adjustment problems such as retailing, distribution, and insurance.

The Austrian labour movement was generally less enthusiastic than industry, mainly because of its concern that integration could diminish the influence that it exerted on Austrian economic policy through the social partnership.[39] Still, labour in general backed further integration, provided its interests were respected in the EC. This position was consistent both with the labour movement's support for liberal trade policies as the best guarantee of international competitiveness, economic growth, and jobs, and with the belief that the workers' interests as consumers were not served by protecting Austrian industry. Labour's prointegration stance was undoubtedly made easier by the release of studies which indicated that further integration with the EC would have only modest effects on Austria's labour markets,[40] as well as by the EC's clear commitment to a social dimension that would protect workers' interests. In a change from the first period of integration, agriculture opposed new initiatives, most likely because Austria's subsidies were now higher than the EC's.

Austria's New Integration Policy

The shift in the EC was quickly reflected in the parties' European policies, which acknowledged both the economic and political pressures that '1992' placed on Austria. The SPÖ departed rapidly from its aloofness vis-à-vis the EC during the Kreisky era. The government's foreign policy review for 1985 outlined EC developments and commented: 'The geographic expansion of the EC, its economic dynamism, and its development in the direction of a European Union have necessarily enlivened the discussion in Austria regarding the relationship with the EC as well'.[41] The change began under Chancellor Fred Sinowatz, but the decisive shift in SPÖ policy came when Austria's current chancellor, Franz Vranitzky, assumed this position in 1986. Vranitzky strengthened the party's market-orientated wing, represented by Peter Jankowitsch, Foreign Minister in Vranitzky's short-lived coalition with the FPÖ, Rudolf Streicher, Minister for Public Economy and Transportation, and Finance Minister Ferdinand Lacina. This new team abandoned Kreisky's policy of relying on the nationalised industries, interventionist industrial policy, and stimulative fiscal deficits to secure full employment.[42] They looked instead to integration with the EC to discipline Austrian industry and guarantee Austria's long-term international competitiveness, industrial future, and employment prospects.

The SPÖ's new approach was further reinforced when the ÖVP returned to government in the grand coalition established after the 1986 election. The ÖVP had long used its pro-EC policy to distinguish itself from the SPÖ, and was able to pursue aggressively closer integration with the Community with Alois Mock as Vice-Chancellor (until 1989) and Foreign Minister. Other domestic political considerations played an important role in ÖVP enthusiasm: Mock saw a pro-EC stance as a vehicle that could be used to repair the damage done to the party and his standing in the eyes of the public – and especially the business community – by the controversy surrounding President Kurt Waldheim, whose candidacy Mock had initiated. The SPÖ was to an extent dragged along by the ÖVP's enthusiasm for a closer relationship with the Community, since it could not afford to abdicate such a significant area to its coalition partner.

For these reasons, the grand coalition's first government declaration referred to the 'great challenge' in integration policy and affirmed:

> One of the principal barriers to Austria's economic development is the small size [*Enge*] of the domestic market. Through consistent efforts towards integration and internationalisation, the government will ensure that Austrian business will be able to participate in the dynamic of the large European market and the technology

programmes of the EC, and that existing or threatened discrimination will be dismantled or averted.

The government asserted that 'it is beyond doubt that an uncoupling of Austria from this [EC] development would necessarily have serious economic and social consequences for Austria and the future of its youth'.[43]

At least until late-1988, these considerations generated agreement between the coalition partners that their policy would have to ensure Austria's full integration into the Community's internal market on a comprehensive basis, going well beyond trade matters to include most areas of the Single Market: agriculture, transportation, research and development, monetary, and economic policies. The government even committed itself to co-ordinate foreign policies with the EC, insofar as neutrality permitted, in areas such as South Africa and development assistance. To achieve this, the government's initial strategy was first to exhaust the opportunities within the existing agreements through bilateral talks with the Community and its members, multilateral contacts between EFTA and the EC, and unilateral action through the autonomous assumption of Community regulations. Although the government carefully did not exclude the possibility of membership in the EC, it also consistently avoided describing its goal in institutional terms. This was a pragmatic policy designed to achieve the effects of full membership in the Community, even as Austria remains an outsider.

Although the Global Approach was championed by Andreas Khol (ÖVP Member of Parliament, influential foreign-policy commentator and close associate of Mock), at least up to mid-1988 this strategy had bipartisan support. Khol suggested that a closer relationship with the EC could be developed in stages. In the first stage, Austria would unilaterally assume Community regulations where practicable and negotiate agreements with the EC in other areas. Later, these would be translated into a comprehensive treaty, that might also give Austria decision-making rights in the EC.[44] Full membership would follow some time later. Several considerations recommended this approach. By avoiding formal negotiations, the government could proceed immediately, it would avoid a neutrality debate, and it would deprive domestic interests of a focal point for their claims for preferential treatment. This last consideration ensured a comprehensive arrangement, a necessity both to avoid the charge that Austria is attempting to 'pick the raisins from the cake' and to capture fully integration's anticipated benefits.

Neutrality in the New Context

In these circumstances, a new interpretation of neutrality gained ground. Many now suggested that existing integration made classical interpretations of sovereignty and neutrality irrelevant, and the politically mainstream position became that while joining the Community would formally diminish Austria's sovereignty, the country would be better able to protect its neutrality in the EC than outside but still subject to decisions over which Austria had no control. Proponents of this position also held that certain fundamental political changes made it easier to reconcile Austrian neutrality with EC membership than in the first stages of integration. Since 1958 the EC had diversified politically by including neutral Ireland, which broke the Community's close identification with Nato; relations between the EC and the Eastern Bloc had improved dramatically; the Community was apparently moving from supranational tendencies to a more confederate approach; and, finally, the 1966 Luxembourg Compromise ensured that no Community action could be imposed on a member against what it saw as its vital interests.

The perception that political conditions had changed fundamentally since the 1960s so that EC-membership was now consistent with neutrality cut across the parties. The FPÖ, ÖVP, and VÖI supported this position; they had long argued that satellisation was a more serious infringement on Austria's sovereignty than EC-membership would be.[45] It was more surprising that the SPÖ's leadership adopted this view, as shown in comments by Jankowitsch, Vranitzky, and even Kreisky.[46] For Kreisky to change his position is remarkable, but in the early 1960s he had already anticipated that a relaxation of Cold War tensions could make neutrality an anachronism.[47] In 1988 the government's international law bureau invoked this argument in its analysis of neutrality and integration.[48] Also at this time, an influential interpretation of neutrality by Waldemar Hummer and Michael Schweitzer concluded that there were no legal barriers to Austria joining the EC that could not be surmounted if both sides showed the flexibility to come up with provisions that would avoid the possibility − or appearance − of conflicts between membership and neutrality.[49]

Despite the consensus on the legal and political compatibility of neutrality and integration, it was equally generally accepted that it would be better not to force the issue. There were strong domestic reasons for avoiding a neutrality debate. Potential domestic opponents of further integration could latch on to the neutrality argument. This included not only fringe groups such as the Greens and Communists, who used neutrality to argue against EC membership, but also a significant element on the SPÖ's left-wing and vulnerable business interests, such as the nationalised industries and the service sector.

For its part, the Soviet reaction to talk in Austria of closer integration with the EC was reserved – even understanding – but the Soviet Union also consistently reminded the Austrians of their obligations to remain neutral and avoid integration with West Germany. The Soviet Union became more vocal only when Austrians dismissed Soviet interest too flagrantly by insisting that Austria alone could interpret its neutrality obligations since these had been assumed autonomously by its parliament.[50] The Global Approach circumvented these problems by using the existing institutions that required no special arrangements or concessions to accommodate Austria's neutrality until very late in the process, after Austria had achieved its important agenda.

The EC's position

The flaw in the Global Approach ultimately proved to be the EC's discouraging response. Although the Community had expressed its willingness to consider a membership application from Austria at any time, the Community and its member governments also voiced misgivings at entering into membership negotiations with any applicant before '1992' was completed. Willy de Clercq, then the EC's Commissioner for external relations, rejected expansion in the near future, citing the Community's need now to 'gain strength through depth' after having expanded rapidly to 12 members.[51] Another problem was ambivalence towards more neutral members since it was feared that this might impede the Community's closer co-operation in foreign policy and military areas. Austrians did little to allay the EC's fears of obstructionism when, to solve their own neutrality problem, they argued that any member could veto Community policies that it felt jeopardised vital national interests. The Community was also reluctant even to consider an application from a neutral state because this would force it to define its own long-term goals in foreign and military policy. The EC was – and is still – divided over to what extent co-operation in this area should take place inside the EC or in other institutions such as the West European Union.

For these reasons, the most promising avenue for closer integration with the EC was initially the EFTA-EC project to extend the EC internal market into the EEA that would encompass EFTA and the EC. The agenda was substantially the same as the Single Market. The two sides pledged to:

- harmonise norms and standards;
- simplify trade administration;
- eliminate unfair trade practices and government subsidies, and liberalise government procurement;
- co-operate in research and development;

– consult on transport, agriculture, fisheries, energy, labour, cultural, consumer and environmental protection, tourism, and intellectual property policies.

Progress was made in these areas, and both groups heralded the project as a significant step in EFTA's relations with the EC, since it established multilateral co-operation in non-trade areas. However, although this was a shift away from the EC's previously rigid position that philosophical divisions over the goal of European integration had to be resolved before practical progress could be made, the Community left no doubt that there were limits to this approach. The EC still insisted on the principles outlined in the Birkelbach report: (a) that co-operation with EFTA could not lead to the EC 'dissolving into a large free-trade area'; (b) that co-operation with the EFTA could not complicate the Community's decision-making or its prospects for further integration by extending decision-making rights to EFTA-states; and (c) that there must be an equal distribution of costs and benefits.

Thus, although the Global Approach could solve some threats of uncoupling that '1992' posed for Austria, over time the strategy's limitations became apparent. Unilateral harmonisation was inadequate, because it could not overcome administrative barriers against Austrian exports, nor could it establish active *participation* in the Community's decision-making. EFTA-EC co-operation proved difficult since there were many different interests involved on both sides. The most contentious issue, however, has been the EC's uncompromising stand against allowing outsiders influence on Community decisions. This reduces co-operation with the EC to merely an invitation to outsiders to harmonise their policies with the Community's without having any influence over these. Indeed, Willy de Clercq forthrightly remarked that Austria, as a non-member, 'will be informed of developments, progress, and decisions in as much detail as possible. You can, if you consider it appropriate, assert your position. Still, anything beyond this would imply involvement in the decision-making process, and that is beyond consideration'.[52] Thus, while the Global Approach could solve some economic threats that '1992' posed for Austria, the challenge of retaining some control over industrial and economic policy-making remained.

The Membership Application

An Austrian government working group on integration weighed the economic and political considerations that Austria faced in deciding its future integration policy in a June 1988 report. The report reviewed the limitations on the Global Approach and concluded:

The question that Austria now faces is, therefore, if consultation and decision-making rights inside a broad — and, therefore, also pluralistic — amalgamation of states such as the EC does not afford more creative possibilities in the sense of scope for negotiations and options than does remaining outside while being bound to developments by compulsion and harmonisation.[53]

The report also argued that Austria's integration problem involved more than the difficulty of maintaining political control: it was also an information problem, which no amount of *ad hoc* co-operation could solve. A reactive policy, such as the Global Approach necessarily was, could not provide the Austrian government and economic interests with the timely information they needed for policy and investment planning. Since Austria could only acquire this information by participating in EC policy-making in the initial stages, the committee concluded that only full membership in the Community would achieve all that Austria now required.

The Committee's report was significant not merely for its analysis of the integration problem, but also for who was speaking, namely representatives of relevant government ministries, the social partners, the VÖI, and the central bank. The report was, therefore, the definitive policy-statement on which the Austrian government proceeded. This consensus was then reaffirmed in the social partners' report on integration that was released in March 1989. Encouraged by the social partners' positions, from autumn 1988 the ÖVP spoke out more vigorously for a formal membership application, but the government would not take the decisive step out of deference to the SPÖ's sceptical left wing. This obstacle was finally overcome in the spring of 1989 when the SPÖ's left wing agreed to support the membership application, most likely as a tactical move to see where negotiations with the EC would lead without committing itself to accept the final product, which it expected would be an association agreement rather than full membership. With support from across the political spectrum and the major interest groups secured, the coalition partners pledged to pursue a joint integration policy until Austria is a member of the EC. Austria's application was finally submitted to the EC in July 1989.[54]

OUTLOOK AND CONCLUSION

Austria's foreign policy agenda and options have been to a great extent determined by the opportunities made available to it by external circumstances. Cold War politics and Soviet security policy defined neutrality and its implications for Austrian politics; the EC's policy on association with third states set the parameters for Austria's integration policy. This pattern will continue.

Since July 1989 Austria's application has also been overtaken by the changes in Europe, which have altered the fundamentals on which the application was based. First, the queue of states looking for closer relations with the Community has lengthened. Although EFTA-EC negotiations on the EEA were concluded, the EEA is still impeded by the EC's position that it will not accord EFTA decision-making rights in the Community, as well as the EFTA states' desire not to subordinate themselves completely to EC regulations and authority. The EEA is partly due to the EFTA-EC negotiations' slow progress, Sweden applied for EC membership in summer 1991, to piggy-back on the EC's negotiations with Austria, and EC-membership is also being seriously discussed in Norway, Switzerland, and Finland. The eastern European states, including Russia, have also said they will apply for membership as soon as their economic restructuring is far enough advanced.

This growing interest in EC membership has important implications for Austria's policy. Each time an EFTA member moved from the EFTA-EC framework towards membership, the EEA became a less viable option as the Community's and EFTA's incentives to participate in what promises to be a complicated arrangement diminish. Although new applications may prompt the EC towards negotiations, as in the 1970s, the possibility also increased the likelihood that Austria's application would again be caught up in the larger question of how the Community deals with other non-member European countries. Unless the EC altered its concern with maintaining its decision-making autonomy and developing a tighter union, and admitted another five or more members – or unless it was prepared to distinguish between Austria and other applicants – it was possible that Austria's application was submitted too late. The EC could closed its doors and forced Austria to accept the second-best solution of the EES.[55]

Initially, the Community held Austria's application in abeyance as it strove to complete the Single Market and embark on the next stages of monetary and political union. However, the EC has recently shifted its approach and selected Austria for special attention. The motive is transit traffic through Austria. The EC has realised that Austria's border controls prevent free movement overland to Italy and thus impede the Single Market. Some in the EC now suggest that Austria be given preferential participation by making its borders internal EC borders before full membership. A possible vehicle is the Schengen Treaty, which includes Germany, Italy, France, and the Benelux countries, and commits its signatories to abolish border controls *vis-à-vis* each other. Austrians are interested in participating in the Single Market from the outset, although there is concern at being asked for advance payment before membership terms are settled. Again, though, the EC's interests and agenda are setting the relationships's parameters.

The momentous changes in Eastern Europe caused this new dynamism in EC–Austrian relations. Despite the Austrians' claim that their parliament autonomously formulates neutrality policy, the relaxation of this constraint on integration policy depended ultimately on the Soviet Union's new attitude to the EC in the late 1980s and, ultimately, on the Soviet Union's collapse. Without liberalisation in the east and the relaxation of tensions that this brought, Austria would not have been able to consider membership, since the more lenient interpretation of the neutrality constraint would have been difficult to sustain domestically, as well as *vis-à-vis* the Soviet Union and the EC. Whether or not the Soviet Union could now veto Austria's application by opposing the membership plans, the pro-membership position at least would have been seriously weakened.

While Austrians made much – politically and economically – of their bridging function between east and west during the Cold War, they are gaining even more from the development of market economies in countries with which they have long-standing links. Thus, the development of a normal political environment in Europe not only facilitates Austria's closer integration with western Europe, but paradoxically opens opportunities that reduce the pressing need for this closer integration.

On the domestic side, it must be emphasised that agreements for either the EEA or EC membership must still be accepted in Austria. Membership would constitute a total revision (*wesentliche Änderung*) of the constitution, which requires approval of two-thirds of the parliament and a referendum; EES membership may be subject to the same approval process. Though the SPÖ and ÖVP are both strongly committed to the membership negotiations, the outcome may not be acceptable to one or the other. Initially, the main opposition was the SPÖ's left wing, but now the SPÖ sees that the EC could weaken the power of conservative groups, mainly in agriculture, and provide a push towards Austria's modernisation. The ÖVP has moved in the other direction. Under opposition from farmers and politicians in the western provinces who fear lower agricultural prices and loss of control over land, the ÖVP is wavering. The FPÖ may likewise temper its support under this populist pressure. The Cabinet had agreed to attach conditions to Austria's application specifying respect for Austria's neutrality, its federal system, social policies, environmental standards, and protection of the agricultural sector.[56] Sufficient scope exists in which to find an agreement unsatisfactory.

Assuming, though, that agreement is reached, what are the implications for Austrian politics? Several contributions to this volume have argued that domestic developments will lead Austria away from the archetypical consociational patterns. Further integration with the international environment will reinforce this. The examination of neutrality policy showed that an external threat to Austria's integrity played a decisive role in moving the political parties and their constituents towards co-operation. As international tensions decline, so too do the parties' incentives to develop common domestic and foreign policies. Just as important, the consociational system ultimately depends on centralised decision-making and disciplined groups so that bargains between them can be achieved and implemented. Advancing integration with the EC is inconsistent with this, since it would move the locus of decision-making and policy implementation to Brussels and bring other states and groups into the bargaining. This would make it difficult to balance the costs and benefits of political power between Austria's groups. The internationalisation of Austrian politics should also help weaken of Austrian's identification with one of two traditionally hostile political subcultures.[57] Each of these tendencies undermines the foundations of consociationalism in Austria. Therefore, inasmuch as Austria's distinctive domestic political arrangements are facilitated by isolation and external threat, further integration promises to lead to normal politics in Austria.

NOTES

The author thanks Wolfgang C. Müller for his constructive comments on an earlier draft of this article. Parts appeared in the author's doctoral thesis, submitted at Oxford University in November 1989. The author also thanks his supervisors, Jim Sharpe and Vincent Wright of Nuffield College, Oxford, and Georg Winckler of the Department of Economics of the University of Vienna for their constructive comments on the thesis. Remaining errors and omissions are, of course, the author's responsibility.

1. For consistency, this article uses EC also to refer to the European Economic Community before 1967.
2. P. J. Katzenstein, 'Dependence and Autonomy: Austria in an Interdependent World', *Österreichische Zeitschrift für Aussenpolitik* [ÖZAP], Vol. 19, No. 4 (1979), pp. 243–56, here pp. 252–54; idem, *Small States in World Markets* (Ithaca, NY: Cornell UP, 1985), pp. 34–5, 95; and M. G. Schmidt, 'Politische Steuerung der Ökonomie in Kleinstaaten', *Österreichische Zeitschrift für Politikwissenschaft* [ÖZP], Vol. 10, No. 1 (1981), pp. 77–89, here pp. 83–4.
3. 'Nationalism' is used here to denote the sense of an Austrian nation distinct from Germany, and not pan-Germanism.
4. R. Hiscocks, *The Rebirth of Austria* (London: OUP, 1953), p. 9.
5. L. Toncic-Sorinj, 'Die Entwicklung der österreichischen Außenpolitik seit dem zweiten Weltkrieg', *Europa-Archiv*, Vol. 9, No. 17 (1954), pp. 6850–1; Hiscocks, *Rebirth of Austria*, pp. 30–6, 240; and T. O. Schlesinger, *Austrian Neutrality in Postwar Europe* (Vienna: Braumüller, 1972), pp. 13–15, 140–1.
6. Schlesinger, pp. 20–35; G. Stourzh, *Geschichte des Staatsvertrages 1945–1955*, 2nd ed. (Vienna: Styria, 1980); and F. Ermacora, *20 Jahre österreichische Neutralität* (Frankfurt: Alfred Metzner, 1975), pp. 35–57.

7. E. Wallrapp, 'Die Verhandlung auf der Berliner Konferenz', *Europa-Archiv*, Vol. 9, No. 8–9 (1954), pp. 6517–22.
8. Statements by Fritz Bock, ÖVP Minister for Trade and Reconstruction in *Österreich und die EWG: Das Salzburger Expertengespräch* (Vienna: Gerold, 1964), pp. 79 and 87; and Karl Czernetz, SPÖ integration spokesman in *Arbeiter-Zeitung [AZ]*, 10 Nov. 1957, p. 2.
9. See statements by Raab to parliament during the EFTA-debate, 26 Nov. 1959, quoted in H. Mayrzedt and W. Hummer (eds.), *20 Jahre Österreichische Neutralitäts- und Europapolitik* (1955–1975), Vol. 1 (Vienna: Braumüller, 1976), p. 36; and Bock and Foreign Minister Leopold Figl (ÖVP) to the OEEC Council of Ministers, 12 Feb. 1957 in *10 Jahre österreichische Integrationspolitik: 1956–1966* (Vienna: Österreichische Staatsdruckerei, 1966), pp. 16–19.
10. *Salzburger Nachrichten*, 31 Dec. 1963, p. 4; B. Kreisky, *Die Herausforderung: Politik an der Schwelle des Atomzeitalters* (Vienna: Europa Verlag, 1965), p. 51 quoted in P. J. Katzenstein, 'Trends and Oscillations in Austrian Integration Policy Since 1955: Alternative Explanations', *Journal of Common Market Studies*, Vol. 14, No. 2 (1975), pp. 171–97, here p. 193; and *Salzburger Nachrichten*, 29 Jan. 1964, p. 2.
11. Österreichsiches Institut für Wirtschaftsforschung [WIFO], 'Zollvergleich Österreich-EWG', *Monatsberichte*, Vol. 34, No. 10 (1961), pp. 431–6; and WIFO, 'Import- und Zollschutz der österreichischen Industrieproduktion', *Monatsberichte*, Vol. 36, No. 11 (1963), pp. 416–22.
12. See comments by FPÖ leader Friedrich Peter in *Salzburger Nachrichten*, 28 Jan. 1964, pp. 2, 8; and ÖVP Economics Committee Chairperson Otto Mitterer in *Salzburger Nachrichten*, 3 Jan. 1964, p. 2.
13. Katzenstein, 'Trends and Oscillations', pp. 184–5; and A. Pelinka, 'Integration als gesellschaftliche Steuerung: Wechselwirkungen zwischen ökonomischer und politischer Integration innerhalb der EWG', *Quartalshefte der Girozentrale*, Vol. 8, No. 1–2 (1973), pp. 83–92.
14. Katzenstein, 'Trends and Oscillations', pp. 190–94.
15. 'Österreich braucht Europa', *AZ*, 10 Nov. 1957, p. 2.
16. Kreisky, *Die Herausforderung*, p. 51, quoted in Katzenstein, 'Trends', p. 193.
17. 3 Oct. 1964, quoted in *10 Jahre österreichische Integrationspolitik*, p. 210.
18. See Ermacora, *20 Jahre österreichische Neutralität*, pp. 133–4, for a comprehensive list of Soviet pronouncements on Austrian integration policy.
19. Kreisky to parliament, *Stenographisches Protokoll des Nationalrates*, 26 Nov. 1959, pp. 270–2; Raab to parliament, 23 March 1960, in Mayrzedt and Hummer (eds.), *20 Jahre*, pp. 343–4.
20. Raab to parliament, 23 March 1960, in Mayrzedt and Hummer (eds.), *20 Jahre*, p. 341.
21. Kreisky and Raab to parliament on 5 and 26 Nov. 1959, respectively, in Mayrzedt and Hummer (eds.), *20 Jahre*, pp. 332, 354.
22. 'Die politischen und institutionellen Aspekte des Beitritts zur Gemeinschaft oder Assoziierung mit ihr', doc. 122, 15 Jan. 1962. Selections reprinted in *ÖZAP*, Vol. 2, No. 3 (1962), pp. 159–68.
23. *ÖZAP*, Vol. 2, No. 5 (1961–62), pp. 288–294.
24. *Österreich und die EWG*, pp. 79–80, 85.
25. Government's 13th integration report at III-17, *Beil. z. d. Sten. Prot. des NR, XI. GP.* (1966), pp. 4–7.
26. M. Fitz, 'Die österreichische Integrationspolitik', in F. Butschek (ed.), *EWG und die Folgen* (Vienna: Fritz Molden, 1966), pp. 48–52.
27. W. Zeller, 'Die bisherige Haltung der EWG gegenüber den Neutralen', in H. Mayrzedt and H. C. Binswanger (eds.), *Die Neutralen in der Europäischen Integration: Kontroversen, Konfrontation, Alternativen* (Vienna: Braumüller, 1970), pp. 217–18.
28. Austria concluded four agreements with the European Communities: an Interim Agreement and a Comprehensive Agreement with both the EC and the European Coal and Steel Community (ECSC). For the agreements, see *Official Journal of the European Communities*, L223/1972 (EC Interim Agreement); L300/1972 (EC Comprehensive

Agreement); L228/1972 (ECSC Interim Agreement); L350/1973 (ECSC Comprehensive Agreement). All references are to the terms of Global Agreement with the EC. The agreements with the ECSC required Austrian producers to publish their prices and sales terms, submit these to the ECSC for monitoring, and to adhere to these; prohibited price discrimination (e.g. lower domestic prices); required the Austrian government to reduce Austria's production capacity through industry rationalisation; and extended tariff reductions in this 'sensitive' sector to 1980. See, e.g., J. Stankovsky 'Die österreichischen Integrationsverträge mit den Europäischen Gemeinschaften', *Monatsberichte*, Vol.47, No. 2 (1974), p. 84.
29. Origin rules specify the minimum local value-added a product must contain to be allowed duty-free movement in the free-trade area. In a multi-state free-trade area, the cumulation system defines what value of inputs sourced in one state in the area can be considered local value-added in goods produced in a second state for export to a third. Stankovsky, 'Die österreichischen Integrationsverträge', pp. 87–90 gives a detailed analysis of these rules.
30. *Sten. Prot. des NR*, 25 July 1972, passim.
31. A. Khol – ÖVP member of parliament and foreign affairs spokesman – 'Österreich und die Europäische Gemeinschaft', *Europa-Archiv*, Vol. 41, No. 24 (1986), p. 699.
32. M. Scheich, 'The European Neutrals After Enlargement of the Communities – The Austrian Perspective', *Journal of Common Market Studies*, Vol. 12 (1973), pp. 246–7.
33. 'Zur österreichischen Aussenpolitik: Vortrag vom BM für Auswärtige Angelegenheiten, Dr Willibald Pahr, am 13. Dez. 1978', *ÖZAP*, No. 4 (1979), p. 321.
34. Alois Mock [ÖVP] at *Sten. Prot. des NR*, 25 July 1972, p. 3512.
35. G. Mutz in 'Die rechtlichen Probleme der EG-Abkommen', in *Probleme der Abkommen zwischen Österreich und der Europäischen Gemeinschaft* (Vienna: Bundeskammer der gewerblichen Wirtschaft, 1973), passim; T. Öhlinger, 'Institutionelle Grundlagen der österreichischen Integrationspolitik im rechtlichen Sinn', and G. Kucera, 'Langfristige Aspekte der österreichischen Integrationspolitik', both in *Institutionelle Aspekte der österreichischen Integrationspolitik* (Vienna: Verlag der österreichischen Akademie der Wissenschaften, 1976/7), pp. 96–7, 306–8, respectively; and F. Esterbauer, 'Die Stellung Österreichs im Europäischen Integrationsprozess und die Möglichkeit einer EG-Mitgliedschaft', in F. Esterbauer and R. Hinterleitner (eds.), *Die Europäische Gemeinschaft und Österreich* (Vienna: Braumüller, 1977), p. 124.
36. Mutz, 'Die rechtlichen Probleme der EG-Abkommen' p. 51.
37. *Sten. Prot. des NR*, 25 July 1972, p. 3528.
38. 5 April 1975, in Mayrzedt and Hummer, *20 Jahre*, pp. 496–7.
39. The Social Partners are the Federal Chambers of Business and Labour, the Austrian Federation of Trade Unions (Österreichischer Gewerkschaftsbund), and the Presidents' Conference of Chambers of Agriculture. They influence government economic and social policy, primarily through the Parity Commission for Prices and Wages, which includes the Social Partners together with representatives of the responsible government ministries. See the contributions of P. Gerlich and V. Lauber in this volume.
40. See the contribution of V. Lauber to this volume.
41. F. Breuss *et al.* (eds.), *Österreichische Optionen einer EG-Annäherung und ihre Folgen* (Vienna: WIFO, 1988), pp. 139–46.
42. E.g. *Aussenpolitischer Bericht, 1985*, III-126, Beil z. d. sten. Prot. des NR, XVI. GP., pp. 42–8. Cf. the 1977 Report at III-116, Beil z. d. sten. Prot. des NR, XIV. GP., which expressed satisfaction with the status quo and foresaw little change.
43. 'Eine neue Partnerschaft für Österreich', 27 Jan. 1987, reprinted in *Pd-Aktuell*, Vol. 21, No. 1 (1987), no page.
44. A. Khol, 'In Dreisprung nach Europa: Kooperation-Assoziation-Union', *Europäische Rundschau*, Vol. 13, No. 3 (1985), pp. 29–45.
45. Khol, 'Österreich und die Europäische Gemeinschaft', pp. 703–4.
46. P. Jankowitsch, 'Österreich und Europa', *AZ*, 3 Jan. 1986, p. 8; *Süddeutsche Zeitung*, 4 Nov. 1987, p. 4; and B. Kreisky in 'Vrantizky macht uns zu einem Greisslerstaat', *Wochenpresse*, No. 1 (8 Jan. 1988), p. 18.

47. Interview, *New York Times*, 27 Nov. 1961, cited in Ermacora, p. 224.
48. *Die Presse*, 26 Nov. 1988, p. 3; and Khol, 'Österreich', p. 702.
49. *Österreich und die EWG* (Vienna: Signum, 1987). A brief version of their argument also appeared as 'Möglichkeiten und Grenzen der Dynamisierung der Beziehungen Österreichs zu den Europäischen Gemeinschaften', *Europa-Archiv*, Vol. 12 (1987), pp. 343–50.
50. E.g. comments by Soviet spokespersons cited in *AZ*, 1 Dec. 1987, p. 6; *Die Presse*, 9 Dec. 1987, p. 2, 20 May 1988, p. 2, and 14 Oct. 1988, p. 2.
51. *Die Presse*, 25 March 1987, p. 3.
52. *Die Presse*, 25 March 1987, p. 3. E. Rhein, 'Auf dem Weg zu einem westeuropäischen Wirtschaftsraum', *Europa-Archiv*, Vol. 40, No. 14 (1985), pp. 417–24.
53. *Der Bericht der Arbeitsgruppe für Europäische Integration*, selections reprinted in *Die Presse*, 24 June 1988, p. 2.
54. M. Rotter, 'Mitgliedschaft, Assoziation, EFTA-Verbund. Optionen der österreichischen EG-Politik', *ÖZP*, Vol. 18, No. 3 (1989), pp. 197–208.
55. O. Schulmeister, 'Wien und die deutsche Wiedervereinigung', *Europa-Archiv*, Vol. 45, No. 4 (1990), pp. 146–7.
56. Rotter, 'Mitgliedschaft, Assoziation, EFTA-Verbund', p. 200.
57. See the contribution of F. Plasser *et al.* in this volume.

Austrian Consociationalism: Victim of Its Own Success?

KURT RICHARD LUTHER AND WOLFGANG C. MÜLLER

Austria was long considered the prime example of consociational democracy and undoubtedly came closest to resembling that type of political system between 1945 and 1966, which we have thus termed the 'classic' phase of Austrian consociationalism. The aim of this volume was to establish whether it is still appropriate to label the Austrian political system consociational. To evaluate the extent of change, it was necessary to identify the central features of Austrian politics during 'classic' consociationalism and to trace their subsequent development. When deciding which features to investigate, we did not restrict ourselves solely to what might be deemed quintessentially consociational structures and processes, over which there is in any event some dispute. Instead, we examined six interrelated 'core characteristics' of Austrian politics up to the mid-1960s. They include what one might term both 'primary' and 'secondary' features of consociationalism and were chosen because together they determined not only the actual conduct of Austrian politics during this period, but also the characterisation of the Austrian polity by the international academic community. The six features were:

1. the persistence of encapsulated subcultures held together by a *Lagermentalität* which helped ensure very stable and predictable voting behaviour;
2. two-party dominance by the SPÖ and ÖVP of Austrian politics and of large parts of Austria's socio-economic system, in both of which the *Lager* elites' interaction was characterised by accommodation;
3. a lack of political salience of formal governmental institutions, which were limited mainly to the ritual endorsement of decisions made elsewhere, namely, primarily in intra-party and inter-party caucuses, as well as within corporatist institutions;
4. corporatism; that is to say, there was wide-ranging co-operation between Austria's large, *Lager*-based interest groups and between them and the state, above all in social and economic policy;
5. a distinctive approach to economic policy that was governed first, by a commitment to the costs and benefits of Austria's economy being

shared more equitably among the various segments of the population than had been the case during the First Republic and second, by all major political forces agreeing to eschew distributive conflicts and to pursue an economic policy designed to produce above-average economic growth;
6. foreign relations severely constrained by Austria's external circumstances. Its location at the Cold War fault-line of post-war Europe obliged it to assume a neutral foreign policy and severely limited the scope for economic integration with the European Community (EC). On the other hand, the external threat posed by Austria's geopolitical position militated in favour of domestic political co-operation.

As this volume has shown, substantial changes have occurred in all six core characteristics. First, the contribution by Plasser, Ulram and Grausgruber has established that encapsulated subcultures characterised by *Lager*-mentality and mutual hostility are no longer predominant. The socio-structural and cultural foundations of the *Lager* have been significantly eroded. In turn, this has led to much greater electoral volatility and a new pattern of electoral competition in which traditional appeals to *Lager* loyalty are much less effective. The *Lager* have not (yet) disappeared, but have become much smaller and less cohesive.

Second, Kurt Richard Luther's analysis has shown first, that the two major Austrian *Lager* parties' intra-subcultural linkages have undergone significant change, with a decline in the SPÖ and ÖVP's organisational penetration, mobilisation and hierarchical control of their respective subcultures. As organisational depillarisation has progressed, these traditional parties of mass integration have assumed a more catch-all role. Second, important changes have occurred within the *Lager* parties' intersubcultural interaction. There has been a decline in two-party concentration, in *Proporz*, in segmental autonomy and in the ubiquity of party influence. Moreover, the style of party interaction in now more competitive.

Third, Wolfgang C. Müller has clearly demonstrated that formal governmental institutions are now no longer to be regarded as mere reflections of Austria's *Lager* politics, as structures to provide formal legitimation of decisions by the two main subcultures in extra-constitutional fora. Formal rules and procedures are much more significant than they used to be. Indeed, governmental institutions appear to be becoming political actors in their own right. Fourth, the political influence of Austria's corporatist structures has passed its peak and is in decline. As Peter Gerlich argues in his essay, increasing party competition and the greater role assumed by formal governmental institutions have resulted in numerous issues being removed from corporatist intermediation. Moreover, the most fundamental organising principles of the large economic interest groups are now under serious and sustained attack while Austria's integration into the European Community will further reduce the scope and impact of its corporatist structures.

Fifth, Volkmar Lauber's analysis of developments in Austria's political economy has shown that while commitment to the traditional goals of economic policy remains, the altered economic circumstances from the mid-1980s decisively changed the instruments of that policy. In particular, there is now a far greater reliance upon market forces and a concomitant reduction in the emphasis on government intervention.

Finally, Mark Schultz's account of changes in Austria's external relations has documented two key developments. First, Europe has during recent years seen substantial changes in international trade, with perhaps the most significant being the creation of a single European economic space. In order to maintain its economic prosperity, Austria has felt obliged to renew its attempts at EC integration. Second, the end of the Cold War and the collapse of the Soviet Union has removed the last major obstacles to Austria's integration into the EC. Membership will undermine Austria's traditional consociational structures in at least two ways: the internationalisation of Austrian society will further weaken *Lager* ties, whilst EC regulations will narrow the scope for two-party control of decision-making, as well as for the main *Lager*'s capacity to maintain segmental autonomy.

Many would attribute the changes experienced by the Austrian polity since 'classic' consociationalism primarily to a fundamental transformation since the 1960s in the country's political culture, which they would in turn regard as a result largely of general socio-economic and cultural change. The argument goes as follows: processes such as urbanisation, secularisation, de-ideologisation and reduced levels of deference have combined to undermine *Lager* mentality and *Lager* cohesion. As a consequence, Austria has witnessed depillarisation and the emergence of new, party-politically much less committed population groups, many of whom reject values most central to 'classic' consociationalism. They include the so-called 'new middle classes', an as yet small group of post-materialists, as well as protest voters.

The appearance of these groups and their values has prompted important changes in the behaviour of Austria's political class. First, the traditional *Lager* elite have been forced to act more competitively. From the mid-1960s until the early 1980s, their electoral competition was no longer directed almost exclusively at mobilising their own previously loyal subcultural clientele, but at trying to win support from the growing reservoir of floating voters. The greater potential pay-offs of party competition now included absolute majorities and single party governments which ruled Austria throughout this period. Co-operation between the two main *Lager* was reduced, but two-party dominance remained. From the mid-1980s, however, increasing competition from the Third *Lager* and from the newly established Greens has resulted in a substantial decline in two-party dominance also.

Second, changes in Austria's political culture have helped enhance the country's formal political institutions. A significant proportion of the new, politically uncommitted sections of the population (and in particular of the new middle classes) are much more inclined to couch their demands in terms of classic constitutional principles such as limited government, the rule of law, public scrutiny and public accountability. As Wolfgang Müller's essay has shown, Austria's politicians and public servants are now having to take these new emphases into account when performing their roles. Moreover, some state institutions are themselves increasingly staffed by persons from the new middle classes. Institutions in which constitutional norms have become more important include the judiciary, the constitutional court and the bureaucracy.

Third, value change has mattered in corporatism's decline and in the re-orientation of Austria's economic policy. For one, the new middle classes' more participatory orientation conflicts with the secretive and oligarchic practices of the old corporatist structures. Furthermore, many values pursued by the large, *Lager*-based interest groups, that dominated the corporatist system in which much of Austria's economic policy was traditionally formulated, stand in direct contrast to the new values espoused by the new middle classes. These include higher levels of commitment to deregulation and market competition, as well as to environmentalism, or ecology.

However, change to Austrian politics since 'classic' consociationalism cannot adequately be explained solely by Austria's political sociology, however significant the accompanying value changes might have been. Instead, one must assess the key role which Austria's political elites have played and continue to play. Indeed, the capacity of political leaders to overcome the assumed constraints of an existing political culture is crucial to consociational theory. First, in 1945, when Austria's political elites decided to engage in overarching political accommodation, the country's political culture was still dominated by *Lager* hostility. The accommodative structures and procedures of Austrian politics for at least the two subsequent decades were thus arguably adopted in spite Austria's political culture, rather than because of it.

Second, the maintenance of *Lager* encapsulation owed much to the deliberate behaviour of the subcultural political elites, whose highly efficient organisational penetration of their respective subcultures facilitated the political system's petrification around the two main *Lager*. Moreover, the 'propaganda battles' of elections during the Second Republic's first two decades helped ensure that *Lager* hostility remained higher than might otherwise have been the case. Third, two decades of co-operation between the leaders of Austria's two main subcultures none the less reduced *Lager* distrust and itself contributed much to the reform of Austrian political culture.

Fourth, the accommodative practices which stabilised the political system in the early post-war years relied upon hierarchical subcultural organisations and oligarchic decision-making. Lacking effective accountability, the *Lager* elites became increasingly remote from the grassroots of their subcultures. The high-handed and in part corrupt behaviour of certain members of Austria's elite cartel has resulted in many Austrians being alienated from the political class as a whole and has thus also contributed to a decline in *Lager* mentality.

To summarise, the transformation of the Austrian polity which this volume has documented is mainly the result of a complex interplay between on the one hand Austria's political sociology and value system and on the other the behaviour of its political elites. Value change certainly has altered the bases of political competition, but has in turn been influenced by elite behaviour. How Austria's political elites have chosen to respond to the altered domestic political environment has itself affected the speed and direction of change. Finally, alterations to Austria's external environment have also mattered in Austrian politics, albeit in a manner beyond Austria's immediate control. In particular, the external threat and economic isolation which originally facilitated Austrian consociationalism no longer apply. The result has been a move towards greater European integration, which will further increase pressures for domestic political reform.

The distinguishing features of a consociational democracy are the coexistence of first, a vertically fragmented social structure with encapsulated and mutually hostile subcultures and second, overarching elite behaviour designed to stabilise a political system, the viability of which would otherwise be under threat. The overall message of this volume is that the cumulative changes to Austrian politics since the 1960s have radically transformed their consociational nature. First, the attitudinal and organisational bases of pillarisation have been fatally undermined. Austrians are no longer as deferential and encapsulated, while the *Lager* parties' hierarchical control of their subcultures has diminished.

Second, elite political behaviour has become more competitive and such co-operation as persists is no longer governed by a perceived need to prevent a potential imminent collapse of the political system. For its survival is no longer threatened by such competition. For example, the prime rationale of the present grand coalition is not system maintenance. Instead, the SPÖ and ÖVP are co-operating to minimise the electoral fallout from the current re-orientation of Austria's economic policy. Moreover, grand coalition government and other traditional practices of consociational co-operation are being challenged from both neo-liberal and populist perspectives, which despite their differences both reject principles and practices of the elite cartel that dominated most of post-war Austrian politics. Reduced deference and increasingly critical orientations have meant a substantial growth in protest voting. The main beneficiary has of late been the FPÖ, which has attacked central features of 'classic' consociationalism, including two-party concentration, mutual veto, *Junktim*, and other expressions of *Lager* accommodation, as well as corporatism, *Proporz* and segmental autonomy.

Austrian consociationalism undeniably produced undesirable side effects, including inefficiency, a lack of democratic accountability and recurrent political corruption. These and other legacies of rule by Austria's elite cartel continue to pose a challenge for the Austrian polity. However, very real successes were achieved by Austrian consociationalism both during its 'classic' phase and since. It provided the country with levels of economic prosperity and political stability that compare very favourably with not only the post-war experience of most other advanced Western nations, but above all with the crises of distribution, incorporation and legitimacy within the first, interwar Austrian republic (see the opening chapter of this volume).

As long ago as 1977, Lijphart characterised consociational democracy as a 'passing phase' and argued that change in Austrian consociationalism was coming about not because consociationalism had failed, but 'because consociationalism by its very success has begun to make itself superfluous' (*Democracy in Plural Societies*, p.2). That process is now virtually complete. The consociational structures and techniques practised during 'classic' consociationalism and since have changed the Austrian polity so fundamentally that Austrian consociationalism has indeed made itself redundant. It has become the victim of its own success.

Appendix 1: Distribution of Votes at National Council Elections (1945–1990)

	1945	1949	1953	1956	1959	1962	1966	1970	1971	1975	1979	1983	1986	1990
SPÖ[1]	44.6	38.7	42.1	43.0	44.8	44.0	42.6	48.4	50.0	51.0	51.0	47.6	43.1	43.0
ÖVP[2]	49.8	44.0	41.3	46.0	44.2	45.4	48.3	44.7	43.1	43.0	41.9	43.2	41.3	32.1
FPÖ[3]	–	11.7	11.0	6.5	7.7	7.1	5.4	5.5	5.5	5.4	6.1	5.0	9.7	16.6
KPÖ[4]	5.4	5.1	5.3	4.4	3.3	3.0	0.4	1.0	1.4	1.2	1.0	0.7	0.7	0.5
Greens													4.8	4.5
VGÖ[5]												1.9	–	1.9
ALÖ[6]												1.4		
DFP[7]							3.3	0.4						
Others	0.2	0.5	0.4	0.1	0.1	0.5	0.1	0.1	0.04	0.03	0.1	0.1	0.3	1.2
Turnout	94.3	96.8	95.8	96.0	94.2	93.8	93.8	91.8	92.4	92.9	92.2	92.6	90.5	86.1
Rae (Fe)	0.55	0.64	0.64	0.60	0.60	0.59	0.58	0.56	0.56	0.56	0.56	0.58	0.63	0.68

Sources: Election results 1949–86: Bundesministerium für Inneres (ed.), *Die Nationalratswahl vom 23 November 1986* (Vienna: Österreichische Staatsdruckerei, 1987), p. 59; 1990: Bundesministerium für Inneres *Nationalratswahl 1990. Endgültiges Ergebnis* (Vienna: computer print-out dated 18 Oct. 1990). Index based on own calculations.

Notes:
1. *Sozialistische Partei Österreichs* (Socialist Party of Austria)
2. *Österreichische Volkspartei* (Austrian People's Party)
3. *Freiheitliche Partei Österreichs* (Freedom Party of Austria); 1949 and 1953: *Verband der Unabhängigen* (League of Independents)
4. *Kommunistische Partei Österreichs* (Communist Party of Austria)
5. *Vereinte Grünen Österreichs* (United Green Party of Austria)
6. *Alternative Liste Österreichs* (Alternative List of Austria)
7. *Demokratische Fortschrittspartei* (Democratic Progress Party)

Appendix 2: Distribution of National Council Seats (1945–1990)[1]

		1945	1949	1953	1956	1959	1962	1966	1970	1971	1975	1979	1983	1986	1990
SPÖ	(abs)	76	67	73	74	78	76	74	81	93	93	95	90	80	80
	(%)	46	41	44	45	47	46	45	49	51	51	52	49	44	44
ÖVP	(abs)	85	77	74	82	79	81	85	78	80	80	77	81	77	60
	(%)	52	47	45	50[2]	48	49	52	47	44	44	42	44	42	33
FPÖ[3]	(abs)	–	16	14	6	8	8	6	6	10	10	11	12	18	33
	(%)	–	10	8	4	5	5	4	4	5	5	6	7	10	18
KPÖ	(abs)	4	5	4	3										
	(%)	2	3	2	2										
Greens	(abs)													8	10
	(%)													4	5
Rae Index (F_p)		0.52	0.61	0.60	0.55	0.54	0.54	0.53	0.53	0.55	0.55	0.55	0.56	0.62	0.67

Sources: As in Appendix 1.
Notes: 1. Total number of seats rose in 1971 from 165 to 183. Due to rounding, percentages do not always total 100.
2. Significantly, the ÖVP had one seat short of an absolute majority (49.7 per cent before rounding up).
3. 1949–1953: *Verband der Unabhängigen* (League of Independents).

Appendix 3: Presidential Elections in Austria since 1945

Candidates	Nominating parties	Number of votes	Percentages of votes
First ballot			
6 May 1951 (turnout 96.8 per cent)			
Dr Burghard Breitner	VdU	662,502	15.41
Gottlieb Fiala	KPÖ	219,969	5.12
Dr Heinrich Gleissner	ÖVP	1,725,451	40.14
Ludovica Hainisch	–	2,132	0.05
Theodor Körner	SPÖ	1,682,881	39.15
Dr Johannes Ude	–	5,413	0.13
Second ballot			
27 May 1951 (turnout 96.9 per cent)			
Dr Heinrich Gleissner	ÖVP	2,006,332	47.94
Theodor Körner	SPÖ	2,178,631	52.06
5 May 1957 (turnout 97.2 per cent)			
Dr Wolfgang Denk	ÖVP-FPÖ	2,159,604	48.88
Dr Adolf Schärf	SPÖ	2,258,255	51.12
28 April 1963 (turnout 95.6 per cent)			
Dr Josef Kimmel	FPÖ	176,646	4.0
Dr Julius Raab	ÖVP	1,814,125	40.6
Dr Adolf Schärf	SPÖ	2,473,349	55.4
23 May 1965 (turnout 96 per cent)			
Dr Alfons Gorbach	ÖVP	2,260,888	49.3
Franz Jonas	SPÖ	2,342,436	50.7
25 April 1971 (turnout 95.3 per cent)			
Franz Jonas	SPÖ	2,487,239	52.8
Dr Kurt Waldheim	ÖVP	2,224,809	47.2
23 June 1974 (turnout 94.1 per cent)			
Dr Rudolf Kirchschläger	SPÖ	2,392,367	51.7
Dr Alois Lugger	ÖVP	2,238,470	48.3
18 May 1980 (turnout 91.6 per cent)			
Dr Norbert Burger	–	140,741	3.2
Dr Wilfried Gredler	FPÖ	751,400	16.9
Dr Rudolf Kirchschläger	SPÖ	3,538,748	79.9
First ballot			
4 May 1986 (turnout 89.5 per cent)			
Freda Blau-Meissner	Greens	259,689	5.5
Dr Otto Scrinzi	–	55,724	1.2
Dr Kurt Steyrer	SPÖ	2,061,104	43.7
Dr Kurt Waldheim	ÖVP	2,343,463	49.6
Second ballot			
8 June 1986 (turnout 87.3 per cent)			
Dr Kurt Steyrer	SPÖ	2,107,023	46.1
Dr Kurt Waldheim	ÖVP	2,464,787	53.9

Source: *Österreichisches Jahrbuch für Politik* 1986, p. 839.
Note: The first president of the Second Republic, Dr Karl Renner, was not directly elected by the people but by the two houses of parliament in 1945.

Appendix 4: Austrian Cabinets since 1945

Cabinet	Date in	Date out	Duration (in years)	Party composition
Renner	27.4.1945	20.12.1945	0.6	SPÖ-ÖVP-KPÖ
Figl (I)	20.12.1945	20.11.1947	1.9	ÖVP-SPÖ-KPÖ
Figl (II)	20.11.1947	8.11.1949	2.0	ÖVP-SPÖ
Figl (III)	8.11.1949	2.4.1953	3.4	ÖVP-SPÖ
Raab (I)	2.4.1953	29.6.1956	3.2	ÖVP-SPÖ
Raab (II)	29.6.1956	16.7.1959	3.0	ÖVP-SPÖ
Raab (III)	16.7.1959	11.4.1961	1.7	ÖVP-SPÖ
Gorbach (I)	11.4.1961	27.3.1963	2.0	ÖVP-SPÖ
Gorbach (II)	27.3.1963	2.4.1964	1.0	ÖVP-SPÖ
Klaus (I)	2.4.1964	19.4.1966	2.0	ÖVP-SPÖ
Klaus (II)	19.4.1966	21.4.1970	4.0	ÖVP
Kreisky (I)	21.4.1970	4.11.1971	1.5	SPÖ
Kreisky (II)	4.11.1971	28.10.1975	4.0	SPÖ
Kreisky (III)	28.10.1975	5.6.1979	3.6	SPÖ
Kreisky (IV)	5.6.1979	24.5.1983	4.0	SPÖ
Sinowatz	24.5.1983	16.6.1986	3.0	SPÖ-FPÖ
Vranitzky (I)	16.6.1986	21.1.1987	0.6	SPÖ-FPÖ
Vranitzky (II)	21.1.1987	17.12.1990	4.0	SPÖ-ÖVP
Vranitzky (III)	17.12.1990	?	?	SPÖ-ÖVP

Source: W. C. Müller, 'Regierung und Kabinettsystem', in H. Dachs *et al.*, *Handbuch des politischen Systems Österreichs* (Vienna: Manz, 1991), p. 119.

Note: To define a cabinet the criteria 'same chancellor', 'same party composition' and 'between parliamentary elections' were used.

Appendix 5: English Language Sources for the Study of Austrian Politics

INTRODUCTORY REMARKS

Despite the fact that Austria had been held by many political scientists writing on themes such as electoral behaviour, consociationalism and corporatism to constitute a fascinating, in many respects almost archetypical case study, there is a surprising and regrettable paucity of political science literature on Austrian politics. In particular, there are relatively few English-language sources. Moreover, much of the most interesting English language material takes the form of journal articles, or is secreted in contributions to thematic edited volumes and is thus not always easy for the non-specialist to locate.

The intention of the following bibliography is to assist non-specialist English language readers interested in investigating Austrian politics during the Second Republic (i.e., since 1945), though it also contains a number of key publications on aspects of Austrian history which the editors consider to be important for an understanding of more recent political developments. The bibliography is limited in the main to materials published in English. Relevant German-language publications on themes covered in this volume are contained in the endnotes accompanying its individual contributions, as well as in the bibliographical sources listed under 1.1 below.

This bibliography excludes conference papers and similar materials. Readers wishing to pursue such possible sources further are advised to consult lists of papers read since the 1960s at the conferences of the American Political Science Association and the International Political Science Association, at both of which a number of interesting papers on Austria have been delivered. There have also been a number of papers on Austrian politics read at the annual Joint Sessions of the European Consortium for Political Research, from which lists of papers and copies of those read since 1973 can be obtained. (The ECPR's secretariat is located at the University of Essex, Colchester, England).

1. GENERAL SOURCES

1.1 Bibliographies

None in English. Some specialised bibliographies in German language books include the relevant English language publications. See, for example: A. Pelinka and F. Plasser (eds.), *Das österreichische Parteiensystem* (Vienna: Böhlau, 1988), pp. 753–68 on parties; P. Gerlich, E. Grande and W. C. Müller (eds.), *Sozialpartnerschaft in der Krise* (Vienna: Böhlau, 1985), pp. 367–95 on corporatism; and *Handbuch des politischen Systems Österreichs*, ed. by H. Dachs, P. Gerlich, H. Gottweis, F. Horner, H. Kramer, V. Lauber, W. C. Müller and E. Tálos (Vienna: Manz, 1991) on a variety of subjects.

International Political Science Abstracts

1.2. Periodicals

The *Österreichische Zeitschrift für Politikwissenschaft* publishes German language articles, but they are all accompanied by English language abstracts.

Politics and Society in Germany, Austria and Switzerland
German Politics, a three times a year journal founded in 1992, includes articles on Austria.

1.3. Surveys of Austrian Political Science

P. Gerlich, E. Tálos and K. Ucakar, 'Austria', in W.G. Andrews (ed.), *International Handbook of Political Science* (Westport, CT: Greenwood Press, 1982), pp. 85–92.
F. Karlhofer and A. Pelinka, 'Austrian Political Science: The State of the Art', *European Journal of Political Research*, Vol. 20 (1991), pp. 399–411.

1.4. Textbooks

K. Steiner, *Politics in Austria* (Boston, MA: Little, Brown, 1972).

1.5. General Works

H. Siegler, *Austria. Problems and Achievements 1945–1963* (Bonn: Siegler & Co., 1967).
K. Steiner (ed.), *Modern Austria* (Palo Alto, CA: SPOSS, 1981).
—— (ed.), *Tradition and Innovation in Contemporary Austria* (Palo Alto, CA: SPOSS, 1982).
J. Sweeney and J. Weidenholzer (eds.), *Austria: A Study in Modern Achievement* (Aldershot: Gower, 1988).
M. A. Sully, *A Contemporary History of Austria* (London: Routledge, 1990).
J. Fitzmaurice, *Austrian Politics and Society Today* (London: Macmillan, 1991).

1.6. Government Publications

Austrian Foreign Policy Yearbook (Vienna: Bundesministerium für Auswärtige Angelegenheiten).
Statistisches Handbuch für die Republik Österreich (Vienna: Österreichisches Statistisches Zentralamt).
Die Nationalratswahl (Vienna: Bundesministerium für Inneres).
Die Bundespräsidentenwahl (Vienna: Bundesministerium für Inneres).

2. HISTORY

2.1 Bibliographies and Periodicals

Austrian History Yearbook (1965ff) contains a bibliography.
Österreichische Historische Bibliographie.

2.2. General Texts

E. H. Buschbeck, *Austria* (London: OUP, 1949).
K. R. Stadler, *Austria* (London: Ernest Benn, 1971).
E. Barker, *Austria 1918–1972* (London: Macmillan, 1973).
W. M. Johnston, *The Austrian Mind – An Intellectual and Social History 1948–1938* (Berkeley, CA: Univ. of California P., 1972).
B. Jelavich, *Modern Austria. Empire and Republic, 1815–1986* (CUP, 1987).

2.3. Monarchy (until 1918)

R. J. W. Evans, *The Making of the Habsburg Monarchy 1550–1700* (OUP, 1979).
R. A. Kann, *A History of the Habsburg Empire 1526–1918* (Berkeley, CA: Univ. of California P., 1974).

C. A. Macartney, *The Habsburg Empire 1790–1918* (London: Weidenfeld & Nicolson, 1968).
H. J. Gordon and N. M. Gordon, *The Austrian Empire: Abortive Federation?* (Lexington, MA: Heath, 1980).

2.4. First Republic (1918–1934)

Ch. A. Gulick, *Austria. From Habsburg to Hitler*, 2 vols. (Berkeley, CA: Univ. of California P., 1948).
F. L. Carsten, *The First Austrian Republic 1918–1938* (Aldershot: Gower, 1986).
C. A. Macartney, *The Social Revolution in Austria* (London, 1926).
—— 'The Armed Formations in Austria', *Journal of the Royal Institute of International Affairs*, Vol. 8 (1929), pp. 617–32.
—— 'Austria Since 1928', *Slavonic and East European Review*, Vol. 7, No. 20 (1929), pp. 288–307.
M. Macdonald, *The Republic of Austria 1918–1934: A Study in the Failure of Democratic Government* (London: OUP, 1948).
K. R. Stadler, *The Birth of the Austrian Republic 1918–1921* (Leiden: A. W. Sijrhoff, 1966).
D. F. Strong, *Austria (October 1918–March 1919). Transition from Empire to Republic* (NY: Columbia UP, 1939).
W. B. Simon, 'Democracy in the Shadow of Imposed Sovereignty: The First Republic of Austria', in J. J. Linz and A. Stepan (eds.), *The Breakdown of Democratic Regimes. Europe* (Baltimore, MD: Johns Hopkins UP, 1978), pp. 80–121.

2.5. Austrofascism and Nazism

M. Kitchen, *The Coming of Austrian Fascism* (London: Croom Helm, 1980).
F. L. Carsten, *Fascist Movements in Austria – From Schönerer to Hitler* (London: Sage, 1977).
A. G. Whiteside, 'Austria', in H. Rogger and E. Weber (eds.), *The European Right* (Berkeley, CA: Univ. of California P., 1965), pp. 308–63.
—— *The Socialism of Fools. Georg Ritter von Schönerer and Austrian Pan-Germanism* (Berkeley, CA: California UP, 1975).
B. F. Pauley, 'Nazis and Heimwehr Fascists: The Struggle for Supremacy in Austria, 1918–1938', in S. U. Larsen, B. Hegtvet and J. P. Myklebust (eds.), *Who Were the Fascists* (Bergen: Universitetsforlaget, 1980), pp. 226–38.
—— *Hitler and the Forgotten Nazis. A History of the Austrian National Socialism* (Chapel Hill: Univ. of North Carolina P., 1981).
G. Botz, 'The Changing Patterns of Social Support for Austrian National Socialism (1918–1945)', in Larsen, Hegtvet and Myklebust (eds.), *Who Were the Fascists*, pp. 202–25.
—— 'Austria', in D. Mühlberger (ed.), *The Social Basis of European Fascist Movements* (London: Croom Helm, 1987), pp. 242–80.
G. Brook-Shepherd, *Anschluss: The Rape of Austria* (London: Greenwood Press, 1977).
R. V. Luza, *The Resistance in Austria, 1938–1945* (Minneapolis: Univ. of Minnesota P., 1984).
F. Molden, *Fires in the Night. The Sacrifices and Significance in the Austrian Resistance 1938–1945* (Boulder, CO: Westview Press, 1989).
G.-K. Kindermann, *Hitler's Defeat in Austria 1933–1934: Europe's First Containment of Nazi Expansionism* (London: Hurst, 1988).

2.6. Special Studies

A. Diamant, *Austrian Catholics and the First Republic* (NJ: Princeton UP, 1960).

J. W. Boyer, *Political Radicalism in Late Imperial Vienna. Origins of the Christian Social Movement 1848–1897* (Univ. of Chicago P., 1981).

C. E. Edmondson, *The Heimwehr and Austrian Politics 1818–1936* (Athens, GA: Univ. of Georgia P., 1978).

P. J. Katzenstein, *Disjoined Partners. Austria and Germany since 1915* (Berkeley, CA: Univ. of California P., 1976).

P. Pulzer, *The Rise of Political Anti-Semitism in Germany and Austria*, rev. ed. (London: Peter Halban, 1988).

R. Bassett, *Waldheim and Austria* (London: Penguin Viking, 1988).

G. Botz, *The Waldheim Case: Analysis of Austria's Nazi Past* (Boulder, CO: Westview Press, 1989).

J. Dixon, *Defeat and Disarmament: Allied Diplomacy and the Politics of Military Affairs in Austria, 1918–1922* (Cranbury, NJ: Univ. of Delaware P., 1986).

K. Harms et al. (ed.), *Coping with the Past: Germany and Austria after 1945* (Madison, WI: Univ. of Wisconsin P., 1991).

H.-G. Heinrich and S. Wiatr, *Political Culture in Vienna and Warsaw* (Boulder, CO: Westview Press, 1991).

J. Lewis, *Fascism and the Working Class in Austria 1918–34* (Oxford: Berg, 1991).

P. Pulzer, 'Three Themes on Austrian Politics', *West European Politics*, Vol. 9, No. 2 (April 1986), pp. 298–306.

P. J. Katzenstein, 'The Last Old Nation: Austrian National Consciousness Since 1945', *Comparative Politics*, Vol. 1 (1977), pp. 147–71.

F. Fellner, 'The Problem of the Austrian Nation after 1945', *Journal of Modern History*, Vol. 60 (1988), pp. 264–89.

R. H. Keyserlingk, *Austria in World War II: An Anglo-American Dilemma* (Univ. of Toronto P., 1988).

3. POLITICAL INSTITUTIONS

3.1. Political Institutions: General

The Austrian Constitution has been translated into English, though, this translation does not include the more recent amendments:

The Austrian Federal Constitution, 2nd ed. (Vienna: Manz, 1983).

The classical English text is:
K. Steiner, *Politics in Austria* (Boston, MA: Little, Brown, 1972).

Chapters on most institutions are included in:
K. Steiner (ed.), *Modern Austria* (Palo Alto, CA: SPOSS, 1981).

3.2. Parliament

O. Kirchheimer, 'The Waning of Opposition in Parliamentary Regimes', *Social Research*, Vol. 24 (1957), pp. 127–56.

R. Preston, 'Austrian Parliamentary Democracy', *Parliamentary Affairs*, Vol. 10, No. 3 (1957), pp. 344–52.

F. C. Engelmann, 'Austria: The Pooling of Opposition', in R. A. Dahl (ed.), *Political Opposition in Western Democracies* (New Haven, CT: Yale UP, 1966), pp. 260–83.

H. Fischer, 'Elections and Parliament', in K. Steiner (ed.), *Modern Austria* (Palo Alto, CA: SPOSS, 1981), pp. 251–59.

A. Pelinka, 'The Case of Austria: Neo-Corporatism and Social Partnership', in V. Bogdanor (ed.), *Representatives of the People?* (Aldershot: Gower, 1985), pp. 184–98.

P. Gerlich, 'Theories of Legislation: Some Austrian Evidence and General Conclusions', *European Journal of Political Research*, Vol. 14 (1986), pp. 357–68.

The formation of one government coalition is dealt with in:

F. C. Engelmann, 'Hagging for the Equilibrium: The Renegotiation of the Austrian Coalition, 1959', *American Political Science Review*, Vol. 56 (1962), pp. 651–62.

3.3. Cabinet

P. Gerlich, W. C. Müller, 'Austria: Routine and Ritual', in J. Blondel and F. Müller-Rommel (eds.), *Cabinets in Western Europe* (London: Macmillan, 1988), pp. 138–50.

P. Gerlich, W. C. Müller, W. Philipp, 'Potentials and Limitations of Executive Leadership: the Austrian Cabinet since 1945, *European Journal of Political Research*, Vol. 16 (1988), pp. 191–205.

H. P. Secher, 'Coalition Government: The Case of the Second Austrian Republic', *American Political Science Review*, Vol. 52 (1958), pp. 791–809.

J. Dreijmanis, 'Austria – the "Black" – "Red" Coalitions', in E. C. Browne and J. Dreijmanis (eds.), *Government Coalitions in Western Democracies* (NY: Longman, 1982), pp. 237–59.

W. C. Müller and H. A. Bubendorfer, 'Rule-Breaking in the Austrian Cabinet: Its Management and its Consequences', *Corruption and Reform*, Vol. 4 (1989), pp. 131–45.

3.4. Presidency

E. C. Kollmann, 'The Austrian Presidency, 1918–1959', *Austrian History Yearbook*, Vol. 1 (1965), pp. 90–117.

M. Duverger, 'Iceland, Ireland and Austria: The Sterilization of the Presidential Election by the Party System', in R. L. McCormick (ed.), *Political Parties and the Modern State* (NY: Rutgers UP, 1984), pp. 87–107.

3.5. Bureaucracy

R. F. Kneucker, 'Austria: An Administrative State. The Role of Austrian Bureaucracy', *Österreichische Zeitschrift für Politikwissenschaft*, Vol. 2 (1973), pp. 95–117.

—— 'Public Administration', in K. Steiner (ed.), *Modern Austria* (Palo Alto, CA: SPOSS, 1981), pp. 261–78.

3.6. Constitutional Court

The history of this institution is dealt with in

W. R. Dallmayr, 'Background and Development of the Austrian Constitutional Court', *Journal of Central European Affairs*, Vol. 21 (1962), pp. 403–33.

Its structure and functioning is analysed in

M. Welan, 'Constitutional Review and Legislation in Austria', in C. Langfried (ed.), *Constitutional Review and Legislation* (Baden-Baden: Nomos, 1988), pp. 63–80.

3.7. Federalism

C. Altenstetter, 'Intergovernmental Profiles in the Federal Systems of Austria and West Germany: A Comparative Perspective', *Publius*, Vol. 5 (1975), pp. 89–116.
T. Öhlinger, 'Centralizing and Decentralizing Trends in the Austrian Constitution', in C. L. Brown-John (ed.), *Centralizing and Decentralizing Trends in Federal States* (Lanham, MD: UP of America, 1988).
P. Pernthaler, *Federal Fiscal Relations in Austria* (Canberra: Occasional Paper No. 30, Centre for Research on Federal Financial Relations, Australian National Univ., 1983).
F. C. Engelmann and M. A. Schwartz, 'Perceptions of Austrian Federalism', *Publius*, Vol. 11 (1981), pp. 81–93.
R. Luther, 'The Revitalization of Federalism and Federation in Austria', in M. D. Burgess (ed.), *Federalism and Federation in Western Europe* (London: Croom Helm, 1986), pp. 154–86.

3.8. Regional and Local Government

W. Crane, Jr., *The Legislature of Lower Austria* (London: Hansard, 1961).
—— 'The Errand-Running Function of Austrian Legislators', *Parliamentary Affairs*, Vol. 15 (1962), pp. 160–69.
P. Gerlich, 'Orientations to Decision-Making in the Vienna City Council', in S. C. Patterson and J. C. Wahlke (eds.), *Comparative Legislative Behavior: Frontiers of Research* (NY: Wiley-Interscience, 1972), pp. 87–106.

4. PARTIES

4.1. Parties and the Party System: General

In chronological order of publication:
W. B. Simon, *The Political Parties of Austria* (Michigan: Ann Arbor repr. of Columbia Univ. Diss., 1957).
H. P. Secher, 'Austria's Survival', in J. S. Roucek (ed.), *Contemporary Political Ideologies* (NY: Philosophical Library, 1961), pp. 345–78.
P. Pulzer, 'The Legitimizing Role of Political Parties: The Second Austrian Republic', *Government and Opposition*, Vol. 4 (1969), pp. 324–44.
—— 'Austria', in S. Henig and J. Pinder (eds.), *European Political Parties* (London: Allen & Unwin, 1969), pp. 282–319.
M. Mommsen-Reindl, 'Austria', in P. H. Merkl (ed.), *Western European Party Systems* (NY: Free Press, 1980), pp. 278–97.
M. A. Sully, *Political Parties and Elections in Austria* (London: Hurst, 1981).
M. J. E. Král, 'Austria', in V. E. McHale and S. Skowronski (eds.), *Political Parties of Europe*, Vol. 1 (Westport, CT: Greenwood Press, 1983), pp. 21–54.
P. Gerlich, 'Consocialism to Competition: The Austrian Party System since 1945' in H. Daalder (ed.), *Party Systems in Denmark, Austria, Switzerland, the Netherlands and Belgium* (London: Pinter, 1987), pp. 61–106.
F. C. Engelmann, 'The Austrian Party System: Continuity and Change', in S. B. Wolinetz (ed.), *Parties and Party Systems in Liberal Democracies* (London: Routledge, 1988), pp. 84–104.
A. Pelinka and F. Plasser (eds.), *The Austrian Party System* (Boulder, CO: Westview Press, 1989).
K. R. Luther, 'Dimensions of Party System Change: The Case of Austria', *West European Politics*, Vol. 12, No. 4 (Oct. 1989), pp. 3–27.

F. Jacobs, 'Austria', in F. Jacobs (ed.), *Western European Political Parties. A Comprehensive Guide* (Harlow: Longman, 1989), pp. 478–99.

4.2. Parties and the Party System: Specific Features

A number of studies in:
A. Pelinka and F. Plasser (eds.), *The Austrian Party System* (Boulder, CO: Westview Press, 1989).

Other specialised studies are:
F. Horner, 'Austria 1949–1979', in I. Budge, D. Robertson and D. Hearl (eds.), *Ideology, Strategy and Party Change: Spatial Analyses of Post-War Election Programmes in 19 Democracies* (CUP, 1987), pp. 270–93.
W. C. Müller and D. Meth-Cohn, 'The Selection of Party Leaders in Austria: A Study in Intra-Party Decision-Making', *European Journal of Political Research*, Vol. 20 (1991), pp. 39–65.
W. C. Müller and F. Plasser, 'Austria: The 1990 Campaign', in S. Bowler and D. M. Farrell (eds.), *Electoral Strategies and Political Marketing* (London: Macmillan, 1992).
W. C. Müller, 'Austria, 1945–1990', in R. S. Katz and P. Mair (eds.), *The Development of Party Organizations in Western Democracies, 1960–1990: A Data Handbook* (London: Sage, 1992).

4.3. Individual Parties and Ideological Groupings

Socialists

V. J. Knapp, *Austrian Social Democracy 1889–1914* (Washington, DC: UP of America, 1980).
J. Buttinger, *In the Twilight of Socialism: A History of the Revolutionary Socialists of Austria* (NY: Praeger, 1953).
A. Rabinbach, *The Crisis of Austrian Socialism. From Red Vienna to Civil War* (NY: Univ. of Chicago P., 1983).
—— (ed.), *The Austrian Socialist Experiment. Social Democracy and Austromarxism, 1918–34* (Boulder, CO: Westview Press, 1985).
W. F. Hahn, 'The Socialist Party of Austria: Retreat from Marx', *Journal of Central European Affairs*, Vol. 15 (1955), pp. 115–33.
H. P. Secher, 'The Socialist Party of Austria: Principles, Organization, and Policies', *Midwest Journal of Political Science*, Vol. 3 (1959), pp. 277–99.
K. L. Shell, *The Transformation of Austrian Socialism* (State Univ. of NY Press, 1962).
M. A. Sully, 'Austrian Social Democracy', in W. E. Paterson and A. H. Thomas (eds.), *The Future of Social Democracy* (Oxford: Clarendon Press, 1986), pp. 153–71.
—— *Continuity and Change in Austrian Socialism* (NY: Columbia UP, 1982).

Conservatives

W. C. Müller, 'Conservatism and the Transformation of the Austrian People's Party', in B. Girvin (ed.), *The Transformation of Contemporary Conservatism* (London: Sage, 1988), pp. 98–119.
—— 'The Catch-All Party Thesis and the Austrian Social Democrats', *German Politics*, Vol. 1, No. 2 (Aug. 1992).

German-Nationals/Freedom Party

M. E. Riedlsperger, *The Lingering Shadow of Nazism: The Austrian Independent Party Movement since 1945* (NY: Columbia UP, 1978).

K. R. Luther, 'The Freiheitliche Partei Österreichs: protest party or governing party?', in E. J. Kirchner (ed.), *Liberal Parties in Western Europe* (CUP, 1988), pp. 213–51.

F. Parkinson (ed.), *Conquering the Past. Austrian Nazism Yesterday & Today* (Detroit, MI: Wayne State UP, 1989).

Communist

D. Devlin, 'Czechoslovakia and the Crisis of Austrian Communism', *Studies in Comparative Communism*, Vol. 2 (1969), pp. 9–37.

Greens

H. Dachs, 'Citizen Lists and Green-Alternative Parties in Austria', in A. Pelinka and F. Plasser (eds.), *The Austrian Party System* (Boulder, CO: Westview Press, 1989), pp. 173–96.

C. Haerpfer, 'The "United Greens" and the "Alternative List/Green Alternative"', in F. Müller-Rommel (ed.), *New Politics in Western Europe* (Boulder, CO: Westview Press, 1989), pp. 23–37.

M. Kreuzer, 'New Politics: Just Post-Materialist? The Case of the Austrian and Swiss Greens', *West European Politics*, Vol. 13, No. 1 (Jan. 1990), pp. 12–30.

5. THE MEDIA, INTEREST GROUPS, CORPORATISM AND NEW SOCIAL MOVEMENTS

H. Feichtlbauer, 'The Media', in K. Steiner (ed.), *Modern Austria* (Palo Alto, CA: SPOSS, 1981), pp. 279–98.

A. Diamant, 'The Group Basis of Austrian Politics', *Journal of Central European Affairs*, Vol. 18 (1958), pp. 134–55.

H. P. Secher, 'Representative Democracy or "Chamber State": The Ambiguous Role of Interest Groups in Austrian Politics', *Western Political Quarterly*, Vol. 13 (1960), pp. 890–909.

F. Fürstenberg, 'Wage Setting in the Austrian System of Social and Economic Partnership: Structure and Functioning of Social Contracts', in R. Blandy and J. Niland (ed.), *Alternatives to Arbitration* (N. Sydney: Allen & Unwin, 1986), pp. 201–18.

P. Gerlich, E. Grande and W. C. Müller, 'Corporatism in Crisis: Stability and Change of Social Partnership in Austria', *Political Studies*, Vol. 36 (1988), pp. 209–23.

U. Kitzinger, 'Austria: The Corporatist Coalition', in *Britain, Europe and Beyond: Essays in European Politics* (Leiden, 1964), pp. 84–106.

S. W. Arndt (ed.), *The Political Economy of Austria* (Washington, DC: American Enterprise Inst., 1982).

A. Pelinka, 'Austrian Social Partnership: Stability versus Innovation', *West European Politics*, Vol. 10, No. 1 (Jan. 1987), pp. 63–75.

H. Gottweis, 'Modernization Conflicts, New Democratic Culture, and Shifts of Power in Austrian Politics', *German Politics and Society*, Issue 21 (1990), pp. 48–62.

More specialised studies include:

W. C. Müller, 'Issue Transfer and Symbolic Legislation: A Case Study of the

Austrian Equal Treatment Act', *European Journal of Political Research*, Vol. 14 (1986), pp. 63–80.

R. Bauböck and H. Wimmer, 'Social Partnership and "Foreigners Policy": On Special Features of Austria's Guest-Worker System', *European Journal of Political Research*, Vol. 16 (1988), pp. 659–81.

6. ELECTIONS

6.1. Elections and the Electoral System

Brief descriptions of the current electoral systems are contained in:

H. Fischer, 'Elections and Parliament', in K. Steiner (ed.), *Modern Austria* (Palo Alto, CA: SPOSS, 1981), pp. 241–59.

M. A. Sully, *Political Parties and Elections in Austria* (London: Hurst, 1981), pp. 146–55.

A. M. Carstairs, *A Short History of Electoral Systems in Western Europe* (London: Allen & Unwin, 1980), pp. 123–34.

The electoral system before the 1970 reform is described in:

U. W. Kitzinger, 'The Austrian Electoral System', *Parliamentary Affairs*, Vol. 12 (1959), pp. 392–404.

J. Dreijmanis, 'Proportional Representation and Its Effects: The Austrian Experience', *Parliamentary Affairs*, Vol. 24 (1970), pp. 43–52.

For details of election results see for example:

T. Mackie and R. Rose, 'Austria', in *The International Almanac of Electoral History*, 3rd ed. (London: Macmillan, 1991), pp. 23–37.

All Austria's national, *Land* and presidential election results are contained in the *Österreichisches Jahrbuch für Politik* (Vienna: Verlag für Geschichte und Politik, 1977ff).

For other data sources see:

R. Stiefbold, 'Ecological Data on Austria', in M. Dogan and S. Rokkan (eds.), *Quantitative Ecological Analysis in the Social Sciences* (Cambridge, MA: MIT. Press, 1969), pp. 567–79.

6.2. Electoral Analysis

Specific elections are discussed in journals such as *West European Politics* and *Electoral Studies*, e.g.:

U. Kitzinger, 'The Austrian Election of 1959', in *Political Studies*, Vol. 9 (1961), pp. 119–40.

M. A. Sully, 'The Austrian Parliamentary Election of 1975', *Parliamentary Affairs*, Vol. 29 (1976), pp. 293–309.

—— 'The Austrian Election of 1979: A Socialist Victory', *Parliamentary Affairs*, Vol. 32 (1979), pp. 437–47.

P. Pulzer, 'The Austrian General Election of 1983', *Electoral Studies*, Vol. 2 (1983), pp. 275–80.

A. Scott, 'The Austrian General Election of 1986', *Electoral Studies*, Vol. 6 (1987), pp. 154–60.

P. Pulzer, 'The Austrian Presidential Election of 1986', *Electoral Studies*, Vol. 5 (1986), pp. 302–4.

K. R. Luther, 'Austria's Future and Waldheim's Past: The Significance of the 1986 Elections', *West European Politics*, Vol. 10, No. 3 (July 1987), pp. 376–99.

D. Meth-Cohn and W. C. Müller, 'Leaders Count: The Austrian Elections of October 1990', *West European Politics*, Vol. 14, No. 2 (April 1991), pp. 183–88.

On the 1979 'Zwentendorf' nuclear power referendum see:

E. Gehmacher and F. Plasser, 'The Austrian Nuclear Power Referendum and Its Influence on the Austrian General Elections in May 1979', in ESOMAR, *Political Opinion Polling* (Amsterdam, 1980).

A. Pelinka, 'The Nuclear Power Referendum in Austria', *Electoral Studies*, Vol. 2, No. 3 (1983), pp. 253–61.

Some electoral studies are included in:

A. Pelinka and F. Plasser (eds.), *The Austrian Party System* (Boulder, CO: Westview Press, 1989).

6.3. Cleavages and Dimensions

K. Liepelt, 'The Infra-Structure of Party Support in Germany and Austria', in M. Dogan and R. Rose (eds.), *European Politics: A Reader* (London: Macmillan, 1971), pp. 183–202.

F. C. Engelmann and M. A. Schwartz, 'Austria's Consistent Voters', *American Behavioral Scientist*, Vol. 18 (1974), pp. 97–110.

—— 'Partisan Stability and the Continuity of a Segmented Society: The Austrian Case', *American Journal of Sociology*, Vol. 79 (1974), pp. 948–66.

C. Haerpfer and E. Gehmacher, 'Social Structure and Voting in the Austrian Party System', *Electoral Studies*, Vol. 3 (1984), pp. 25–46.

C. Haerpfer, 'Austria', in I. Crewe and D. Denver (eds.), *Electoral Change in Western Democracies* (London: Croom Helm, 1985), pp. 264–86.

7. CONSOCIATIONALISM

G. Lehmbruch, 'Consociational Democracy in the International System', *European Journal of Political Research*, Vol. 3, No. 4 (1975), pp. 377–91.

—— 'A Non-competitive Pattern of Conflict Management in Liberal Democracies: The Case of Switzerland, Austria and the Lebanon', in K. D. McRae (ed.), *Consociational Democracy. Political Accommodation in Segmented Societies* (Toronto: McClelland & Stewart, 1974), pp. 90–7.

V. Lorwin, 'Segmented Pluralism, Ideological Cleavages and Political Cohesion in the Smaller European Democracies', in *Comparative Politics*, Vol. 13 (1971), pp. 141–75.

G. B. Powell, Jr., *Social Fragmentation and Political Hostility. An Austrian Case Study* (CA: Stanford UP, 1970).

—— with L. W. Powell, 'The Analysis of Citizen-Elite Linkages: Representation by Austrian Local Elites', in S. Verba and L. W. Pye (eds.), *The Citizens and Politics: A Comparative Perspective* (Stamford, CT: Greylock, 1978), pp. 197–217.

—— 'Political Cleavage Structure, Cross-Pressure Processes, and Partisanship: An Empirical Test of the Theory', *American Journal of Political Science*, Vol. 20 (1976), pp. 1–23.

—— with R. P. Stiefbold, 'Anger, Bargaining, and Mobilization as Middle-Range Theories of Elite Conflict Behavior', *Comparative Politics*, Vol. 9 (1977), pp. 379–89.

W. T. Bluhm, 'Nation Building. The Case of Austria', *Polity*, Vol. 1 (1968), pp. 149–77.
—— *Building an Austrian Nation* (New Haven, CT: Yale UP, 1973).
R. P. Stiefbold, 'Elites and Elections in a Fragmented Political System', in R. Wildenmann (ed.), *Sozialwissenschaftliches Jahrbuch für Politik*, Vol. 4 (Munich: Olzog, 1975), pp. 119–227.
—— 'Segmented Pluralism and Consociational Democracy in Austria: Problems of Political Stability and Change', in M. O. Heisler (ed.), *Politics in Europe. Structures and Processes in Some Postindustrial Democracies* (NY: McKay, 1974), pp. 117–77.
—— 'Political Change in a Stalemated Society: Segmented Pluralism and Consociational Democracy in Austria', in N. J. Vig and R. P. Stiefbold (eds.), *Politics in Advanced Nations* (Englewood Cliffs, NJ: Prentice Hall, 1974), pp. 425–77.
J. J. Houska, *Influencing Mass Political Behavior. Elites and Political Subcultures in the Netherlands and Austria* (Berkeley, CA: Inst. of Int'l Studies, 1985).

8. ECONOMIC AND SOCIAL POLICIES

8.1. Economic Development and Structure

Several chapters on the Austrian economic development and structure can be found in:
K. Steiner (ed.), *Modern Austria* (Palo Alto, CA: SPOSS, 1981).

8.2. Labour Relations and Corporatism

M. Edelman, *National Economic Planning by Collective Bargaining. The Formation of Austrian Wage, Price, and Tax Policy after World War II* (Urbana, IL: Univ. of Illinois Inst. of Labor and Industrial Relations, 1954).
J. Barbash, 'Austrian Trade Unions and the Negotiation of National Economic Policy', *British Journal of Industrial Relations*, Vol. 9 (1971), pp. 371–87.
T. Prager, 'Austria's "Social Partnership" – A View From Within', *Monthly Review*, Vol. 34, No. 6 (1982), pp. 49–64.
R. J. Flanagan, D. W. Soskice and L. Ulman, 'Austria', in R. J. Flanagan, D. W. Soskice and L. Ulman, *Unionism and Incomes Policies: European Experiences* (Washington, DC: Brookings, 1983), pp. 40–82.
H. Duda and F. Tödtling, 'Austrian Trade Unions in the Economic Crisis', in R. Edwards, P. Garonna, F. Tödtling (eds.), *Unions in Crisis and Beyond* (Dover, MA: Auburn House, 1986), pp. 227–68.
P. J. Katzenstein, *Corporatism and Change: Austria. Switzerland and the Politics of Industry* (Ithaca, NY: Cornell UP, 1984).
B. Marin, 'Austria – The Paradigm Case of Liberal Corporatism?' in W. Grant (ed.), *The Political Economy of Corporatism* (London: Macmillan, 1984), pp. 89–125.
—— 'From Consociationalism to Technocorporatism: The Austrian Case as a Model-Generator', in I. Scholten (ed.), *Political Stability and Neocorporatism* (London: Sage, 1987), pp. 39–94.
A. Pelinka, 'Austrian Social Partnership: Stability versus Innovation', *West European Politics*, Vol. 10, No. 1 (1987), pp. 62–75.
P. Gerlich, E. Grande and W. C. Müller, 'Corporatism in Crisis: Stability and Change of Social Partnership in Austria', *Political Studies*, Vol. 36, No. 2 (1988), pp. 209–23.

8.3. Economic Policy

S. W. Arndt (ed.), *The Political Economy of Austria* (Washington, DC: American Enterprise Inst., 1982).

W. C. Müller, 'Economic Success without an Industrial Strategy: Austria in the 1970s', *Journal of Public Policy*, Vol. 3 (1983), pp. 119–30.

W. Hankel, *Prosperity Amidst Crisis. Austria's Economic Policy and the Energy Crunch* (Boulder, CO: Westview Press, 1981).

G. Chaloupek, 'The Austrian Parties and the Economic Crisis', *West European Politics*, Vol. 8, No. 1 (1985), pp. 71–81.

L. G. Stauber, *A New Program for Democratic Socialism. Lessons from the Market-Planning Experience in Austria* (Carbondale, IL: Four Willows Press, 1987).

W. C. Müller, 'Privatising in a Corporatist Economy: The Politics of Privatisation in Austria', *West European Politics*, Vol. 11, No. 4 (Oct. 1988), pp. 101–16.

P. Gerlich, 'Deregulation in Austria', *European Journal of Political Research*, Vol. 17 (1989), pp. 209–22.

—— and W. C. Müller, 'Austria: A Crisis Resolved or a Crisis Postponed?', in E. Daamgard, P. Gerlich and J. J. Richardson (eds.), *The Politics of Economic Crisis* (Aldershot: Averbury, 1989), pp. 146–62.

9. FOREIGN POLICY – AUSTRIA'S INTERNATIONAL POSITION

C. T. Grayson, Jr., *Austria's International Position 1938–1953* (Genéva: Librairie E. Droz, 1953).

W. T. Stearman, *The Soviet Union and the Occupation of Austria* (Bonn: Verlag für Zeitarchive, 1961).

W. B. Bader, *Austria Between East and West, 1945–1955* (CA: Stanford UP, 1966).

D. R. Whitnah and E. L. Erickson, *The American Occupation of Austria: Planning and Early Years* (Westport, CT: Greenwood Press, 1985).

K. Gruber, *Between Liberation and Liberty* (London: Deutsch, 1955).

P. J. Katzenstein, 'Domestic Structures and Political Strategies: Austria in an Interdependent World', in R. L. Merritt and B. R. Russett (eds.), *From National Development to Global Community, Essays in Honour of Karl W. Deutsch* (London: Allen & Unwin, 1981), pp. 252–78.

G. Lehmbruch, 'Consociational Democracy in the International System', *European Journal of Political Research*, Vol. 3, No. 4 (1975), pp. 377–91.

O. Höll and H. Kramer, 'The Process of Internationalization and the Position of Austria. Problems and Current Development Trends of the "Austrian Model"', in O. Höll (ed.), *Small States in Europe and Dependence* (Vienna: Braumüller, 1983), pp. 184–219.

B. Unger, 'Possibilities and Constraints for National Economic Policies in Small Countries: The Case of Austria', *German Politics and Society*, Issue 21 (1990), pp. 63–77.

J. P. Katzenstein, 'Trends and Oscillations in Austrian Integration Policy since 1955: Alternative Explanations', *Journal of Common Market Studies*, Vol. 14 (1975), pp. 171–97.

T. O. Schlesinger, *Austrian Neutrality in Postwar Europe: The Domestic Roots of a Foreign Policy* (Vienna: Braumüller, 1972).

R. A. Bauer, *The Austrian Solution* (Charlottesville: UP of Virginia, 1982).
A. Pelinka, 'The Politics of Neutrality', *German Politics and Society*, Issue 21 (1990), pp. 19–32.
A. K. Cronin, *Great Power Politics and the Struggle over Austria, 1945–1955* (Ithaca, NY: Cornell UP, 1986).
K. R. Stadler, 'The Kreisky Phenomenon', *West European Politics*, Vol. 4, No. 1 (Jan. 1981), pp. 5–18.

ABSTRACTS

Consociationalism and the Austrian Political System
Kurt Richard Luther and Wolfgang C. Müller

This essay first considers the origins and nature of Austria's traditional subcultures, or *Lager*. Second, it outlines the crises of national identity, democratic legitimacy and economic distribution that fatally undermined the First Austrian Republic of 1918–34 and resulted in a short civil war, authoritarian rule and fascism. Third, it highlights the coexistence in the Second Republic of segmentation (albeit considerably attenuated) and social, economic and political stability, a combination that led to Austria being labelled an example of consociational democracy. The consociational literature's assertions on Austria were based in the main on developments between 1945 and 1966, which is thus termed the 'classic' phase of Austrian consociationalism. The essay concludes by identifying six 'core characteristics' of Austrian politics during this period.

The Decline of *'Lager* Mentality' and the New Model of Electoral Competition in Austria
Fritz Plasser, Peter A. Ulram and Alfred Grausgruber

This article commences by sketching out the subcultural underpinning of Austria's consociational system, namely, the so-called *Lager*. By reference to a wealth of empirical data it then identifies processes, such as the decline of *Lager* mentality, by which Austria's encapsulated subcultures have been eroded. Attention is then given to the implications of these ongoing developments for the previous hyperstability of Austrian electoral behaviour and explanations are offered as to how and why Austria's electorate has of late become increasingly volatile. By detailed analysis of the 1990 general election the authors first demonstrate the declining salience of traditional determinants of voting behaviour. Second, they identify eight new 'clusters' or 'segments' of voters which may constitute the bases for a restructuring of party competition and thus also for a possible realignment of the Austrian party system.

Consociationalism, Parties and the Party System in Austria
Kurt Richard Luther

This article provides a detailed analysis of changes since 'classic' consociationalism (1945–66) within and between Austria's *Lager* parties. First, their intra-subcultural linkages are examined (organisational penetration and mobilisation of their respective subcultures; the degree of party hierarchical control over the *Lager*). Second, the article investigates the *Lager* parties' role in inter-subcultural interaction in the party system's various arenas. This involves changes to both structure of the *Lager* parties' interaction (traditionally characterised by high levels of concentration, pervasiveness of party activity, as well as by prevailing *Proporz* and segmental autonomy) and to its style. Various indicators of change to Austria's parties and party system since are identified, including depillarisation, declining levels of organisational penetration, of hierarchical control and of the *Lager* parties' mobilisational capacity. Emphasis is placed upon organisational factors as explanations of *Lager*-based politics' persistence, as well as upon likely further and possibly quite rapid change in parties and party system.

Austrian Governmental Institutions: Do They Matter?
Wolfgang C. Müller

This essay examines the relevance of the formal powers of the main Austrian governmental institutions (parliament, president, cabinet, administration, constitutional court, judiciary, audit office, federalism and direct democracy). It focuses on developments since 'classic' consociationalism (1945–66), during which Austria's political 'core institutions' were largely determined by the country's two main political subcultures, the elites of which staffed key positions within them. Austria's institutional framework thus reflected rather than constrained the subcultures' accommodative interaction and lacked the political salience envisaged by the constitution. However, institutions previously under control of *Lager* elites or practising 'self restraint' are now far less inclined merely to reflect the wishes of those subcultures. Austria's formal institutional framework has thus become more salient and many constituent institutions now comprise arenas, the rules of which are highly relevant for the political process. Moreover, formal governmental institutions' tendency to become actors in their own right has made the political process more complex and less predictable.

A Farewell to Corporatism
Peter Gerlich

Traditionally, social partnership has held an important position within the Austrian political system, making it one of the prime examples of corporatism. But the period of corporatism is now drawing to an end. The traditional principles of social partnership concerning organisations, political style and inherent stability are being called into question, introducing potentially sweeping changes in the country that would bring it in line with the rest of Western Europe. There are various scenarios for future development, all of which agree that social partnership will become less important. Both the political and economic spheres are becoming more competition orientated and hopefully also more competitive. In retrospect corporatism may be viewed as an intermediate stage in the modernisation process of Austrian society.

Changing Priorities in Austrian Economic Policy
Volkmar Lauber

The basic features of 'Austrokeynesian' economic policy took shape in the 1950s. Corporatist co-operation and support were one of its pre-conditions. Its instruments consisted of a hard currency policy, investment promotion, wage moderation and deficit spending, with the overall goal of achieving maximum economic growth and stability. After 1975, deficit spending expanded considerably; this secured both 'Austrokeynesianism's' apotheosis and its downfall. In 1985–86 a major policy reversal initiated budget consolidation, a substantially greater reliance on market mechanisms and thus a cutback of corporatist (and to some extent state) power over economic policy.

Austria in the International Arena: Neutrality, European Integration and Consociationalism
D. Mark Schultz

This article discusses the relationship between Austria's international environment and its distinctive pattern of centralised, co-operative politics dominated by the political parties and the major interest groups. Through an examination of Austria's neutrality and integration policies, the author suggests that external factors – and particularly Austria's location on a faultline of the Cold War – were instrumental in the development of consociational politics and the main determinants of Austrian foreign policy. Reduced East-West tensions and further integration with the European Community will increase Austria's foreign policy options, but will also promote the decline of consociationalism by reducing the social cohesiveness on which it is based.

Index

accommodation, 7–8 (in First Republic); 9, 10, 18, 46, 63, 65, 72, 77, 78, 81–82, 91, 136–137, 168, 173, 174, 196–197, 201, 205
administration, 18, 19, 88–91, 112–115
advisory committees, 86, 135, 143
Advisory Council for Economic and Social Affairs, 135, 141, 149–150, 152
age (and voting), 31, 35, 36, 39, 40, 41, 56
Agrarian League (*Landbund*), 4
Alford Index, 34
Allied occupation, 34, 46–47, 115–116, 174
Andics, Hellmut, 6
Anschluss, 5, 7, 9, 14, n.27, 147
Association of Austrian Industrialists (VÖI), 133, 134, 188, 191, 194
attitudes, 16, 18, 23, (see also ideology)
Audit Office, 120–122, 143
austerity, 159, 160, 164, 167, 169
Austrian Club for Automobilists, Motorbikers and Cyclists, 54
Austrian People's Party (see ÖVP)
Austrofascism, 7, 76, 88, 112–113, 134
Austrokeynesianism, 11, 15, n.35, 147–152, 153, 163, 164
Austromarxism, 6, 61
auxiliary associations, 1–2, 51–55, 59, 65–71
Benya, Anton, 136
Bernhard, Thomas, 132
Bielka, Erich, 186
Birkelbach report, 180, 181, 182, 193
Bock, Fritz, 178, 182
budget deficit, 150, 151, 152, 153, 156, 157, 158–160, 163, 164
Bundesrat (Federal Council), 78, 102, 123–124, (see also parliament)
bureaucracy, 88–91, 112–113, 114–115, 204
cabinet, 79–82, 103, 106, 108–112, 118–119, 210
candidate-orientated voting, 30, 31, 32–33, 34, 35–37, 39, 70, 76
Catholic-conservative *Lager*, 2–3, 6, 10, 63, 71, 112, (see also ÖVP)

Central Association of Austria's Small Gardeners, Homecrofters and Pet Breeders, 54
central bank (*Nationalbank*), 88, 194
Chamber of Agriculture (LWK), 83, 88, 133, 134, 139, 148, 149
Chamber of Business (BWK), 83, 84, 85, 87, 88, 133, 134, 135, 136, 139, 148, 149, 188
Chamber of Labour (AK), 83, 84, 85, 86, 88, 133, 134, 135, 148
chambers, 52, 53, 66, 82–88, 132–145, 148, 162, 166–167; obligatory membership thereof: 53, 83, 88, 91, 133, 134, 136, 139–40, 145, 148, 166–167; elections within: 83–86
chancellor, 79–81, 82, 86, 109, 110, 111, 135
Christian-Social Party, 1, 2, 4, 6, 12, n.4, 13, n.22
church attendance, (see religiosity)
civil service, 88–91, 112–115
civil war (1934), 7, 45
classic consociationalism, 8–12, (defined: 10–12)
class voting, 20–21, 34–34, 35, 36, 39, 40
cleavage structure, 16–19, 26–27
clientelism, 63–65, 67, 92, 141, (see also patronage and *Proporz*)
consensus, (see accommodation)
co-operation, (see accommodation)
Coalition Committee, 82, 103, 109–110
coalitions, 4 (in First Republic), 74, 79, 103
Cold War, 174, 175, 191, 194, 195, 202, 203
Communist Party of Austria, (see KPÖ)
competition, economic: 162, 177–78; electoral: 37–42, 73–77, 202, 203; party: 37–42, 72–91, 142, 149, 202, 203, 204, 205
consociational theory, 9–10, 14, n.28–30, 45–46, 47, 72, 93–94, n.6–7
consociationalism, 8–12, 14, 45, 46, 47, 79, 91–93, 126–127, 145, 173–174, 196–197, 201–206

and European integration, 127, 173–200, (see also European Community)
and party system, 45–98
constitution, First Republic: 4, 7; Second Republic: 8, 100, 101, 109, 112, 115–118, 124, 125, 126, 128, n.7, 138, 139, 196, 204
constitutional court, 115–118, 124, 140, 163, 204
core characteristics of Austrian politics, 10–12, 201–206
corporatism, 11, 15, n.33, 19, 45, 53, 82–88, 100, 132–146, 152, 163, 168, 169–170, legitimacy of: 139, 141, 169–170, 201, 202, 204, 206, (see also interest groups and social partnership)
corruption, 65, 77, 119, 205, 206, (see also clientelism and patronage)
Council of Europe, 185
Creditanstalt, 88
crisis of distribution, (in First Republic) 5–6, 64, 206
crisis of legitimation, (in First Republic) 6, 64, 206
Czernetz, Karl, 177, 178
de Clercq, Willy, 192, 193
de-alignment, 16, 23–26, 30, 32, 33, 93
deference, 60–61, 67, 77, 96, n.32, 115, 139, 205, 206
deficit spending 150, 151, 153, 164, 189
denazification, 113
Denmark, 180, 183
depillarisation, 22–23, 31, 51, 59, 65, 83, 91, 202, 203, 205
depoliticised democracy, 11
deregulation, 156, 162, 168, 169, 188, 204
Diamant, Alfred, 6
direct democracy, 101–103
Duverger, Maurice, 3
economic growth, 63, 147, 148–149, 150, 151, 152, 158, 159–160, 170, 202
economic policy, 11, 61–62, 63, 64, 81–82, 137, 147–142, 147–172, 201–202, 203, 204, 206
economy, 5–6 (First Republic); 8, 11, 147–72
education, 22, 29, 36, 35, 40, 41, 56, 57, 58, 138
EFTA (European Free Trade Area), 153, 180, 181, 182, 185, 186, 190, 192, 193, 195
election campaign, 156
elections, 74, 83–88 (to chambers), 100, 207, 208
electoral arena, 73–77
electoral behaviour, (see voting behaviour)
electoral competition, 37–42, 73–77, 202, 203
employment policy, 153, 158
encapsulation (see segmentation)
EURATOM, 181
European Coal and Steel Community, 181
European Economic Area (EEA), 180, 195, 196
European Community, (European integration) 64, 138, 142, 143–144, 152–153, 160, 162, 163, 169, 170, 175–197, 202, 203, 205
exports, 149, 150, 153, 160, 176, 178, 185
factionalism, 71, 80
farmers, 17, 20, 26, 39, 40, 56, 57, 58, 63, 134, 139, 142,
Federal Assembly (*Bundesversammlung*), 129, n.16
Federal Civil Servants' Representative Body (*Bundespersonalvertretung*), 89–90
federal president, 101, 105–108, 109, 115, 118, 129, n.16
federalism, 70–71, 122–126, and distribution of competences: 122–123, 124
Figl, Leopold, 174
Finland, 180, 185, 195
First Austrian Association of Worker Stamp-collectors, 54
First Republic (1918–34), 4–8, 88, 100, 106, 112, 134
floating voters, 27, 30, 31, 32–33, 76, 203
foreign policy, 11, 173–200, 202
FPÖ (*Freiheitliche Partei Österreichs*, Freedom Party of Austria), 11, 17, 22, 30, 33, 34, 35, 38, 39, 40, 41, 42, 47, 49, 50, 51, 52–53, 55, 57–58, 62, 63, 69, 70, 75, 77, 78, 80, 81, 85, 89, 90, 104, 105, 107, 120–121, 138–139, 160, 168, 178, 184, 186, 191, 196, 206, (see German-national *Lager* also)
France, 182, 183, 188, 195

INDEX

Fraktion of Socialist Trades Unionists, (see FSG)
free trade agreements, 153, 183–185, 186, 187, 188
Freedom Party of Austria, (see FPÖ, as well as German-national *Lager*)
Freier Wirtschaftsverband Österreichs (Free Business Association of Austria), 52
FSG (*Fraktion Sozialistischer Gewerkschaftler* Fraktion of Socialist Trades Unionists), 52
functionaries, 18, 53, 55–57, 58, 59, 66–67, 136, 137, 142
GATT (General Agreement on Trade and Tariffs), 181, 185
German-national *Lager*, 3–4, 7, 13, n.9 & 15, 47, 55, 59, 94, n.11, 112, (see also FPÖ)
Germany, 5, 7, 8, 9, 174, 175, 176, 179, 183, 192, 195
Geyer, Walter, 122
government, 79–82
governmental institutions, 11, 99–131, 169–170, 201, 202
governor (*Landeshauptmann*), 71, 81, 123–124, 124–126
governors' conference (*Landeshauptmännerkonferenz*), 72, 125
grand coalition, 7 (First Republic); 11, 18, 62, 63, 79, 80, 81–82, 104, 108, 122–127, 132, 157, 158, 159, 160, 167, 169, 174, 206
Greater German People's Party (*Großdeutsche Volkspartei*), 4
Green Party, 29–30, 33, 35, 40, 73, 77, 138, 191, 204
Haider, Jörg, 30, 35, 58, 62, 69, 70, 81, 157, 167, 168
Hainburg, 142
hard currency policy, 148, 149, 150–151, 152, 163
Hummer, Waldemar, 191
ideology, 1–2, 3, 6, 17, 18, 23, 24, 47, 58, 61–63, 69, 76, 205
incomes policy, 11, 149, 163–164, 169
indirect federal administration, 124–126
inflation, 148, 149, 152, 165
interest groups, 18, 52, 82–88, 132–146, 148, 169, 201, 202, 188 (and European integration), (see also corporatism and social partnership)
investment promotion, 149, 153, 163
Ireland, 183, 191
issue voting, 30, 31, 32, 33, 35, 37, 42
Italy, 176, 182, 183, 195
Jankowitsch, Peter, 189, 191
Joint Commission, 86, 134–135, 137, 140, 141, 144, 149, 150, 152
Jonas, Franz, 8
judiciary, 116, 118–120
Junktim (log-rolling), 72, 77, 82, 87, 91, 206
Kamitz, Reinhard, 150
Katzenstein, Peter, 173
Kelsen, Hans, 112
Khol, Andreas, 190
Kirchschläger, Rudolf, 184
Klaus, Josef, 109
Körner, Theodor, 106
KPÖ (*Kommunistische Partei Österreichs*, Communist Party of Austria), 6, 49–50, 51, 57, 59, 68–69, 178, 191
Kreisky, Bruno, 29, 70, 109, 113, 156, 164, 166, 177, 178, 181, 184, 185, 191, 189
labour, (see ÖGB also) 17, 20, 39, 40, 41, 133, 148, 151, 152, 153, 165–166, 177, 189
Lacina, Ferdinand, 157, 167, 168, 189
Lager, (see also subcultures/subcultural)
Lager, 1–8 (historical origins of), 16, 18, 19, 20, 34, 37, 46, 126–127
culture, 34, 37
factionalism, 62, 68, 71, 80
mentality, 10, 16, 18, 22–28, 29, 36–37, 43, n.3, 60, 76–77, 93, 201, 202, 203, 205
oligarchy, 65–71, 67, 86, 87, 91
parties' inter-subcultural interaction, 18–19, 72–91, 92, 202
parties' intra-subcultural linkages, 18–19, 46–71, 91–92, 202
radicalisation, (First Republic) 56
theory, 12, n.3, 42, n.2, 94, n.8
values, 59, 61–65
laissez-faire economics, 1, 5
Lanc, Erwin, 185
Länder, 115, 120, 122–126
Länderbank, 88

Landeshauptmann, (see governor)
Landtag (Land parliament), 78, 124, 126; elections: 70–71 73–75
late deciders, 30, 33
League of Independents, (see VdU)
League of Socialist Freedom Fighters and Victims of Fascism, 54
Leagues (*Bünde* of the ÖVP), 52, 68, 71, 80
left-right self-placement, 23–24
legislation, 78, 104, 116, 135, 138, 140, 142
legitimacy, 1 (in Monarchy); 4–6 (of First Republic); (Second Republic) 88, 91
Lijphart, Arend, 206
Lijphart index, 34
log-rolling, (see *Junktim*)
Luxembourg Compromise, 191
Marshall Plan, 9
mass parties, 3, 68, 202
media, 22, 23, 32, 111, 121, 139, 141
McAllister, Ian, 37
ministerial cabinets, 114
ministers, (role of) 108–111, 135
mobilisation, (subcultural mobilisation)
mobility, social and geographic, 2, 22, 61
Mock, Alois, 186, 189
monarchy (pre-1918), 1–3, 134
mutual veto, 72, 77, 82, 87, 91, 206
Mussolini, Benito, 6
national identity, 4–5, 17, 21–22, 43, n.8, 45, 59, 94, n.3
National Socialism, 3, 6–7, 88, 112–113, 147
nationalised industries, 64, 148, 155, 156, 161, 164, 166, 168, 188, 189, 191
Nationalrat (National Council), 73–74, 77–79, 102, 120, 123 (see also parliament)
NATO (North Atlantic Treaty Organisation), 178, 191
neutrality, 173–175, 178–179, 181, 183, 186, 191–192
Neutrality Act, 175
new institutionalism, 99–100
Norway, 180, 183, 185, 195
occupation, (see social structure)
OEEC, (Organisation for European Economic Co-operation), 180
oligarchic control, 65–71
ombudsman's office, 131, n.52

ÖGB (*Österreichischer Gewerkschaftsbund*, or Austrian Trade Union Federation), 83, 86, 87, 133, 134, 135, 136, 148, 149, 156, 166, (see also labour)
organisational density, 48–51, 91
Österreichischer Arbeiter- und Angestelltenbund (Austrian League of Workers and Salaried Employees, or ÖAAB), 52, 62
Österreichischer Bauernbund (Austrian Farmers' League, or ÖBB), 52
Österreichischer Wirtschaftsbund (Austrian Business League, or ÖWB), 52, 62, 81
overlapping leadership, 52, 53, 67–68, 69, 70, 72–73, 86, 138, 142
overlapping membership, 67–68, 69, 70, 91
ÖVP (*Österreichische Volkspartei*, Austrian People's Party), 9, 10, 11, 17, 19, 21, 23, 24, 25, 27, 28, 29, 31, 33, 34, 35, 37, 38, 39, 40, 42, 48–50, 51, 52, 55–59, 61–62, 68, 69, 72, 75, 102, 104, 105, 108, 109, 122, 138, 142, 150, 152, 153, 156, 160, 167, 168, 169, 177, 178, 182, 184, 186, 189, 191, 194, 196, 206
Pahr, Willibald, 185
paramilitary organisations, 6–7
Paritätische Kommission, (see Joint Commission)
parliament, 73–74, 77–79, 102, 103–105, 106, 120, 121, 123–124, 128, n.12, 135, 140, 207, 208
parties, and European integration, 177–179, 184–186, 189–190, 191, 196–197
and hierarchy, 65–71
and interest groups, 142
internally- vs. externally-created, 2, 3
and inter-subcultural interaction, 18–19, 72–91, 92, 202
and oligarchy, 65–71, 77
organisational density, 48–50
social composition, 55–59
vulnerability of, 32, 142
partisan attachment (partisanship), 10, 18, 19, 26, 28, 31, 35, 45, 60, 65, 67, 76
party, competition, 16, 37–42, 72–91
discipline, 78, 102, 103
functionaries, (see functionaries)

INDEX

identification, 19, 24–26, 30, 31, 36, 37, 42, 45, 60
loyalties, 27–28, 31, 32, 39, 40
members, 18, 19
membership (density), 10, 25–26, 48–51, 53, 55–59, 66, 68
networks, 19, 23
newspapers, 19, 22
of notables, 3, 68, 69
supporters, 21, 60
weariness, 27
party system 16, 29, 201, 202, 206, (concentration); 32, 45–98 (esp. 72–91), 118
patronage, (see also *Proporz* and clientelism), 19, 63–65, 68, 88–91, 160, 166
pillarisation, 9–10, 18, 37, 45, 46–71
Pilz, Peter, 122
Pittermann, Bruno, 177, 178
political information, 22
political participation, 19, 60–61, 67
political stability, 16, 19, 46, 206
popular sovereignty, 100
Portugal, 180
postmaterialism, 203, 204
presidential elections, 209
privatisation, 156, 157, 158, 161, 164, 168
Proporz, 18, 57, 64, 72, 77, 79, 86, 88, 90, 91, 103, 113, 115, 120 (see also patronage and clientelism)
protest (voting), 27, 31, 34, 35, 36–37, 62, 77
public debt, 154, 156, 158
public sector, 64, 88–89, 148, 152, 156, 157, 161, 163, 164
recession, 150, 151, 153, 156, 164
recruitment, 33, 46, 55, 66, 69, 70
referendum, 101–103, 196
religion, 1, 2, 58, 59, 61; and voting: 21, 33, 34, 36, 39, 40, (see also secularisation)
religiosity, 19, 21, 33, 34, 35, 36, 58, 59
Renner, Karl, 8, 174
Republikanischer Schutzbund (Republican Defence League), 7
Ring Freiheitlicher Studenten (Circle of Free Students), 55
Ring Freiheitlicher Wirtschaftstreibender (Circle of Free Businesspersons, or RFW), 53
Rose, Richard, 37
Sallinger, Rudolf, 136
Sartori, Giovanni 72, 74, 79
Schärf, Adolf, 106–107, 174
Schleinzer, Karl, 184
Schönerer, Georg von, 3
Schweitzer, Michael, 191
SDAP (*Sozialdemokratische Arbeiterpartei*, Social Democratic Workers' Party), 1–2, 4, 6, 7, 12, n.5, 106
Second Control Agreement, 116
sectionalism, (see also segmental autonomy), 97, n.51
secularisation, (see also religion), 21, 26, 60
segmental autonomy, 64, 72, 75, 79–80, 86–87, 88, 89, 90, 91, 97, n.51, 113, 202, 203, 206
segmentation, (see pillarisation)
self-employed, 17, 56, 57, 58, 83, 167
Single Market, 187, 188, 190, 192–193, 195
Sinowatz, Fred, 167, 185, 189
social democratic consensus, 165, 166
social partnership, 82–88, 100, 128 n.5, 132–146, 147, 150, 188, 194; historical origins: 7, 134; organising principles: 136, 139–140; procedural principles: 136–137, 140, 202; legitimising principles: 137, 141, prospects of: 143–145; (see also corporatism and interest groups)
social structure, 20, 26, 51, 55–59, 60–61, 202, 203
socialist *Lager*, 2–3, 10, 112, (see also SPÖ)
Socialist Party of Austria, (see SPÖ)
Socialist Youth of Austria, 54
South Tyrol, 182, 183
Soviet Union, 148, 174, 175, 178, 179, 182, 183, 192, 194, 196, 203
SPÖ (*Sozialistische Partei Österreichs*, Socialist Party of Austria), 10, 11, 17, 19, 21, 22, 23, 24, 25, 27, 28, 29, 31, 33, 34, 35, 37, 38, 39, 40, 41, 47, 48–49, 51, 52, 55–58, 61–62, 68, 69, 75, 102, 106, 108, 109, 119, 138, 152, 160, 166, 167, 157, 168, 177, 178, 185, 186, 189, 191, 194, 196, 206, (see also socialist *Lager*)

SPÖ-Bauern (SPÖ-Farmers), 52
SPÖ-FPÖ government, 11, 16, 110, 156–157
Ständestaat (see Austrofascism)
Staribacher, Josef, 184, 186
state prosecutors, 119
State Treaty, 174, 175, 179, 183
state-building, 4, 9, 13, n.13, 45, 106
Steger, Norbert, 69, 80, 157
Steyrer, Kurt, 107
Stockholm Treaty, 182
Streicher, Rudolf, 189
student organisations, 55, 59
subcultural
  bureaucratisation, 65–66, 87
  cohesion, 19, 59, 63, 65, 91, 67–71
  encapsulation, 1–2, 18, 22, 45, 46, 51, 61, 65 67, 92, 201, 202, 204, (see also pillarisation)
  fragmentation, 45 (see also *Lager* factionalism)
  hierarchy, 65–71, 202, 205
  hostility, 5–6, 7, 18, 45, 58, 197
  incorporation 10, 46, 53–54, 47–49, 91
  integration, 2–3, 19, 31, 54, 62, 91
  interaction, 18–19, 72–91, 92, 202
  mobilisation, 2–3, 13, n.8, 32, 46, 50, 59–65, 76, 91
  penetration, 2–3, 10, 47–49, 26, 53, 91, 93, 202, 204
  sociology, 1–3, 20–21, 55–59
subcultures, (see also *Lager*), 18, 22, 46
subsidies, 64, 156, 158–159, 160, 161–162, 168, 188
supply-side policies, 148–149, 156, 158–159, 160, 161
Sweden, 180, 195
Switzerland, 180, 195
tax policy, 64, 148–149, 152, 156, 158–159, 161–162
technocratic values, 66–67
Third *Lager*, (see FPÖ and German-national *Lager*)
Third Republic, 127
trade, policies: 173; with EC: 175–177
Trade Union Federation, (see ÖGB)
trade union membership, 33, 166
trade union state (*Gewerkschaftsstaat*), 127
Treaty of Rome, 180, 181
turnout, 28–29, 30, 32, 60
Umfeld, 54
unemployment, 148, 152, 153, 155, 156, 159, 165
union voting, 33, 34, 39, (see also voting behaviour)
United Kingdom, 180, 182, 183
VdU (*Verband der Unabhängigen*, League of Independents), 47, 175
vice-chancellor, 77, 80, 81, 110, 111
VOEST, 157, 161
volatility, 28–29, 30, 31, 60, 76, 96, n.30, 202
Vorfeld, 54, 55
voter alignments, 31
voter clusters, 37–42
voting behaviour, 10, 16, 24, 27, 28–42, 29, 30, 32, 33, 44, n.17, 49
voting behaviour, determinants of, 24, 26–27, 30, 31–36, 37–42
VÖI, (see Association of Austrian Industrialists)
Vranitzky, Franz, 35, 70, 109, 111, 129, n.22, 157, 167, 168, 189, 191
Waldheim, Kurt, 44, n.19, 107–108, 189
West European Union, 192, 195
Working Group for Sport and Body Culture in Austria, 54
Zwentendorf, 142